Praise for *Wired Differently*

"Management books come and go, and most are not remembered. This book, as the title implies, is different. It is a *tour de force* by a genuine servant leader. This is a book about what cooperation really means, about what ethical leadership really means and about what it means to put people before profit. Above all, *Wired Differently* has made an important contribution to the philosophy of cooperative management that has profound implications for how organizations can and should operate in the future."

— *Martin Lowery, Executive Vice President, Member and Association Relations, National Rural Electric Cooperative Association; U.S. elected representative, International Co-operative Alliance Board of Directors*

"Vern Dosch is not only wired differently, he is a masterful storyteller. This is an influential book, a must read for anyone who wants to do the right thing in business and in life."

— *Ted Case, author of* Power Plays: The U.S. Presidency, Electric Cooperatives, and the Transformation of Rural America

"*Wired Differently* captures the living, breathing spirit of what it means to work cooperatively for the good of others. Unlike many who share their theories on service and leadership, Vern, along with NISC employees, always walks the walk and is the first to find ways to promote collaboration and partnership."

— *Shirley Bloomfield, CEO, NTCA – The Rural Broadband Association*

"*Wired Differently* is much more than the story of a technology cooperative. It is a carefully crafted tribute to what's best in human nature, gathering into its pages beautiful insights about leadership, service, values and happiness. For all who are honored to know him, Vern Dosch is remarkable for his humility, his integrity and his generosity of heart. If you would have told me those qualities could be captured in the written word, I wouldn't have believed it. I just finished *Wired Differently*, and I'm a believer now!"

— *Monsignor James Shea, President, University of Mary*

"*Wired Differently* is the perfect and refreshing antithesis to Wall Street greed. The book is filled with remarkable stories of servant leadership, service to a calling higher than self and a desire to give back to one's community. Good solid values of giving and caring dance through the pages with a marvelous felicity. But so too does success—good solid success in software development, deployment and re-development. *Wired Differently* will make a valuable contribution to the history of NISC, as well as to a new way (for much of the business world) of looking at the bottom line and leadership."

— *Larry Skogen, PhD, Interim Chancellor, North Dakota University System*

"I can't think of a more important book for people interested in the cooperative business model. *Wired Differently* makes the case that values matter by illustrating the connection between what we value and how we act. Reading this book will inspire you, and I bet it will change how you view the organizations in your life."

— *Bill Patrie, Executive Director, Common Enterprise Development Corporation*

"What a great book! Vern Dosch convincingly makes the case (along with the supporting data) for the power of servant leadership, company values and building a collaborative culture. For me, the credibility of the book also comes from personally knowing the author, who is the real thing—one of the very best servant leaders I know!"

— *James C. Hunter, author of* The Servant: A Simple Story About the True Essence of Leadership *and* The World's Most Powerful Leadership Principle: How to Become a Servant Leader

"*Wired Differently* is a truly inspirational and magnificent book. I love that [it] combines real stories of challenges and successes with some of the best management and leadership ideas of our time. The book's focus on servant leadership, putting others first and always doing the right thing is [an approach that is] desperately needed in business today. *Wired Differently* should be required reading by all who care about aligning values with business success. If read and acted upon, the message of *Wired Differently* would be transformative in its impact."

— *Rich Larochelle, retired Senior Vice President, Rural Utilities Cooperative Finance Corporation*

"Collaboration, compassion, integrity, shared values and service are table stakes for servant-led organizations. In *Wired Differently*, Vern Dosch ups the ante. He offers a multitude of compelling stories for developing and nurturing a culture with a soul; lessons that can be applied to any organization, regardless of its corporate structure. One of the markers of a servant-led organization is the number of servant leaders it produces. The rich experiences shared in this book show that NISC not only attracts but grows an abundant number of servant leaders with spirit and verve and quiet dedication. If you want to see how servant leadership works at the organizational, policy and personal levels, read this book in all its gratifying detail."

— *Don M. Frick and James Sipe, PhD, licensed psychologist; co-authors of* Seven Pillars of Servant Leadership

"While *Wired Differently* is about the impressive growth of NISC through and by its employees, the compelling management prescriptions offered clearly tell you how your business can emulate the success of the National Information Solutions Cooperative. Yes, it's that good."

— *Mark Glaess, Founder and CEO, InnerG; former General Manager, Minnesota Rural Electric Association*

"What a pleasure it was to read *Wired Differently*. It very effectively integrates modern business theory with NISC's experiences and the key elements of the cooperative business model. Great job."

— *Michael A. Goodroe, President and CEO, Sawnee Electric Membership Corporation*

"This book is a remarkable montage of firsthand accounts of a rare courage, born of deeply held shared values. These behaviors permeate the cooperative at all levels, from the front lines to the boardroom, and they create a vibrant, healthy culture that is the most critical determinant of a high-performing business. *Wired Differently* is a powerfully compelling story for others to follow and provides a roadmap to create success by 'doing the right thing, always.'"

— *Melvin D. Nelson, author, President and CEO, Executive Management Systems, Inc.*

"*Wired Differently* is, much like the Gospels, a continuous journey to a deeper reality. It speaks the truth. It speaks the truth from every perspective—member, staff, management, subscriber and partners. It speaks the truth from the experience of many years of practice and from the commitment that results from paying the price and living the gamble. In *Wired Differently,* the author doesn't talk you into believing what he says, he walks you into living it."

— *Father Paul D. Becker, Pastor, Church of Corpus Christi*

"This is an inspirational read—whether you've worked for cooperatives for decades or you are just reading about them for the first time. *Wired Differently* is proof that a corporate mission, vision and values really do make a difference when practiced on a daily basis. *Wired Differently* tells how NISC has become an enduring success when measured against financial metrics and what really matters: service, ethics, professionalism and commitment to members and to each other. The world would be an even better place if more corporations were wired differently."

— *Dennis Hill, Executive Vice President and General Manager, North Dakota Association of Rural Electric Cooperatives*

"*Wired Differently* provides a great blueprint for other organizations and leaders to consider! If I picked a single word that strikes to the heart of NISC's story it would be 'always.' It's one thing to 'often' do the right thing, it's one thing to 'usually' listen to customers, it's one thing to treat co-workers and colleagues with decency 'most of the time,' but it's another thing to 'always' do such. NISC has come as close to 'always' as any organization I know! I believe all who read *Wired Differently* will enjoy and find true value."

— *Marv Athey, former General Manager and CEO, Trico Electric Cooperative, and author of* Chaff: Proven Leadership Concepts that Will Add to an Organization's Success

WIRED
DIFFERENTLY

How to Spark Better Results with
a Cooperative Business Model,
Servant Leadership
and Shared Values

VERN DOSCH
WITH WALLY GOULET
AND TRACY FINNEMAN

**M MILNER &
ASSOCIATES INC**
· EDITING · PUBLISHING · COMMUNICATIONS · CONSULTING ·

Library and Archives Canada Cataloguing in Publication Data

Dosch, Vern, 1953-, author
    Wired differently : how to spark better results with a
cooperative business model, servant leadership and shared values
/ Vern Dosch with Wally Goulet and Tracy Finneman.

Includes index.
Issued in print and electronic formats.
ISBN 978-0-9938557-9-5 (bound).—ISBN 978-0-9939990-0-0 (pbk.).
—ISBN 978-0-9939990-1-7 (epub)

    1. Servant leadership. 2. Cooperation. 3. Organizational
effectiveness. I. Goulet, Wally, 1948-, author II. Finneman, Tracy
, 1963-, author III. Title.

HM1261.D68 2015   658.4'092   C2014-908436-6
                                          C2014-908437-4

Production Credits
Editor: Karen Milner
Copy editing and proofreading: Lindsay Humphreys
Interior design and typesetting: Adrian So
Cover design: Adrian So — adriansodesign.com
Cover photo: Igor Ovchynnikov/Thinkstock
Printer: Dickinson Press Inc.

Published by Milner & Associates Inc.
www.milnerassociates.ca

Printed in the United States
10 9 8 7 6 5 4 3 2 1

Contents

Contents

Foreword

If you believe *Wired Differently* is just a book about the history of National Information Solutions Cooperative (NISC), you will miss its essence. This book does tell the story of an amazing group of people and their dream to create a very special cooperative family; however, it goes well beyond the company history. As you read the book, I ask you to open your heart and mind to a fundamentally different way of thinking about business. If you do, you will realize the power of what can happen when people who love life and their communities come together to create a servant leader enterprise.

In 1998 Steve Collier, an engineering and technology visionary, asked me to help him on a special project that he had been asked to do for Central Area Data Processing (CADP). CADP was based in St. Louis, Missouri, and it was one of three regional IT cooperatives serving rural electric and telecommunications cooperatives in the United States. Its board of directors wanted Steve to help them assess their strategy, and Steve wanted me to join him on that project. This was the beginning of my sixteen-year relationship with what has become NISC.

When we completed our strategic analysis of CADP's customers, industry and competitors, we concluded that CADP had to embrace a major strategic pivot if it was going to survive. We did not believe that the three regional data processing cooperatives, which had actually begun to compete with each other over time, had the scale and financial strength to make it independently in a rapidly changing market. Large publicly traded software firms were attempting to get rural electric cooperatives to switch software vendors. For these reasons, we advised CADP to consolidate with one or both of its regional cooperative competitors.

When we shared our analysis and recommendation with CADP, we weren't sure how CEO Gary Hobson, the senior leadership or the board of directors would respond. This wasn't the first time I had told a client their business model was broken, but it ended up being the first and, to this day, only time the client was more concerned about their customers than their own jobs. Their number one concern was about what would happen to CADP's cooperative customers if the only software they could buy was from large for-profit firms. That says a lot about the core values of a cooperative right there.

I did not know Vern Dosch or his team at North Central Data Cooperative (NCDC) when we recommended that CADP reach out to them. All I knew was that NCDC was a well-respected cooperative, and, quite frankly, that was all I needed to know. By that time, I had become a believer in the special human magic that is at the heart of all great cooperatives. CADP did reach out to NCDC, and eventually the two merged to become one cooperative: NISC. Today, I am honored to call Vern and the NISC team dear friends.

This book will move you. It tells a humbling, inspiring and wonderful story of what can happen when people strive to live a life of meaning and service to others. It will show you the power of putting organizational values into action, and perhaps it will even wake up corporate America to the cooperative model and a whole new way of doing business.

I was born in California, but I've been a Texan since 1989. Texas is a big state, and one that is largely rural. As such, we have more rural electric cooperatives than any other state in the nation. We have a saying in Texas that speaks volumes about why NISC is such a special organization: "Your actions are making so much noise that I can't hear what you are saying." NISC employees consistently act in a manner aligned with the organization's proclaimed shared values. In fact, their reputation for living these shared values precedes any conversation you might have with them. NISC exists because the people of CADP and NCDC believed that their customers were more important than their jobs, and NISC is thriving today because its actions have turned the concept of the servant leader and cooperative shared values into reality.

I live and work in Austin, Texas, and have been blessed to consult with clients in thirty countries around the world. They range from a client that generates more than $1 billion in revenue a day to governments that are trying to change the direction of their economies to entrepreneurs who are trying to turn their dreams into viable business-es. I have never, ever, seen a more amazing group of people than those who I have met at NISC. The people of NISC are in a different league. NISC is not a company—it is a community; it is a movement. It's a co-operative. Simply put, working with the people of NISC has been one of the greatest blessings that God has given me in my life.

When you finish reading this book, you will have a deeper ap-preciation for the power of the cooperative way of doing things and a greater understanding of the meaning of being a servant leader. It is my hope that the message of this book will spread beyond the cooperative world and influence corporations of all types.

John N. Doggett
McCombs School of Business
The University of Texas at Austin
November 2, 2014

Preface

I work at a special place. National Information Solutions Cooperative (NISC) has been my home for most of my thirty-nine-year career, and it is an honor and a privilege to serve as Chief Executive Officer for the company's one thousand employees and nearly seven hundred member systems.

In the earlier part of my career, I was like everyone else holding down a job and "working for the man." Now I shudder to use those words, especially when I think of the millions of men and women who have this same mindset, because I know now that there is another path—a rewarding journey where your individual contributions are recognized because they really matter.

The two technology cooperatives that consolidated in 2000 to form NISC were founded in the 1960s. Now nearly fifty years old, NISC has evolved from being just a place to earn a paycheck to being a collaborative organization that strives to truly make a difference in the lives of our employees and our member/customers.

For my part, I've been blessed with a remarkable, challenging career and exceptional mentors who have pushed me harder and farther than I imagined possible. These mentors presented to me a powerful case for the cooperative business model and the role it can, and should, play in our free-enterprise economy. They nudged me, not so gently at times, to consider the importance of commonly shared values that everyone within the organization can understand, interpret and act upon. And they have helped to build a culture of collaboration at NISC that breathes life into the work we do, the products we develop and the people we serve.

As a company, NISC has traveled far, and not so far, from its early roots when it was formed as a cooperative to meet the technology needs of end users in rural America. Far in the sense that today we serve millions of people across forty-nine states and across Canada, and we store billions of bits of information in a place you can't see called the *cloud*. Not so far in that we still honor the intrinsic value of each individual and we always strive to do the right thing, as we always have done.

Preserving our cultural development and the critical elements that led us to it is one of the prime motivations for this book. *Wired Differently* is an apt name. We've come to expect more of ourselves and our organization over the decades. There are tangible reasons why so many of our employees choose to grow their careers at NISC rather than consider us merely as a stop along their journey.

To the best of our ability, through story and example, *Wired Differently* offers NISC as a business, cultural and leadership model for your consideration. Let me be clear: I do not believe cooperatives are the only way, nor in every circumstance are they the best way. Not one penny of any NISC employee's retirement funds is invested in a cooperative. That is to say, we are betting our retirement on the success of our free-market economy and the corporate business model. At the same time, cooperatives are a different way, and I've spent my adult life learning about their place in society and the value they add.

Take what you read in the pages that follow and tweak it so it works for you; modify our best practices so that they deliver even better results in your organization. My hope is that by reading this book, your knowledge of cooperatives grows; your respect for servant leadership expands; and your desire to create a collaborative culture for employees that encourages them to live out their values is sparked. Because then you, too, will be wired differently.

Take good care,

Vern Dosch, CEO
National Information Solutions Cooperative

For more information about NISC, visit www.nisc.coop.

PART I

LEADERSHIP THROUGH SERVICE

Leadership through service has a powerful impact on your organization's culture and the level of collaboration that individuals working in that culture realize. The person who leads through service recognizes that leadership is a choice, not a position. Indeed, servant leadership is a philosophy and set of practices that enriches the lives of individuals, builds better organizations and, ultimately, creates a more just and caring world. At NISC, we've found there to be specific, learned traits that help ensure employees have a mindset to serve first and lead second. By hiring, training and nurturing these traits at all levels in the organization, servant leadership becomes the desired result and the natural outcome.

Chapter 1

Not Your Everyday Merger

To give real service you must add something which cannot be bought or measured with money, and that is sincerity and integrity.
— Douglas Adams

There are few examples that better contrast the cooperative business model with the investor-owned corporation than the true story of an attempted take-over where money is no object and, ultimately, not the governing value.

It was a crisp October day in 2006 when our team of five executives from National Information Solutions Cooperative (NISC) sat in the boardroom of our corporate suitor. A take-over was in the making for the nearly fifty-year-old software cooperative we represented.

The gathering that day was the culmination of three other meetings we'd had with the mergers and acquisitions team, whose due diligence had led them to the belief that NISC was possibly the best intellectual property gem of its kind. They had been looking far and wide for a software company like NISC, and in their considered opinion, NISC would fit in nicely with their portfolio of companies.

Our suitor's chief executive officer cut to the chase: "Today we are here to consummate a business deal with NISC. I have a checkbook in my hand, Vern," he said as he looked at me, "and I am asking you to fill in the amount it will take to buy NISC and make it a very integral part of our corporation."

Talk about an icebreaker!

As a cooperative, NISC was not my company to sell. Those of us from NISC's executive team were only acting as fiduciaries whose responsibility it was to gather the specifics of the offer and deliver them to our board and then to the membership as a whole. It was our duty to entertain the proposed acquisition, but, paradoxically, no member of our management team had any financial stake in the outcome. We wouldn't profit from the company being sold, as none of us held any stock or stock options. The profit would return to the cooperative's members, who also own the cooperative.

As it was not my blank check to sign, I told the CEO and his team, "On behalf of NISC, we are humbled by your remarkable offer. Our board policies require a three-quarters supermajority approval from the board members in order for them to recommend the sale of NISC to the membership. We will then need the separate approvals of both our board and the membership before NISC can be sold. We will convene a meeting with our board as soon as we can."

In the weeks that followed, we confirmed that, should the acquisition go through, NISC would have all of its debt retired with the purchase. In addition, all of the capital credits (profit) would be paid to our members, and members would receive guaranteed, price-capped service contracts for up to ten years. We also confirmed that our employees would receive continued employment assurances for a minimum of three years.

A sale price from $500 million to upwards of $1 billion was discussed. It was without question a good financial deal for all at NISC and a well-thought-out one with respect to its structure and terms. Most companies would jump at such an attractive offer. But in this case, a number was never filled in on the waiting check and NISC was never sold. The value that our directors and members put on their software cooperative went beyond money and profit. They placed greater importance on service and relationships than on dividend payments or return on investment.

Three Powerful Attributes

To turn down a blank check like that you'd have to be more than unconventional, you'd need to be wired differently, so to speak. The painstaking decision that the NISC board members made hinged on three of the most powerful attributes of the cooperative business model:

1. **Cooperatives encourage long-term strategies rather than short-term gain.** Members of NISC have the opportunity to become highly engaged with the organization, and full engagement takes time. They can serve on the board of directors; they participate in management advisory committees; and they regularly provide input and feedback on how NISC can develop leading-edge software to meet their needs. For example, we currently have over one hundred members involved in a dozen different management advisory committees. Member/owners are more than customers. They are our partners in product and service delivery, and their active inclusion in that process requires a long-term view.

2. **Cooperatives promote a culture that serves others first.** In the cooperative model, it's in the best interest of NISC employees to serve their customers well because customers are also the ones who own the company. This means that employees from NISC and employees from our members' organizations get to know one another well (many even become lifelong friends) and they communicate frequently about what is and isn't working. Collaboration is key to our success, and relationships span years.

3. **Cooperatives support a mindset to seek the greater good for many rather than for just a few.** If NISC had been sold, the cooperative business model would have ended and the mission of the organization would have shifted from serving member/owners to increasing wealth for shareholders. Instead of seeking every possible innovation to hold costs down for people we know and work with regularly, we would

We want to make a difference in the lives of each other and in the lives of our members.

be focusing on innovation for the sake of increased profits and selling our products and services to a wider global audience. A subtle change on the surface, the fundamental shift for employees and our customer/members would be substantial. It would strike at the very heart of why we do what we do: we want to make a difference in the lives of each other and in the lives of our members.

Those who founded NISC in the 1960s set out to fill an industry need at an affordable price. Over the decades we've discovered, sometimes intentionally and other times by accident, that the power of leadership through service, the importance of putting values in action, and the foundational strength of operating as a cooperative combine to deliver a collaborative culture in practice.

COOPERATIVE PRINCIPLES

↓

LEADERSHIP THROUGH SERVICE

↓

VALUES IN ACTION

↓

COLLABORATIVE CULTURE IN PRACTICE

Wired Differently seeks to present a compelling business case for these elements because at NISC we have seen how effective they are at drawing out the best in people, empowering them to consistently deliver positive bottom-line results. In reading this book you will be taken inside a software company where one out of every ten employees has chosen to stay and contribute for more than two decades, and the average tenure of our one thousand employees exceeds ten years. In this book we offer you our insights, our errors and the story of the successful evolution of our organization into the well-respected community partner and industry leader that NISC is today.

A Bit of Background

Two regional technology cooperatives were formed in 1967 and 1968 respectively: one in Missouri and the other in North Dakota. They consolidated in 2000 to become National Information Solutions Cooperative (NISC). (More on this merger and the two cooperatives that formed NISC in chapter 8.) As of January 1, 2015, NISC has just over one thousand employees with four locations in the Midwest: Cedar Rapids,

Iowa; Lake St. Louis, Missouri; Mandan, North Dakota; and Shawano, Wisconsin.

The company is a leading provider of information technology products and services in forty-nine U.S. states as well as in Canada, American Samoa and Palau. We offer billing, accounting, engineering, e-commerce and infrastructure products, including 24-hour support, and we provide consulting to utilities and telecommunications companies. We also serve other infrastructure industries, and our clients include businesses from Fortune 100 and Fortune 500 lists. In a nutshell, NISC's products and services make it easier and more cost effective for our customers to do business with their own customers.

The NISC community comprises members, associate members, customers, partners and employees. Together, we collaborate to provide enterprise business solutions that continue to set the industry standard. Our successes include the following:

- *Computerworld* magazine has recognized NISC as one of the Top 100 "Best Places to Work" in the IT industry for the past eleven years.
- The greatest business growth in NISC's history occurred during 2007–2013—when the rest of the national economy was experiencing a collective downturn.
- HDI (formerly known as Help Desk Institute) named NISC to its 2014 "Elite 50" list, which recognizes businesses worldwide for their outstanding technical service and support.

The Art of Hyperseeing

I distinctly remember taking a family vacation to Mount Rushmore as a ten-year-old. My four siblings, mother, father and I piled into a 1959 Plymouth sedan headed for South Dakota.

Before I go on, let me just quickly note that the five-hour trip from Bismarck, North Dakota, didn't include air conditioning, computer tablets with digital video, iPods or an annoying voice from a constantly recalculating GPS. Rather, the five of us in the back alternated between sleeping on the floor, sitting in our designated seats and bickering, all of which was never encumbered by seatbelts. We survived nicely, thank you.

The "faces" first appeared at nearly thirty miles away. They seemed rather small and disappointingly insignificant from that perspective. But as we pulled into the parking lot and walked the winding path to the observation deck, each of us became increasingly quiet. I remember standing there, staring, mouth open, not sure if I was even breathing. An elderly lady next to me said, "Young man, you could stand in Lincoln's eye."

Stand in Lincoln's eye? My 5'11" frame shook in amazement. How had Mount Rushmore's creator, Gutzon Borglum, envisioned President Lincoln in the original granite expanse?

There's a term that sculptors use to describe an artist's ability to look at a rough piece of stone and see it in its finished, perfected form. They call this "hyperseeing." As leaders, managers and coaches, it's our job to *hypersee* for the organization. We need to look beyond the surface and see what lies inside then diligently work to bring it out.

At NISC, the combination of a cooperative business model with leadership through service and values in action is the right foundation on which to put a collaborative culture into practice. These combined elements give our leaders the tools they need to hypersee the potential of their teams and provide the appropriate coaching, direction and role modeling needed to move the team along a path of success.

Time and again we have seen the value of this foundation demonstrated at NISC, but these elements have the potential to be effective in any environment. Placing others' needs first—servant leadership—can reap benefits in a family setting as well as around the boardroom table. Putting your values into action on a daily basis more clearly aligns who you are with what you do and why it matters to you, whether it be as an individual or as an organizational leader. And when you live and work collaboratively, your circle of influence grows and positive results follow.

In the pages that follow, you will read about how these principles are put into practice at NISC and what the results are. You will be made privy to several of our lessons learned (both good and not so good). In chapter 11, for example, we share a series of best practices that we've tweaked over time to help ensure that every single person in our organization feels connected to our mission and knows how to deliver on it, daily. You will discover in chapter 12 that NISC has achieved positive business results in traditional areas such as gross margin, cash balance and equity. And you will learn that of equal importance to us are the results associated with employee satisfaction and member (or customer) retention.

This doesn't mean, however, that our focus on values diminishes the imperative to meet and exceed financial goals. Businesses of any kind can agree on the importance of the numbers, and NISC is no different. But it is how we get to those numbers that's different, as well as how we accomplish short-term goals and determine measures of success—how we hypersee what our success can look like in the future. Our focus is on the next fifty years of service to our members and to the rural electric and telecommunications industries we serve.

KEY POINTS TO CONSIDER IN THIS CHAPTER

1. When the acquisition proposal was offered to the management team at NISC, it was our duty to entertain it, but, paradoxically, none of us had any financial stake in the outcome. **We wouldn't profit from the proposed sale because none of us held any stock or stock options** in the cooperative. The profit would return to the members, who also own the cooperative.

2. In the cooperative model, it's in the best interest of NISC employees to **serve their customers well because customers are also the ones who own the company.**

3. As leaders, managers and coaches, it's our job to "hypersee" for our organization. **We need to look beyond the surface to what lies inside and then diligently work to bring it out.**

4. At NISC, **the combination of a cooperative business model, servant leadership and shared values is the right foundation on which to build a collaborative culture.**

Chapter 2

A Different Model for Business and Leadership Today

Alone we can do so little; together we can do so much.
— Helen Keller

Wally Goulet, general counsel of NISC, tells the story of working with T-Mobile when the company was signing up for NISC's utility bill payment services. The senior corporate counsel of T-Mobile USA, Inc. told Wally and Tracy Porter, NISC's chief financial officer, that he had been in numerous contract negotiations over the years and, in his experience, the contract process they had just completed was the best he had ever been through.

Wally chided him that such an assessment might not be a compliment to a fellow attorney, as it implied that NISC may have been too easy on T-Mobile in the negotiations. "No," T-Mobile's counsel replied. "You were firm where you needed to be firm, and you weren't lacking in any area of how NISC was represented. That is not what I am saying. The explanations given by your team and the respect and fairness they showed during the contract process were exceptional."

Understanding then that the corporate counsel's response was indeed a compliment, Wally responded, "I think I can explain what you experienced. You were just introduced to our collaborative culture and the cooperative way of doing business. On a daily basis we serve our owner/members. And," he went on to explain, "if every day you are serving and dealing with your owner, you aren't going to come up with extra 'gotcha' or penalty clauses in a contract. You will see us practicing the Golden Rule and treating our owners just the way *we* want to be treated, with no hidden agendas or unreasonable transfers of liabilities. So yes, you better believe we are going to offer all the respect and courtesy we can to our owners."

This wasn't the first time a member or customer commented on our unique way of doing things and how it impressed them. And, as we continue using the cooperative business model, it's certain not to be the last time.

What Is a Cooperative?

What does it mean for NISC to be a cooperative? First of all, it means that NISC is member- or customer-owned rather than investor/stockholder-owned. If you have ever owned a condominium or home that is part of an owner's association, you have the basic idea of how a cooperative works. As a member of the homeowner's association, you pay fees to take care of services that all of the members mutually enjoy or need, such as lawn care, security or the upkeep of a recreation room or outdoor party area. You have a form of shared ownership in the larger association and, therefore, a vested interest in making sure the mutually beneficial services are provided at a reasonable cost. Members of your association are democratically elected to serve on a governing board that sets the policies and fees for the use and maintenance of the shared services.

This model contrasts with an investor-owned apartment complex, where the property owner (or owners) alone determines the rent and all the policies and fees for using common areas and shared services. The owner doesn't necessarily live on the property, and he or she sets the price for all shared services based on what the market will bear rather than on input from other member/owners. Sometimes the relationship between the property owner and renter is favorable, other times it is not. Most times, the relationship isn't important to either party.

So for the sake of comparison, the products and services provided by NISC are similar to the lawn care, security and facility upkeep for the homeowner's association we just discussed. And similar to members of a homeowner's association, at NISC we have member/

owners. These include rural electric and telephone cooperatives, independently owned commercial communications companies and a good number of public power companies, which are described as public power districts, public utility districts and municipally owned power companies. These organizations, many of whom are cooperatives with their own members, provide electric distribution or telecommunications services to their customers. They are also the owners of NISC, and a number of their CEOs and directors are elected to NISC's governing board of directors.

According to the 2009 project *Research on the Economic Impact of Cooperatives* from the University of Wisconsin Center for Cooperatives, Americans hold 350 million memberships in four broad types of cooperatives:

1. **Consumer** – for people who buy goods and services (e.g., credit unions, REI)

2. **Producer** – farmers and others who join together to market their products (e.g., Organic Valley, Land O'Lakes)

3. **Purchasing** – small businesses who pool their resources to be competitive with larger chains (e.g., Ace Hardware stores, Best Western hotels)

4. **Worker** – owned and democratically governed by employees (e.g., Equal Exchange, Rainbow Grocery)

For NISC's part, we are a *consumer* cooperative with four locations in the United States. In 2014, we held $78.5 million in assets and generated nearly $165 million in revenue and $79 million in wages and benefits.

The original seven principles on which every type of cooperative is founded are known as the Rochdale Principles, which were established by the Rochdale Society of Equitable Pioneers in Rochdale, England, in 1844. The principles provide a framework for how cooperatives put their values into practice in seven areas:

- Voluntary and open membership
- Democratic member control
- Member economic participation
- Autonomy and independence

- Education, training and information
- Cooperation among cooperatives
- Concern for community

According to the International Co-operative Alliance, cooperatives are based on the values of self-help, self-responsibility, democracy, equality, equity and solidarity. In the tradition of their founders, cooperative members believe in the ethical values of honesty, openness, social responsibility and caring for others.

In 2009, when the aforementioned *Research on the Economic Impact of Cooperatives* study was conducted, researchers identified nearly 30,000 cooperatives operating at 73,000 locations throughout the United States. These cooperatives owned more than $3 trillion in assets and generated over $500 billion in revenue and $25 billion in wages.

Credit unions fall into the cooperative category and, according to the International Co-operative Alliance, well over 7,500 credit unions provide financial services to one hundred million U.S. consumers. Additionally, insurance companies owned by or closely affiliated with co-ops serve about 233 million people in the United States and more than 50,000 families in the United States use cooperative day-care centers, giving co-ops a crucial role in the care of our children. Cooperatives provide more than one hundred million jobs globally, and over one billion people belong to cooperatives.

Cooperatives Are a Unique Kind of Business

Generally speaking, the cooperative business model is designed to produce goods and services at the lowest possible cost and provide these goods and services to members at a price only slightly over the cost of production, thus making it affordable for the members' advantage. A cooperative model then, stands in contrast to the corporate model, in which the main objective is to increase shareholder wealth or make a profit.

The sale of electricity can be used as a good example of this philosophical difference. Many cooperatives provide off-peak discounts for electricity use during low-demand times, like early in the morning, later at night or on weekends when there is less industrial and commercial use. As household appliances such as clothes dryers, water heaters, dishwashers and car rechargers can all be run more economically at off-peak rates, cooperatives encourage people to shift their usage to those off-peak times. At NISC, we've developed a software technology, known as SmartHub, which allows end users to track their electricity usage in a near real-time environment so that they can shift to off-peak times when the lower rates are available, allowing them to better manage their electric bills. Investor-owned utility companies are interested primarily in selling kilowatts (in other words, making a profit), so you're not likely to see an investor-owned utility promoting conservation, off-peak rates or usage-monitoring technology like a cooperative does.

Another valuable function that cooperatives serve can be illustrated using the example of farmers, who regularly form cooperatives to sell their produce—everything from fruits and grains to dairy products or even sugar beets. Well-known examples of producer cooperatives include American Crystal for sugar, Land O'Lakes for dairy products, Blue Diamond for almonds, Sunkist for oranges, Ocean Spray for cranberries and Sun-Maid for raisins. These cooperative efforts give the individual producers more bargaining power, increased brand/product awareness and greater sustainability in the commodity market through shared marketing and value-added processing.

In general, cooperatives provide products and services that might otherwise be absent from a particular marketplace because the product or service doesn't provide a sufficient return on investment to generate a sustainable profit. This opens the door to a shared-cost model for business. The phrase "necessity is the mother of invention" is truly appropriate when it comes to describing cooperatives.

In the case of NISC, the cooperative was formed to provide technically innovative products and services to meet member/customers' needs in the areas of accounting, billing, engineering, e-commerce and cloud computing at the most economical prices. All of these products and services are basically administrative and their subsequent costs are passed on to the end consumer. By providing these services at the cost of production, our electric and telecommunications members are able to deliver energy and telecom services at a lower cost to the end consumer.

After the cost of production is covered, any excess earnings (referred to variously in a cooperative as margins, patronage or capital credits) are given back to members based on their usage of the products and services. Said another way, margins are distributed among members according to their economic participation rather than according to the value of their capital shareholdings, as is done in the case of stock-holders in an investor-owned company.

Let me explain this concept further by providing you with an example. I live in an area, not far from the nearest city, that is served by a rural electric cooperative. It is Capital Electric that makes it possible for the lights to come on in my home when I flip the bathroom switch in the morning. Capital Electric is also an NISC member and currently uses several of our products and services.

Because NISC provides services to Capital Electric at cost, the rate I pay for my electricity is slightly less than what homeowners in the nearby city pay for their electricity, which is provided by a utility company. Of course, the reduced cost that I and other members pay for electricity can't be attributed only to the cost savings that NISC passes on to Capital Electric, but we certainly contribute. And it goes one step further: In June 2014, Capital Electric held its annual meeting for members, like me, who receive service and own the co-op. According to our electricity usage, we each received a capital credit (or dividend) check following that meeting.

In the investor-owned model, the stockholder isn't required to buy or even use the product that the company they've invested in produces. As a stockholder, you can drive a Chevrolet while owning shares in Ford, Chrysler or Toyota. You never have to consume one latte at Starbucks, but you can own ten thousand shares.

In a cooperative enterprise, ownership, control and beneficiary are vested directly in the hands of the user/customer. Cooperative members own the company. They elect a representative group from their midst to serve as their board of

Cooperative members own the company.

directors, and they receive the direct benefits (patronage, goods and services) as a result of the cooperative's formation. The benefits could be anything from receiving electricity at reasonable prices to realizing cost savings through joint marketing efforts, as is the case with Florida orange growers who are co-op members.

A corporation will often purposely separate duties and relationships between the employee, the customer and the stockholder out of concern over a conflict of interest or inappropriateness. For example, a corporate employee wouldn't typically ask a customer or shareholder to help him or her with a product concept unless the customer was being paid as a consultant. But in the case of cooperative customers, they are also the owners, so their guidance and input are key to the cooperative's success.

Compared with corporations, cooperatives are arguably a more democratic form of organization, allowing one vote per member. This doesn't change no matter how much business a member does with the organization or how much equity he or she holds. In the corporate scenario, voting power is based on one vote for every share owned, so it's possible that a handful of shareholders with a majority of stock could rule a corporation.

In their book *Seven Pillars of Servant Leadership*, James Sipe and Don M. Frick provide an intriguing description of collaboration in business, which has great similarities to the cooperative business model:

> *Collaboration is a mutually beneficial relationship between two or more parties who work toward common goals by sharing responsibility, authority, and accountability for achieving results. Collaboration is more than simply sharing knowledge and information (communication) and more than a relationship that helps each party achieve its own goals (cooperation and coordination). The purpose of collaboration is to create a shared vision and joint strategies to address concerns that go beyond the purview of any particular party.*

Sipe and Frick identify nine attributes of a collaborative culture:

- Trust and respect in everyday situations
- Egalitarian attitudes among members at all ranks
- Power based on expertise and accountability
- Shared leadership where all members take initiative
- Commitment to the success of other members, rather than just one's own success
- Valuing of truth and truth telling
- Commitment to continuous improvement of the whole organization
- Active learning
- Personal responsibility

These attributes could just as well describe how a cooperative does business because they strike at the heart of the relationship between the organization and its customers. The relationship between NISC and our members is one of partnership rather than simply vendor and customer. In a vendor relationship the product is delivered "as is" and the customer has little or no input on the features or functionality of the product. They can take it or leave it. Whereas in a cooperative like NISC, our partnership with our member/owners means that they are actively involved in establishing product priorities and they have a predominate voice in determining where our research and development dollars will be directed. Our member/owners' fingerprints are all over our products.

The magic occurs when you combine the technical expertise of NISC employees with the practical subject matter expertise of the ultimate user of these products. The cooperative business model fosters that kind of collaboration, and it is one of the most important intangible factors in NISC's success. Collaboration between the customer and the company may be the subtle difference that is often overlooked when trying to understand the uniqueness of cooperatives.

Ed Wolff is a member of NISC's vice presidents group and came to us from a Fortune 500 company. Here's what he has to say about his experience working for a corporation and then a cooperative:

I grew up on a farm in a rural community supported by six rural cooperatives, with my father serving as a board member on one of them. By the time I started my undergraduate studies, I had a good idea of what cooperatives were and why they existed.

After graduation I took a job working for a publicly held company. It was a well-run, well-respected organization. About three years later, I considered moving to NISC. That idea was not well received by some of the management at my (then) current employer. While they were professional and encouraging, there were a few who thought this "conservative" (me) had lost his mind.

They argued I would be entering a socialist environment with little or no market pressure to innovate or build on efficiencies. They said there was no competition, and they provided a number of other warnings about going to "the other side."

At the time of the move, I didn't dwell a great deal on the difference between the two organizations, but it didn't take long working at NISC to realize that there was a significant difference.

At NISC our customers are of more importance to us than reaping financial profit, whereas in the three years I worked for the publicly traded company, I didn't hear about customer satisfaction a single time; I never heard the phrase "do the right thing, always"; and I didn't see many efforts to build partnerships. What was important at the corporation, was that my colleagues and I understood stock prices and the impact they had on our quarterly decisions; that we clearly understood the financials; and that we were clear on how our personal contributions impacted the company's overall financial performance. While the corporate experience provided me with a valuable perspective, one I use each and every day in my career, I came to quickly realize at NISC that there are other things worthy of importance.

At NISC we say there is no mission without a margin. We know we need to be fiscally responsible and be good stewards of our members' resources. We know we can't serve in a world-class way if we can't pay the bills. However, we also know we are in business to serve others and that we have a responsibility to our members and our community. I learned early in life that being responsible is motivating, and I feel responsible for more than just a bottom line at NISC. I am convinced I made the right move. It's one I made over twenty years ago, and I hope to be at NISC for many more years.

I've always found our desire to partner with our members to be refreshing and invigorating. I recall an occasion when we hired an employee who had worked for another tech company. After he was through the mentorship program and on the phones, he was amazed to discover that our member/owners actually liked working with us. He immediately recognized the spirit of cooperation and partnership. While I had been immersed in the environment for some time, it was uplifting to see the reaction of someone who wasn't used to that environment.

Despite the warnings from my colleagues at my former employer, I learned quickly that NISC is, indeed, in a very competitive environment. We win and lose business based on our products, services, price, reputation and relationships, just like any other business. When I'm on the phone or in front of a member/owner, I am not only working with a client, I am working for and with an owner. Talk about pressure!

I mean that in a positive way, because it is motivating to have that kind of responsibility. In our environment you are single-handedly representing the good work of a thousand employees. There is a lot of built-in accountability in the cooperative business model. In retrospect, there are bigger differences than I anticipated when I moved to a career at a cooperative, but all are reasons I continue to work here today.

Service . . . and then Some

One of the best-known cooperatives in the United States is Recreational Equipment, Inc. (REI), the outdoor adventure company. Here is an excerpt from the "About Us" section of REI's web site at www.rei.com:

What began as a group of 23 mountain climbing buddies is now the nation's largest consumer cooperative. Our passion for outdoor adventure is clear, whether you visit any of our stores across the country, phone us or interact with us online.

By staying true to our roots, we've earned a place on Fortune magazine's list of the "100 Best Companies to Work For" every year since the rankings began in 1998. We work hard to earn our reputation for quality and integrity every day. Our core purpose guides everything we do: we all work to inspire, educate and outfit for a lifetime of outdoor adventure and stewardship.

What does it mean to be a member of the country's largest consumer cooperative? In straight numbers, it means you pay a one-time fee of $20 to join REI, and you enjoy a discount of, on average, 10 percent on eligible purchases. It means an annual refund much like the margin, patronage or capital credits mentioned earlier, and members can sign up for a credit card and get 5 percent back on purchases made at REI and 1 percent back everywhere else you use the card. In addition to these benefits, as a member of the co-op, you elect your REI Board of Directors each year. But the very best benefit is the level of service the REI members receive. Let me explain.

My family and I have the good fortune of living along the Missouri River. Like many others who live near water, we feel drawn to spending time on it, and we especially enjoy kayaking. In fact, my favorite way to start my day in the summer is to jump in the kayak at dawn, make my way slightly downstream and across the river, drop off my kayak and get on my waiting bike. After cycling the remainder of the five-mile trek to the office, I take a quick shower and feel completely energized for the day.

Several years ago, I stopped in to the REI store outside of Minneapolis, Minnesota. My family and I have been REI members for quite a while, and I was in the market for a new kayak. In fact, I intended to leave the store with a kayak on the roof of my vehicle. We have several great outdoors and sporting goods stores in the Upper Midwest, and I'd already visited a few of them as I was gathering intelligence on the make, model and size kayak I wanted. But I had an additional reason for going to REI: I wanted to compare the level of service I received from its staff with the level of service we provide at NISC. As a firm believer in the cooperative business model, I have high expectations of our NISC staff and of myself. I was hopeful of finding the same to be true at REI. Robert, the sales associate who assisted me, didn't disappoint.

I made my way to the kayak section of the store and was greeted warmly by a twentysomething young man who looked like he'd been out on the water that morning. He had a firm handshake when he introduced himself, and he easily and professionally inquired about my interests in a kayak. Within a few minutes, we were looking at different models and Robert had confirmed information I'd already learned as well as provided me with new insights that I appreciated.

One of the great things about REI is that they want their associates to be more than simply a retail clerk, the likes of which you find in many big-box stores; REI asks associates to think of themselves as subject matter experts. Robert was an avid kayaker who knew the products from personal experience, as REI associates are encouraged to take store equipment on weekends and use it, thus becoming familiar with the products and therefore able to be much more effective in serving their less-experienced customer/members and able to engage at a higher level with more knowledgeable enthusiasts.

Robert spent no less than an hour with me, and I left the store with a kayak I couldn't wait to get in the water. The only downside was the six-hour drive I had ahead of me.

It wasn't until I got home that I discovered a glaring error. In my excitement over the new kayak and great experience working with Robert, I realized a small but very important detail we had overlooked. The fourteen-foot kayak was six inches too short for my body, making it impossible for my long legs to operate the rudder.

I called the REI store to tell Robert what had happened and ask if I could ship the kayak back to the store and possibly get the right-sized kayak shipped out once they had my kayak in hand. Robert wasn't working when I called, so I was transferred to the store manager, Tom. I explained my situation to Tom and let him know how much I appreciated Robert's help in making my purchase, albeit the wrong one. I suggested my solution as Tom listened patiently, although he would have none of it. He said that he would ship out the right kayak that very day and that I could just drop off the other kayak the next time I was in the area.

I remember responding, "Tom, do you realize I'm six hours away from your store, and I might not get back your way for several months?" He didn't miss a beat.

"I'm not worried about you getting the kayak back to me," was his response. "You're a member, and I trust you. What concerns me is that you get the kayak you wanted in the first place and can get out on the water!"

Within two days, I had the right-sized kayak, and it performed exactly as I hoped it would on the water. Considering the great customer/ member service experience that REI had provided, I decided to also keep and pay for the original kayak for my wife. I ended up spending twice as much as I intended; however, the extraordinary service made this a positive experience for my family and for REI.

There is a valuable lesson about customer service in this experience with REI. The level of service that the REI associates provide is directly related to each employee's understanding of their connectedness to the members they represent as a cooperative organization. I'm not saying that every cooperative operates with the same high level of customer service, but in my experience, it's far more common in cooperative-based settings than in consumer-based settings.

In chapter 7, I tell the story of two NISC employees who packed over $100,000 worth of equipment in their vehicle and traveled eight hours one way to help a member cooperative get back online serving their customers after a freak rainfall left the basement of their office flooded and four feet of water on the main floor. Our two employees had no prior authority and every responsibility to walk out the door and do exactly what they did. Their story is one we use at NISC as a model of how we want our employees to care for our member/customers. I feel proud to say that we strive to have the highest customer service standards, just as REI does.

Without hesitation I would tell you that you can ask any of our one thousand NISC employees what our guiding principle is when making decisions, and you will hear these words or something close to them nearly 100 percent of the time: *Do the right thing, always.* When we have a member or customer who is in a bad place, our first priority is to provide solutions and worry about the financial details later. For instance, there have been times in the past when, to help out a member in peril, we advanced hundreds of thousands of dollars in equipment and services without so much as a purchase order.

Critics of this approach ask the question: What about the people who may take advantage of the situation? It's a fair question, but in NISC's nearly fifty-year history I don't believe there has been a single instance in which our members or customers were unreasonable or took advantage of the organization in these situations. We have always been kept whole. But in any case, NISC employees would much rather have a reputation of always doing the right thing and looking after our members when time is of the essence, rather than being more concerned about the business side of things.

NISC's Formation

In the early 1960s, the Rural Electrification Administration pitched the idea of regional IT processing centers that would serve the electric and telephone cooperatives across the nation who were struggling to efficiently and cost effectively bill their customers. The North Dakota association of sixteen rural electric cooperatives liked the idea and formed a separate division called Electronic Data Processing (EDP). After securing its first mainframe computer, EDP began hiring technical staff and developing a billing application.

In 1967, EDP was providing technical expertise for a start-up regional data cooperative in Missouri. That cooperative, Central Area Data Processing (CADP), had incorporated earlier that year. One year later, in 1968, the EDP division was spun off from the North Dakota Association of Rural Electric Cooperatives to become North Central Data Cooperative (NCDC) in North Dakota, also as a regional data cooperative.

The original business model for these data cooperatives was regional by necessity, due to expensive or nonexistent communication circuits at the time. The cooperatives needed to be in close proximity to their customers. But as time passed and technology advanced, close proximity was no longer necessary for data communication, and thus the regional business model was made obsolete. CADP and NCDC found themselves competing for the same member/customers.

In 2000, CADP and NCDC collectively served about four hundred members. The two cooperatives realized that if they banded together they could incorporate better functionality and the latest software technologies, which would effectively vault them into the next century. And so the two organizations merged to tackle a multimillion-dollar rewrite of their enterprise software platforms, which were outdated and needed advancement. This is how NISC was formed. (You will find more on this consolidation in chapter 8.)

National Information Solutions Cooperative has grown from what it was in the early 1960s, two regional cooperatives providing services for a few members, into the mature software company it is today, offering a full enterprise suite of products that serve more than seven hundred electric and telecommunications companies in forty-nine states as well as American Samoa, Palau and Canada. Also worth noting is that NISC has been in business for nearly fifty years without being acquired. Employees are proud to say that their organization came into existence before technology giants such as Microsoft, Oracle, Apple and CISCO were around. Our cooperative business model gives rise to different relationships with our end users as compared to an off-the-shelf vendor of software that is readily purchased from Staples, Best Buy, Walmart or Amazon.com.

Our products are dynamic, not static, in the sense that member/owners provide significant input on changes and product enhancements. Ours is a collaborative effort; our users are heavily engaged and they take a great deal of pride in ownership of NISC products.

The Cooperative Industry that NISC Serves

As the core of NISC's data and software business is with electric and telephone cooperatives and independent companies and municipalities across the country, NISC is an integral partner of those networks. From its formation, NISC began working closely with three national trade associations: the National Rural Electric Cooperative Association (NRECA), which was initially formed in 1942 to represent nine hundred electric cooperatives; the American Public Power Association (APPA), which serves about two thousand community-owned electric utilities; and the National Telecommunications Cooperative Association (NTCA), which represents over eight hundred telecommunications companies.

Taking a closer look at each, NRECA cooperatives cover 75 percent of the U.S. landmass, distributing power over 2.5 million miles of line; however, they serve only about 12 percent of the U.S. population. For APPA's part, it serves about forty-seven million people, which represents 14 percent of the nation's electric customers. Formed in 1954, NTCA's independent telephone systems serve more than 40 percent of the nation's landmass—and less than 5 percent of the nation's telecom subscribers. On average, NTCA member cooperatives serve about seven subscribers per square mile. By contrast, larger telecommunications companies, on average, serve 130 customers per square mile.

So, as you can see, cooperatives often serve just a few customers per rural mile, while investor-owned utilities and municipalities usually serve major cities with dozens and sometimes even hundreds of consumers per square mile. Generally speaking, cooperatives serve more rural customers, and investor-owned utilities and municipalities serve larger urban centers. Cooperatives got their start by electrifying rural America when other power companies wouldn't make the investment to bring electricity to the countryside. In his book *Power Plays*, Ted Case re-tells the moving story of a family returning home the first night their farmhouse was hooked up with electricity in 1939. The mother thought the house was on fire. "No, mama," her daughter said. "The lights are on." The family lived in the Texas Hill Country, an area served then and today by Pedernales Electric Cooperative.

Do What You Do Better than Anyone Else

Best-selling author Tom Peters notes in his book *In Search of Excellence* that successful companies always "stick to the knitting"; they do what they do better than anyone else in the industry.

To date, NISC has operated in the niche of rural and municipal electric and telephone systems, and we have avoided the temptation to move into areas where we don't have the subject matter expertise. You will find that this is the approach taken by most cooperatives. We generally have a clearly defined mission that we follow closely because providing products and services at the lowest possible cost to our intended customers is paramount to our success—venturing into unrelated areas is not.

> "Successful companies always stick to the knitting; they do what they do better than anyone else in the industry."
> – Tom Peters

I vividly remember when, in 2009, Google ventured into the electric industry with its PowerMeter, a product designed to provide extensive energy information to end consumers. At the urging of our members and after numerous discussions with Google representatives, NISC announced a channel partnership with Google to integrate their PowerMeter software into our own new iVUE® Meter Data Management System (MDMS) platform, which was also designed to provide extensive energy usage information.

Google executives attended our 2009 member information conference, where they presented Google's PowerMeter to over fifteen hundred NISC member/customers. After the utility general session, they greeted members and answered questions about the product. Within a month, over thirty-five utility members indicated they would be part of our Google/NISC initiative.

As we continued our partnership with Google, we enhanced our own MDMS platform. We worked closely with our members and sought their advice on how to develop and refine our product so that it offered the greatest benefit to members and their end users. Nearly fifteen months later, on January 12, 2011, we released version 1.4 of MDMS for our members. One of the many features of the new platform was an interface with Google PowerMeter.

David Bonnett, our vice president of Marketing, said this about the deployment at the time: "We have finished development on the system's basic features and have pilot tested it for more than a year. NISC MDMS is solid and ready for prime time. It is with confidence that we are starting commercial deployment at several locations around the nation."

Just six months after the launch of MDMS 1.4, Google's blog informed PowerMeter users of the following:

> We first launched Google PowerMeter as a Google.org project to raise awareness about the importance of giving people access to data surrounding their energy usage. Studies show that having simple access to such information helps consumers reduce their energy use by up to 15 percent; of course, even broader access to this information could help reduce energy use worldwide.
>
> We're pleased that PowerMeter has helped demonstrate the importance of this access and created something of a model. However, our efforts have not scaled as quickly as we would like, so we are retiring the service. PowerMeter users will have access to the tool until September 16, 2011.

For NISC, however, our MDMS platform has been a solid success. It now has similar functionality to PowerMeter and is in use at over 160 utility companies across the country (as of January 2015). We are installing MDMS at a rate of two to three companies each month for the foreseeable future.

We moved forward and deployed MDMS for our members because it clearly aligns with our mission and it provides customers with a level of information about energy usage that is literally reinventing the electric utility industry. What's more, it allows customers to receive monthly, daily and hourly energy consumption information on their smart devices.

We may never fully understand why Google backed away from the PowerMeter initiative. Perhaps the decision makers at Google determined they should follow Tom Peters' advice and stick to their knitting.

What we do know is that rapid scalability isn't a criterion by which cooperatives measure success. Benefit to the end user is.

The cooperative business model is a patient model. Unlike Google, we did not demand immediate success; we sought out the advice of the end users to determine what features and functionality would provide greater value. We enhanced the product and then went back to the members, again requesting advice and feedback. This iterative model of constant and gradual product improvement allows us to refine and perfect a product. It is time-consuming and can be expensive, but in the end we develop quality, focused products that deliver true value to the end consumer.

The Importance of Collaborative Relationships

There is another reason why NISC continues to find success in serving the rural electric and telecommunications markets. In the last decade, we have been displacing large, worldwide software companies like SAP SE and Oracle Corporation; companies with deep pockets and tens of thousands of employees. In the United States, NISC has over 54 percent of the rural electric market compared to SAP and Oracle, who have less than 1 percent of the market share, combined.

Throughout NISC's history in the marketplace, we've done more than build our technical expertise, as demanded by users in the IT field; we have developed some of the most respected industry experts in the nation, and our member/owner/customers know this to be true. They know it because we consistently deliver technically sound products, and we treat our relationship with them as if they are family.

It's common for NISC employees to sit around the table with members—in our office or theirs—and banter like brothers and sisters about what is needed, what is wanted, what is possible and what is a priority. Members will throw down challenges about timelines or features, and NISC employees will take them seriously—we don't like to be told we can't get something done. Who does?

When everyone in your organization has a common vision and understands the shared values, you have a powerful formula for achievement. In his book *The Fifth Discipline: The Art & Practice of the Learning Organization*, Peter Senge makes some profound points about the notion of a shared vision. He states:

This is not to say that visions cannot emanate from the top. Often they do. But sometimes they emanate from personal visions of individuals who are not in positions of authority. Sometimes they just 'bubble up' from people interacting at many levels. The origin of the vision is much less important than the process whereby it comes to be shared. It is not truly a 'shared vision' until it connects with the personal visions of people throughout the organization. . . . A group of people truly committed to a common vision is an awesome force. They can accomplish the seemingly impossible.

What We Do, Why We Do It, How We Do It

A mission statement communicates the fundamental purpose of a business or organization. The more compelling the mission statement, the easier it is to develop an organizational culture of like-minded individuals who support it.

The NISC mission statement is designed to be in alignment with those of our founding cooperatives. Our mission statement calls us "to deliver information technology solutions and services that are member- and customer-focused, quality-driven and value-priced."

One of NCDC's founding cooperative member/owners, Consolidated Telcom in Dickinson, North Dakota, has a simple mission statement that fully advises anyone entering the Consolidated culture what the mission is and what the reason is for going to work each day. It states:

Consolidated Telcom will deliver a state-of-the-art network providing advanced services to our customers.

Consolidated has kept our customers connected to the world with telephone, television and high-speed Internet for more than 50 years. We proudly continue that tradition of commitment and passion to our customers today.

Such straightforward statements point the cooperative compass to true north. At NISC, we know that each day we must focus on our members and that we need to provide innovations that will help them deliver better service to their customers at an affordable price. This is no small task. Our products and services must keep up with the amazing transformation of Consolidated's business model from what we called POTS (Plain Old Telephone Service) to today's world of broadband services.

The NISC vision statement closely parallels our mission statement and provides further guidance for employees. It calls us "to enhance the success of our member/owners by providing world-class information technology solutions while building lasting business relationships."

Cooperative principles, mission statement, vision statement—these elements lay a solid foundation for what we do and why we do it. The missing element is *how* we do it. That's where our shared values come into play: they are what defines how we do our work. These shared values are part of our cooperative DNA.

NISC's Shared Values

At NISC, we believe in striving for excellence with a passion and determination that is guided by our shared values. Following are the values that inspire us, guide us, and determine the manner in which we conduct ourselves in carrying out the business of our organization:

Integrity: We hold ourselves to the highest professional, moral and ethical standards. We are committed to doing the right thing, always.

Relationships: We believe that people are the heart of our organization. We are committed to building, nurturing and preserving lasting relationships with our member/owners, our customers, our partners, our families and friends and with one another. We are passionate about the service we provide, and we demonstrate that by being responsive to the needs of our customers and constantly striving to exceed their expectations. We believe in engaging in honest communication, showing respect for others and treating all people with the dignity they deserve. Because we understand the importance of relationships, we support a healthy balance between work and family.

Innovation: We promote the spirit of creativity and we champion new ideas. We believe that a passion for quality and the desire to constantly improve what we do is critical to our success. We challenge each other to continually strive for excellence and to define new ways to build our future.

Teamwork: We exemplify the cooperative spirit by working together with respect for one another's ideas and contributions. We believe in using both our individual and our collective knowledge and skills in order to improve our organization, and we agree to show support for all decisions once they are made. We know that the combination of our talents allows us to accomplish great things because there is greater potential for success when we share our diverse experiences.

Empowerment: We believe individuals have the power to make a difference. We agree to be accountable and responsible in the decisions that we make, to use good judgment and to take pride and ownership in our work.

Personal Development: We believe that the free exchange of knowledge and information is absolutely necessary to the success of each individual as well as to the organization's success. We agree to work every day to learn new things and are committed to sharing our ideas with one another. We support education and learning and are dedicated to providing opportunities for every individual to grow in their abilities.

A truly unique component of our shared values is that NISC employees created them, defined them and, every day, live by them. Our employees measure whether they always do the right thing under the highest moral, ethical and legal standards. They challenge and remind each other, including those of us in leadership positions, that our relationships with one another and our customers are the highest priority—that fostering trust and respect should be foremost in all of our activities.

A truly unique component of our shared values is that NISC employees created them, defined them and, every day, live by them.

How each employee exemplifies our shared values weighs as heavily in their annual review and coaching sessions as do their competencies, sales and work performance. Each of these values also is carefully intertwined and part of NISC's ethics program. (See chapter 11 for more detail.)

The cooperative business model that NISC follows, combined with the shared values outlined above, is what makes up our core strength.

These elements are what, in large measure, have allowed us to succeed. Any group or organization can emulate the best practice of identifying shared values; putting them into action is the critical element. The evolution of a collaborative culture where individuals actively seek to serve others first is something we've noticed developing at NISC over the last few years. While relatively new to us, everything about the servant leadership style tells us it is one we want to embrace and infuse across our organization.

KEY POINTS TO CONSIDER IN THIS CHAPTER

1. Generally speaking, the **cooperative business model is designed to produce goods and services in such a way that the cost of production is met and the goods and services are made affordable for the member/owners' advantage.** For most investor-owned businesses, the main objective is to increase shareholder wealth or make a profit.

2. Should there be any earnings over the cost of production, these **excess earnings in a cooperative are described as margins, patronage or capital credits, and they are allocated back to members** based on their usage of the products and services. Said another way, margins are distributed among members according to each member's economic participation rather than according to the value of their capital shareholdings, as is the case for stockholders in an investor-owned company.

3. The **original seven principles on which every cooperative is founded are known as the Rochdale Principles.** The Principles were first set out by the Rochdale Society of Equitable Pioneers in Rochdale, England, in 1844, and they have formed the basis for the principles on which cooperatives around the world operate to this day.

4. The important thing about **the vision, mission and shared values of NISC is their role in everything that NISC does. We consider them part of our cooperative DNA.**

Chapter 3

Embracing Leadership through Service to Others

The servant-leader is servant first. . . . [Servant leadership] begins with the natural feeling that one wants to serve, to serve first. Then conscious choice brings one to aspire to lead. That person is sharply different from one who is leader first . . . .

— Robert K. Greenleaf

Sister T and Warren Buffett

In the spring of 2009, several NISC colleagues and I had the privilege of representing our organization at a retirement party for Sister Thomas Welder, who had been serving as president of the University of Mary (known as America's leadership university) in Bismarck, North Dakota, since 1978.

When I think of what it truly means to be a servant leader, Sister Thomas (or "Sr. T" as she is affectionately known) is the first person who comes to mind. Being a servant epitomizes her life, which makes her message even more effective—all that she talks about, she actually lives. Her life is made up of an unlikely blend of religion, politics, business and education. During her thirty-year stint as president, the university grew in size, scope and reputation, under a chosen model of servant leadership. Sr. T served on numerous local and national boards, most notably with MDU Resources Group, Inc., a Fortune 500 company.

At NISC we were lucky enough to have had Sr. T speak to us on servant leadership as part of our leadership development program.

When her retirement was approaching, Sr. T was asked what she would like for her retirement. Her simple response was, "A rocking chair would be nice." This, from a woman whose reputation commanded an unbelievable outpouring of love and respect in the form of a going-away party attended by thirteen hundred people, many of whom had observed, admired and been inspired by Sr. T for three decades. (And the party would have been even larger had the organizers not run out of room and cut off ticket sales!)

As a Benedictine nun and member of a monastic order, Sr. T has never owned a car or a house. Her personal possessions consist primarily of a modest wardrobe, yet she is admired by CEOs of large corporations and is sought after by students, esteemed governors and senators. In fact, she received the coveted Theodore Roosevelt Rough Rider Award in 2004. Sr. T is loved and respected by all. I don't think she ever received the rocking chair, but a $6 million scholarship fund was established in her honor at the University of Mary. What a legacy.

The weekend of the retirement party, I happened to finish reading *The Snowball: Warren Buffett and the Business of Life* by Alice Schroeder. Mr. Buffett is a corporate legend who is annually identified by *Forbes* magazine as one of the richest people in the world, (usually as one of the top five). His estimated net worth in 2014 was well above $60 billion. To put this into perspective, you would have to spend $11,415.53 a minute, 24 hours a day, 365 days a year for the next ten years to spend $60 billion.

It is fascinating that, although Buffett could afford to purchase any number of extravagant estates, he chooses to live in the same modest house in Omaha, Nebraska, where he has lived for thirty years; he can afford the choicest cuts of meat, yet he chooses to eat hamburgers. If he were interested in impressing people, he could have a wine cellar stocked with rare vintages from around the globe. But what is Buffett's choice of drink? Cherry Coke.

In August 2010, Buffett, along with Bill and Melinda Gates, founded the Giving Pledge—an initiative to help address society's most pressing problems by inviting the world's wealthiest people to commit to giving more than half of their wealth to philanthropy or charitable causes either during their lifetime or in their will.

More than 125 individuals and families have signed a Giving Pledge, which is phenomenal.

Living in the United States, it is very easy to get caught in the trap of keeping up with the Joneses and feel like too much is never enough. This is why the modest choices of Sr. T and Mr. Buffett are so remarkable, and it teaches us a profound lesson: Positively affecting people's lives has very little to do with how much we earn, our net worth, the car(s) we drive or the clothes we wear. Our ability to effect positive change has everything to do with our personal integrity, our reputation and the consistency of our actions: not only talking the talk, but also walking the walk.

Leading by example and making certain that our intentions are always pure and aligned with our actions—that is what it takes to be a true servant leader. Renowned author and speaker Wayne Dyer says it this way: "I don't think that Jesus was teaching Christianity. Jesus was teaching kindness, love, concern and peace. What I tell people is, don't be Christian, be Christ-like. Don't be Buddhist, be Buddha-like."

> **"What I tell people is, don't be Christian, be Christ-like. Don't be Buddhist, be Buddha-like."**
> **– Wayne Dyer**

I cannot talk about servant leadership without acknowledging the profound impact that my father had on my life as a servant leader. A self-made man, Adam Dosch worked tirelessly to provide for his wife and five children with little or no concern for himself. The first in his family to earn a college degree, as a father he worked to support an education for his two sons and three daughters, and he made efforts to improve his church and his community. Any financial contributions he made were anonymous. He was a man of few words who was modest and unassuming. One of his most memorable quotes is "the best sermon is a good example."

That is how he lived his life—with integrity, honesty and by unassuming example. Being his children, we knew him well, but my siblings and I had no idea of the lasting impact he had on other peoples' lives until the day of his funeral when a line formed of friends who wanted to tell us their "Adam stories." We were so fortunate to grow up under his mentorship. Without question his example was one of the most profound influences in my life, and for that I will be forever grateful.

I have heard it said that we are simply a melting pot of the people we know throughout our lives. In my case, although Sr. T, Warren Buffett and my father were very different individuals, I have certainly learned a great deal from each of them through their service to others and that knowledge has affected how I live my life. Indeed, their similar approach to living life has heavily influenced my leadership style at NISC and, I believe, also the servant leadership model that is slowly evolving in our cooperative culture.

A Modern Day History of Servant Leadership

The roots of servant leadership reach deep into history. Modern day practitioners recognize Robert K. Greenleaf as the individual who revitalized the idea of leaders in service to others for the twentieth century and beyond. Mr. Greenleaf was born in 1904 in Terre Haute, Indiana. Growing up, he observed his father taking on the role of community steward, and he later said that his father's action of serving his community was his original model for servant leadership.

Greenleaf graduated as a math major in 1926 from Carleton College in Minnesota. One thing that stuck with him from his years in college was one teacher's perspective that large institutions were doing a poor job of looking out for, or serving, individuals and society as a whole. Shortly after graduation, Greenleaf joined AT&T, which at the time was one of the largest companies in the world. He wanted to see if he could quietly influence a complex organization like AT&T from the inside out. He rose quickly through the ranks and spent five years as what, today, we would call a "turnaround specialist" for AT&T as well as for other companies associated with the telecommunications giant. It became apparent to Greenleaf that successful organizations were led by individuals who focused on serving the needs of their employees and their organization.

In 1964, Greenleaf retired and began his second career as a writer, consultant and teacher. He produced several works, including a seminal essay entitled *The Servant as Leader* that was published in 1970. According to Greenleaf, the best leaders were servants first. He believed that the key tools for a servant leader are strong aptitudes for listening and persuasion, access to intuition and foresight, effective use of language and pragmatic measurements of outcomes. Greenleaf forwarded some unpopular ideas among the mainstream business community, including his belief that "the work exists for the person as much as the person exists for the work." He outlined this idea in his essay *On Becoming a Servant Leader.*

Some fifteen hundred years earlier, St. Benedict of Nursia (480–547), who led an expanding network of monastic orders, wrote *The Rule of Saint Benedict*, a book offering practical insights based on his years of managing monastic orders. *The Rule of Saint Benedict* was a masterpiece, combining as it did the best of the Greco-Roman organizational theory with early Christian leadership principles.

Benedict developed and shared with the leaders in his movement twelve steps to be used as a guide for leading a life of humility. According to Benedict the process is like a ladder, the end goal being to reach the deepest level of humility. True humility then, it seems, was the ultimate achievement for abbots (the leaders of the monasteries), and therefore would have been also for everyone else who lived in the community.

Two things are interesting about this: First, a book containing rather simple principles written nearly fifteen hundred years ago still has great applicability today. Second, the thousands of organizations around the globe that have chosen to follow *The Rule of Saint Benedict* and actively practice the twelve steps to humility are, for the most part, alive and prospering today.

Another modern day name that is synonymous with servant leadership is James C. Hunter. Mr. Hunter is the author of two internationally best-selling books: *The Servant: A Simple Story About the True Essence of Leadership* and *The World's Most Powerful Leadership Principle: How to Become a Servant Leader.* His books are used as texts in many MBA programs and other higher education curricula around the world. They have been

> **"Servant leadership is the skill of influencing people to work enthusiastically together toward goals for the common good, with character that inspires confidence."**
>
> **– James C. Hunter**

translated into two dozen languages, selling over 4.4 million copies in total.

Hunter's definition of servant leadership is "the skill of influencing people to work enthusiastically together toward goals for the common good, with character that inspires confidence."

For Hunter, servant leadership is about leading with love. He regularly cites 1 Corinthians 13 from the Bible, feeling it matches the core values that inspired his leadership paradigm. These core values are as follows:

- **Patience**: To show self-control
- **Kindness**: To give others attention, appreciation, encouragement, common courtesy
- **Humility**: To be authentic, not boastful, arrogant or puffed-up
- **Respectful**: To treat others as important people
- **Selflessness**: To meet the legitimate needs of others
- **Forgiveness**: To give up resentment when wronged
- **Honesty**: To be free from deceptive behavior
- **Commitment**: To stick to the choice(s) you have made

"When people begin to serve others and behave in healthy ways," Mr. Hunter says, "they begin to see themselves differently and gain confidence as a result. The process begins with improving yourself a little each day."

Servant Leadership in Action

As mentioned in the opening to Part I, servant leadership is a philosophy and set of practices that enriches the lives of individuals, builds better organizations and, ultimately, creates a more just and caring world.

Servant leaders focus primarily on the growth and well-being of the people they lead and of the communities to which they belong. While traditional leadership involves the accumulation and exercise of power by one at the "top of the pyramid," servant leadership is different. The servant leader shares power, puts the needs of others first, and helps people develop and perform to their highest potential.

Let me give you an example of servant leadership in action. In the summer of 2010, NISC had been working with a prospective member. Even at our first meeting, I remember thinking, "These are people who would truly be good partners." That impression strengthened as we worked through the site visit, the demonstration and the request for information. The personnel at this cooperative were impressive, and our confidence that the cooperative would make a good NISC member was high. In the end though, this prospect chose a competitor over us. To say we were disappointed is an understatement. We searched exhaustively for the tipping point. Was it our product? Was it something we said? Was it a gap in the software functionality we showcased?

There is a cardinal rule by which we live at NISC: We will win with our people, products and processes, and we will never be part of distributing negative information about our competition.

None of us liked to lose, and we had an ace yet to play. A former NISC member who had recently moved on to the same vendor had just been starting the conversion process when the decision makers realized they had made a mistake in their choice. This former member subsequently returned to NISC and, at the time, was attempting to rescind their contract with the other vendor.

When I had visited with the CEO of this returning member, he'd told me, "Vern, we made a poor decision when we decided to leave NISC. We were just looking at price and now, we are paying the price. NISC saved us, and we will be forever grateful. Please, if you ever need a reference, let me help. I would love to share my perspective on the differences between NISC and the competition."

Naturally then, when we received word that our member prospect had selected our competitor, I recalled this conversation and the CEO's offer. I figured that in order to reverse the decision, all it would take is one call; that one reference would tell the rest of the competitor's story and this prospect would become our newest member.

But then my role as a servant leader entered my mind and it became a mental debate. Should I make the call? The discussion between CEOs would not shine a positive light on our competition. Is undermining our competition how NISC wants to be known as a competitor?

There is a cardinal rule by which we live at NISC: We will win with our people, products, and processes, and we will never be part of distributing negative information about our competition.

Needless to say then, the call was never made and, indeed, we lost the prospective member . . . that time. The experience of losing them became the baseline against which NISC measures all of its ongoing interactions with that very same prospect. We lost them once, but this doesn't mean we will lose them the next time. And make no mistake, we will be ready and eager the next time.

Ken Blanchard has a wonderful perspective about employees in organizations and the role that leaders play in helping them achieve greatness. In his Situational Leadership workshops, he says:

> I think people want to be magnificent. It is the job of the leader to bring out that magnificence in people and to create an environment where they feel safe and supported and ready to do the best job possible in accomplishing key goals. This responsibility is a sacred trust that should not be violated. The opportunity to guide others to their fullest potential is an honor and one that should not be taken lightly. As leaders we hold the lives of others in our hands. This hand needs to be gentle and caring and always available for support.

Servant leadership requires humility, and it exudes gratitude for others. While "humble leader" brings to mind an intriguing image worthy of further discussion, "humble boss" seems like an oxymoron: it just doesn't equate. You can see a humble leader anchoring the line on which the entire team is exerting its might; how does a humble boss do the same when he or she is standing behind the team ready to crack the whip or is above the team and acting as a judge? A servant leader is a coach and resource who can interpret the data or lend experience, but the individual or the team makes most decisions.

According to Merriam-Webster, the definition of a boss is "one who makes decisions or exercises authority." To act as a boss means "to give orders to, especially in an arrogant or domineering manner; to be or act as a supervisor or controlling element." In contrast, a leader is "one that leads or guides." To lead is "to show the way by going in advance; to guide the behavior or opinion of another."

A boss can be humble when he or she truly places the needs of customers and employees before his or her own needs. It is so tempting to focus on ourselves and our own aspirations and goals that it takes a true leader to trust that if you do the right thing for others, you will also prosper. Servant leadership is about guiding others on a path to success for themselves and for the organization, and that success effectively benefits all employees, including the servant leader.

Jim Collins operates a management research laboratory in Boulder, Colorado. He is the author of six books including *Good to Great: Why Some Companies Make the Leap . . . and Others Don't.* Mr. Collins has spent the past twenty years trying to understand how some companies are able to sustain superlative performance. The NISC staff has spent a significant amount of time learning from and practicing the insights shared by Collins in *Good to Great*. The concepts are solid and, as an organization, we are committed to the greatness that Collins describes.

He argues in the book that the key ingredient that allows a company to become great is having what he calls a "Level 5" leader: an executive who possesses genuine personal humility blended with an intense professional will. This idea sounded counterintuitive when Collins first wrote about it in 2001 and almost everyone still believed CEOs should be charismatic, larger-than-life figures. *Good to Great* blows that belief out of the water.

From 1996 to 2001, Collins and a team of twenty-two research associates conducted a five-year project searching for the answer to what moves a company from being merely good to being truly great. Based on their research, they concluded that the most powerfully transformative executives possess a paradoxical mixture of personal humility and professional will.

Of the over fourteen hundred companies the research team studied, there were a total of eleven that qualified as having experienced a "good to great" transformation. The criteria that was identified as being responsible for the successful transformation of these companies was not what was expected from observers. It didn't have anything to do with whether companies in the study were in a crisis or in a steady state, nor did it matter how big the transformation was. The determining factor for an organization's success was having a Level 5 leader at the time of the transition from good to great.

The hierarchy of leadership capabilities consists of five levels, and it was created in order to distinguish between the different types of leadership styles and how successful these leadership styles were at the companies included in the study. According to Collins, the capabilities of the five levels of leaders break down like this:

Level 5 leader: This executive (or organization) builds enduring greatness through a unique blend of personal humility plus professional will.

Level 4 leader: This effective leader (or organization) catalyzes commitment to, and vigorous pursuit of, a clear and compelling vision; stimulates the group to high performance standards.

Level 3 leader: The competent manager organizes people and resources toward the effective and efficient pursuit of predetermined objectives.

Level 2 leader: The contributing team member contributes to the achievement of group objectives and works effectively with others in a group setting.

Level 1 leader: A highly capable individual who makes productive contributions through talent, knowledge, skills and good work habits.

As you can see, the Level 5 leader is at the top of this hierarchy of leadership capabilities. This person, according to the research conducted by Collins and his research team, is a necessary factor for transforming a good business into a great business. The research indicates that it is not necessary for an individual to move sequentially through each of the different levels; however, the Level 5 leader requires the capabilities of all the lower levels—plus the special characteristic of humility.

Servant leadership is a combination of many traits, not the least of which are humility and gratitude. In the fall of 2011, I had a once-in-a-lifetime homecoming experience that I hope never to have again. It was joyful, humbling beyond my wildest dreams, and it left me vulnerable to experience gratitude at a level I hadn't known was possible. In my desire to express this gratitude, I blogged about the experience to our NISC employees. Here is that blog post.

The Highest Appreciation to You
September 23, 2011

Last Friday I drove up to our home for the first time in 111 days. No rowing a duck boat, no climbing over a wall of clay and sandbags, no muddy boots or nervous glances at a series of pumps on the interior wall of the dike, looking for signs of breaches and pooled water. As I pressed the button and witnessed the garage door open to welcome me, I felt a rush of emotion. I was home. Our home had survived the wrath of the Missouri River and its mighty 2011 flood.

Over the last four weeks, we've worked to remove the dike, one that was hastily built in just two days by a small army of friends and family. How we built this incredibly resilient structure in such a short time with water lapping at its base and running over the road, I will never know.

There is a long list of people who came to our aid. Some came for an hour, others for days—some whose names I did not even know. I have accepted the fact that I cannot adequately thank or repay all of those who helped us. The accountant in me wants to balance the ledger and make sure everyone who brought equipment, hauled sandbags, provided food or documented the event with pictures is made whole. But I don't even know where I would start.

My family and I have a significant debt to pay forward and, in the future, when opportunities arise for us to lend a hand, we will. And we will do so while remembering the faces of our friends, family, coworkers and new-found friends as they endured aching backs, cramping arms, and sweaty, sunburned faces, placing themselves in harm's way and challenging a raging river to save a single house at the end of a lonely gravel road.

These acts of kindness were repeated again and again by employees of NISC as they came to the aid of people affected by the flood. We recently provided an update on NISC activities at a regional member meeting, and near the end we opened the mic for questions. Bruce Carlson, the CEO of Verendrye Electric, one of our founding member cooperatives in Velva, North Dakota, grabbed the mic. He proceeded to tell all in the room about a group of NISC employees who traveled 120 miles from our offices in Mandan to Velva on one fateful day to help sandbag, move furniture and do whatever was necessary to help his cooperative prepare for the rising waters that were very intimidating.

Bruce expressed how much he appreciated this selfless act of kindness from the NISC employees. "This is an example of people helping people in need for all the right reasons," he said. "It is this culture and the attitude of the NISC employees that have been part of our decision to embrace partnership for the past forty-seven years. . . . And I would happily take the opportunity to tell anyone that NISC is much more than technology and software products; rather, it is an organization with heart, made up of people who care deeply about those they serve."

Humility. Gratitude. This doesn't sound like the stuff of fierce competitors or Fortune 500 executives. As Robert Greenleaf points out in his essay *The Servant as Leader*, the power-hungry person, who relishes competition and is good at it (meaning: usually wins) will probably judge the servant leader to be weak or naïve, or both. The power-hungry individual will not comprehend the value of service to others or the benefit beyond self-serving goals.

If we look past the individual to the institution in which he or she serves, what (or who) is it that makes that institution strong? Mr. Greenleaf contends that the strongest, most productive institution over a long period of time is one in which, other things being equal, there is the largest amount of voluntary action in support of the goals of the institution. These organizations would be those in which employees do the right things at the right time—things that optimize total effectiveness—because the goals are clear and comprehensive, and they understand what ought to be done. They believe they are the right things to do, and they take the necessary actions without being instructed.

At the 2013 NISC Leadership Forum—an annual event for about fifty employee leaders—we discussed several characteristics that NISC leaders should model for others, nurture within their teams and hold one another accountable to. The traits we felt were the most important are an eclectic mix that will help propel NISC forward as we seek to emulate a culture of service for others. These are the five key qualities: compassion, discipline, competence, innovation and inspiration.

> **"NISC is much more than technology and software products; rather, it is an organization with a heart, made up of people who care deeply about those they serve."**
> **– Bruce Carlson**

You will note similarities between our top five leadership characteristics and the five levels of leadership capabilities identified by Jim Collins in *Good to Great*. The five leadership traits we reinforce at NISC are discussed in more detail in chapter 4, and you will find an interesting comparison of these leadership characteristics and the seven pillars of servant leadership in chapter 11.

The five traits serve two major functions at NISC. First, they help us evaluate and coach our supervisors. We don't expect every emerging leader at NISC to necessarily have all five traits, but we look for individuals who are coachable and will be able to develop any lacking traits. Second, we work to continually foster these leadership traits in individuals as we strive to enhance our succession planning.

As part of NISC's feedback process for leaders, we conduct confidential 360-degree surveys that are used on an annual basis to help employees assess what they do well and determine how they can be more effective. The survey process includes self-evaluation, peer evaluation, and direct report and supervisor evaluation. The surveys include the leadership characteristics outlined earlier, aligning them with NISC's shared values (see chapter 2). Reviewers are asked to select a rating that best describes how the employee being evaluated delivers on that trait. This information is compiled and discussed during our one-to-one coaching sessions.

These Are Challenging Times

Without question, the most challenging message to deliver to employees is when we lose a member of the cooperative.

Our stated organizational goal is to have an annual churn rate of less than 1 percent. To put that into perspective, in the software business a churn rate of 25 percent is not unusual. Our churn has actually never put us above 0.5 percent, even during our most vulnerable times of rewriting software. In total, we have lost fifteen members since our merger in 2000. During that same period, our member count has gone from under four hundred to over seven hundred.

Each quarter, we report member wins and member losses to our board of directors and our employees. We have gone months and, at times, years without losing a member, but when it does occur, it's devastating for our organization. There is much soul searching and discussion of lessons learned, and we implement strategies to make certain we do everything we can to prevent future loss. Our culture is more concerned about retaining existing members than we are about gaining a new one.

When we receive word that a member is leaving, we immediately begin the process of winning them back. It starts with a call to their CEO, pledging NISC's commitment to do everything in our power to facilitate a successful de-conversion from our products. These calls are received with quite a bit of astonishment and a good deal of grateful-ness. They are a prime example of our long-term commitment to the welfare of our members and the industry we serve. During the calls, we let CEOs know that while we are disappointed, we respect their deci-sion. Harboring resentment that comes with losing a member poisons not only the recipient but also the sender. Treating our members with dignity and respect is always worth it in the end.

One of our members left us for a competitor in the summer of 2009, at which time their new vendor began working on the de-con-version from NISC. While every conversion has its challenges, let's just say that this particular conversion from NISC to a competitor was not a good experience for the vendor or the member. In fact, the member's staff was so disappointed, they made the decision to pull the plug after being live on the competitor's software for only two months, and return to NISC.

Shortly after this I received a letter from one of the directors of the returning member. It made my day. No—in truth, it made my week. It was an absolute affirmation of the way our organization does business. In the body of the letter, the efforts of two NISC employees were singled out. The care with which they served this member—before, during and after the member's return—is a shining example of servant leadership and an inspiration to anyone seeking to understand the importance of being a servant leader.

There is a prevailing Darwinian approach to business in the marketplace right now. In every industry, across all sectors, service providers are turning over every rock to build their business. Promises are being made that can't always be met in the end. While it is tempting to join in the fray, beat our chests, yell the loudest and use stealth strategies to yield fruitful rewards, it would not be honest and we don't believe it is the way to build a reputation and long-term business relationships. We choose a different path that allows us to stick to our values, even if it costs us some short-term business. We work hard to serve our members by being honest, engaged, innovative, committed and transparent. Most of all, we will always, always, always look out for their best interests.

This approach does not always yield results quickly, and it is not always comfortable. Rather, it is slow and arduous. But it pays long-term dividends to our members and to all NISC employees who have invested their careers in our organization. We firmly believe servant leadership does not rest only with our leadership team. We want it to permeate our organization so that every employee willingly bears the responsibility to serve as well; to serve those with whom they work, and to serve our member/owners who are, after all, our reason for being.

Ours is not a perfect organization, but we strive for it to be a great one. In the years to come, we envision an organization in which leadership through service to others is a natural extension of employment at NISC. We want to enable a culture of compassion and be a place where NISC demonstrates care and concern for our employees, members and customers, and where employees fully engage in their service for members, customers and each other.

KEY POINTS TO CONSIDER IN THIS CHAPTER

1. **Leading by example and making certain that your intentions are always pure and aligned with your actions**—that is what it takes to be a true servant leader. Our ability to effect positive change has everything to do with our integrity, our resulting reputation and the consistency of our actions—not only talking the talk, but walking the walk.

2. **Servant leadership is a philosophy and set of practices that enriches the lives of individuals, builds better organizations and ultimately creates a more just and caring world.** A servant leader focuses primarily on the growth and well-being of people and the communities to which they belong. While traditional leadership generally involves the accumulation and exercise of power by one at the "top of the pyramid," servant leadership is different. The servant leader shares power, puts the needs of others first and helps people develop and perform to their highest potential.

3. There are several **characteristics that NISC leaders strive to model for others, nurture among their teams and hold one another accountable to.** These traits are an eclectic mix that will serve to propel NISC forward as we seek to emulate a culture of service for others. They boil down to five key qualities: compassion, discipline, competence, innovation and inspiration.

Chapter 4

Leadership Traits that Make a Difference

A leader . . . is like a shepherd. He stays behind the flock, letting the most nimble go out ahead, whereupon the others follow, not realizing that all along they are being directed from behind.
— Nelson Mandela

One of the greatest privileges and most humbling tasks that I've had as CEO of NISC was to deliver the eulogy of a dear friend and former employee, Brian Wolf. Brian died from cancer in November 2008, and if ever there was a person who demonstrated the difference one individual can make in an organization, it was Brian.

We can all relate to the concept of wanting to make a difference, whether it be in the life of our spouse or the lives of our children or our colleagues, in our work or in our community or, more ambitiously, the wider world. Well, without question, Brian's short life made a difference.

Some may say, "What a tragedy Brian lived only forty-six years," but a better observation to make is, "What an incredible forty-six years Brian had, filled with love and passion for his family and his work." The man had one speed only, and that was full-out: he read fast, he walked fast, he talked fast, he ate fast—never wasting a second. One of his favorite sayings and one that speaks of how he lived his life, was, "Go big or go home."

Nothing was more invigorating for Brian than a big, audacious challenge. The bigger the better, in fact: the higher the improbability for success was, the more determined he became. And, true to form, that is exactly the way he approached his cancer. When he was undergoing chemotherapy, Brian was disappointed when the doctor recommended he stop taking a drug after eight treatments—even though no one had ever had more than six consecutive doses of this particular drug.

One of the most powerful memories I have of Brian's battle with cancer took place in September 2008 at our annual member conference in St. Louis, Missouri. We pleaded with Brian to allow us to cover for him so that he wouldn't have to participate, but he refused. He was even a bit insulted that we would suggest he relinquish his part in this major event.

And so it was that, just two months before his passing, Brian took center stage to carry out his presentation. His lack of hair and eyebrows and his gaunt face and body did not deter him one bit. He delivered his message with all of the passion and enthusiasm we had come to expect from him. There were almost fifteen hundred people in the room and, as Brian spoke, every one of them sat in thoughtful silence, knowing full well they were witnessing one of the most amazing demonstrations of human determination and dedication one can see. For Brian, it was just another day at the office, and he truly did not see any reason for a fuss to be made.

One of Brian's passions had been fly-fishing, and some of my fondest memories of him are from when he was enjoying the activity on the Yellowstone River in Montana. On one particular trip, we decided that each of us in the group would take turns being responsible for dinner. For most of us, dinner was straightforward: a couple of steaks, a large can of beans, salad in a bag, several bottles of wine, and we were good to go.

Not Brian. On the day appointed for him to make dinner, his preparation began early in the morning as he hand-chopped the garlic and onions and mixed the spices that would garnish the whole pig he had ordered. In an outdoor pit, Brian tended a fire for hours to get the coals just right and then gently wrapped the pig in banana leaves, which he had special ordered from a grocer near the cabin. Next, he buried the pig in his pit for roasting. While the rest of us went fishing for the afternoon,

Brian painstakingly tended his pig. The outcome was an extraordinary feast of roasted pork with all the trimmings. Go big or go home.

In Brian's last position as chief operating officer at NISC, he was responsible for almost three hundred employees and he was an exceptional leader. There were many reasons for this, not least of which was how he cared about, mentored and served his team. Brian was an amazing champion for his employees, and they loved him. He had a way of earning their respect and motivating them to be great.

Even with his go-big-or-go-home approach, Brian was a model servant leader. He didn't consider himself the quarterback for the team, which is what you might expect as that's how many managers consider themselves. Rather, Brian would ask the members of his team, "How can I block or tackle for you?" If his team had a company goal to carry out, he wanted to know how he could clear the path ahead of any obstacles, and he was always asking what additional resources might be needed to reach the goal. Clearly he knew what it meant to be a team player, and he modeled how to volunteer and tackle the tough duties while offering starring roles and accolades to his staff when they reached their goals. By his example, Brian inspired other NISC leaders to think of themselves as linemen who help others to carry the ball; he planted the seeds of servant leadership in a deliberate yet unintentional manner.

When he found out he had cancer, Brian sent an e-mail to those who worked closely with him. In it he said, "I feel that this team is like my second family, and there is nowhere I would rather be to face these professional challenges and personal struggles than here at NISC."

One of Brian's most treasured accomplishments at NISC was that, during his watch, his utility division completed hundreds of software implementations around the country and they never had a failed implementation. Brian would proudly say of it, "Our takeoffs equal our landings, which is a good thing."

Brian wanted NISC to be more than a good software company, and it's he who sparked the desire for NISC to become a great one. He had the unique ability to hypersee for his team as well as for all of NISC. He challenged us to go beyond the immediate answer and seek out a vision of how our technology will serve the future. Those who had the privilege to work with Brian stand in awe of the contribution he is still making to our organization today. He raised the bar for the employees he supervised, and our senior management group realizes that he is still raising the bar for them several years later.

For this reason, while some people refer to their legacy as what they have accomplished in their lifetime, that's not entirely the case for Brian. His legacy is yet to be fully written. Yet to come are the accomplishments of his wife, Kathy; the accomplishments of his talented and gifted children; and the accomplishments of the literally hundreds of individuals who Brian touched, influenced, motivated and mentored during his life.

Traits of People Who Make a Difference

There are five traits you would have witnessed when in Brian's presence on any given day, which is what made his impact so noteworthy. And it's no coincidence that these are the five traits we identified at the leadership forum mentioned in chapter 3. Possessing all five isn't required to make a difference in the workplace or in the world; however, the more traits one has, the more formidable is one's personal and professional tool chest that can be used to effect positive change.

The five make-a-difference traits challenge us to be

- Compassionate,
- Disciplined,
- Competent,
- Innovative and
- Inspirational.

A combination of these five make-a-difference traits is critical to creating an environment of trust in the workplace, whether the traits reside in one leader like Brian or are shared among the members of a leadership team. When these traits are put into practice, they establish credibility for the leader(s); confidence in the organization; and trust among coworkers. (You'll find more on trust and transparency in chapter 10.)

Compassionate

To have compassion is to feel or show empathy and concern for others. Think of it as putting yourself in another person's shoes and seeing the world from his or her view.

Each fall, NISC hosts a member information conference (MIC) where a few thousand of our customers gather in order to take part in shared learning about NISC products and services; achieve better understanding of our processes; increase their knowledge of leading-edge technologies; and, also, have a bit of fun. No single event does more to build NISC's credibility and reputation than the annual MIC. While not every employee is directly involved in the conference preparation or participation efforts, the success of it each year is a tribute to the work of the entire organization.

It's a time for making memories and growing friendships, old and new. One particularly remarkable memory, which few of our employees and even fewer members know about, was made during the 2009 MIC. I'll share it now, as it's an excellent example of the power of compassion, featuring one of our employees who truly went above and beyond the call of duty.

While most people were resting in their rooms following a busy day of MIC sessions, one of the conference attendees fell ill and needed to be transported to the hospital. Ron Alfred, senior manager of NISC shared services, was available and took responsibility for getting the attendee to the hospital. But it didn't stop there. Ron stayed with this attendee to provide assistance and comfort for over six hours, patiently waiting until he was personally able to return the member to the conference hotel to continue recovery.

Ron's actions provide a great example of what it means to serve members (or customers) with compassion. A note to NISC from the member who had been in need captures this sentiment well:

> You say you tell your employees that during the MIC they are to act as our hosts, but I honestly don't think you had something like escorting me to the hospital in mind. Ron's servant heart was greatly felt and appreciated, and I just want to say THANK YOU and let everyone know what a compassionate guy you have on your team!

I am as guilty as the next person: there are a number of little things I could do or should do, at the office and at home, that would demonstrate compassion and make a difference in the lives of those around me. Sometimes it's hard to slow down and take the time, and sometimes it's much easier to rationalize a choice to accomplish the tasks before me. It is a constant challenge to find the balance between the compassion in our hearts and the logic in our brains. Funny thing is though, the two are not exclusive. Showing compassion for others often paves the way for efficiency in our relationships at home and at work. Compassion is a critical factor for make-a-difference leaders.

Disciplined

A disciplined person is one who has established a goal and is willing to make personal sacrifices to achieve the goal. In its simplest terms, if you are disciplined it means you will do what you say you will do. A derivative of the word discipline is disciple, the essential meaning of which is one who grasps or learns. Discipline is a way toward listening, learning, and the freedom to influence others to action or to work toward a common goal. In Brian's case, his seemingly boundless energy was, in large part, a result of the tremendous discipline he demonstrated in helping others achieve their goals, even until his death.

A great true-life example of discipline is told in one of my favorite Disney movies, *Miracle*. It tells the story of the 1980 U.S. Olympic hockey team and their bid to win a gold medal that year at the Olympics in Lake Placid, New York. The "Miracle on Ice," as the game has come to be known, took place on Friday, February 22. It wasn't the gold-medal round, but it was the matchup of the century. The U.S. team was made up of amateur and collegiate players, but incredibly, that day they managed to defeat the Soviet Union national team, which had won nearly every world championship and Olympic gold medal since 1954.

When the U.S. team's coach, Herb Brooks, had interviewed for the position of head coach in 1979, he told the group interviewing him that the only way Team USA could beat the Soviets was to change their game: they had to practice harder, train longer and incorporate a different style of play. Brooks had a tough, confrontational style, skating hard practices to build his players' stamina, often berating them for perceived weaknesses. His goal was to have his team be able to keep up with the Soviet hockey team through all three periods and be mentally tough enough to believe they could win.

The U.S. players endured nearly eight months of agonizing preparation . . . and it paid off. After defeating the Soviets in the semi-finals,

Team USA went on to defeat Finland for the gold medal. In 1999, *Sports Illustrated* named the "Miracle on Ice" the Top Sports Moment of the 20th Century.

Whenever I question whether or not I have the discipline necessary to complete a project, I remember the discipline demanded of Team USA by Herb Brooks and the results of their efforts. It never fails to inspire me.

Competent

Competent people have the necessary abilities, knowledge and skills to do many things successfully. During his time at NISC, Brian Wolf exemplified competency, and he constantly raised the bar within our organization because he modeled a level of competence others wanted to emulate. Brian was a lifelong learner. Academically, he held a master's degree in business, but we considered him to have the equivalent of a PhD in project management based on his accumulated knowledge and experience. To watch Brian as a leader was to see competence in action. Following is an example.

In his role as vice president of our utility division, Brian had the daunting task of completing almost four hundred enterprise software conversions around the country. He recognized that an important part of a conversion was the education process for the utility employees on the new software product that was going to be installed. Brian realized that if NISC was going to look like one company, our processes had to be consistent so that all NISC member/customers fully knew what to expect when it came to time, scope and cost. We had to speak the same language. In order to achieve this level of consistency, a dramatic change was required in how NISC did business. Brian's solution could easily have been to criticize the inconsistent approach currently in place. Or he could have just mandated the change that he felt was needed. Instead, he took it upon himself to teach a three-day course on project management to every NISC employee so that we would all understand the importance of consistent project management.

The classes consisted of between twenty-five and thirty people, so it took a couple of months to complete the task. Brian went well beyond the implementation teams; even accountants, code writers, lawyers and support teams were included, as project management is applied at all levels in an organization.

I can tell you from personal experience that being a student in one of Brian's classes was like drinking water from a fire hose. His well of knowledge was deep, and his delivery was animated and enthusiastic. His training methods mirrored his approach to life and can be epitomized in this quote from Antoine de Saint-Exupéry: "If you want to build a ship, don't drum up the men to go to the forest to gather wood, saw it, and nail the planks together. Instead teach them the desire for the sea."

Project management was only the beginning of Brian's efforts on behalf of employee education at NISC. He realized that the more information our employees and our members' employees had and the more they understood about NISC's software products, the fewer support calls we would have to field and the better the customer experience would be. He also convinced us that developing a team of adult education experts at NISC would be critical to launching our planned online curricula and certification programs. This was how our National IT Learning Center was born. The learning center allows more member employees to take courses without leaving their office or home. Brian was the chief architect of this solution for NISC and, after his death, we fittingly renamed the learning center as the Brian Wolf National IT Learning Center.

Interestingly, Brian once humbly told us that his high school counselor had discouraged him from attending college. The counselor had told Brian that he should look at other trade school or career opportunities, as he really wasn't college material. Thank goodness he didn't take the counselor's narrow-sighted advice or we would have missed Brian's genius. Competency might come from academic learning, or it can be nurtured through the school of hard knocks. To Brian's credit, he drew on both, and he leveraged competency with his innate sense of strategic vision to help position NISC for a bright future.

Innovative

One of NISC's shared values is that a person who wants to make a difference must be able to innovate: he or she needs to be willing to make changes in something established, usually by introducing new methods, ideas or concepts. There's an example of innovation I like to think of, which involves two English mathematicians and the world's first computer.

Charles Babbage first conceived the idea of an advanced calculating machine to calculate and print mathematical tables in the 1820s, when he was a professor of mathematics at Cambridge University. He called his machine the Analytical Engine, and it was designed to evaluate any mathematical formula.

Another remarkable English mathematician, Ada Lovelace, was asked to translate from French to English one of Babbage's presentations on the Analytical Engine. She did so, and her translation was published in 1843. It included her own extensive notes about the invention, how it worked and some of its potential capabilities. She described an algorithm used by the Analytical Engine to compute Bernoulli numbers. That algorithm is considered to be the first ever specifically tailored for implementation on a computer, and Ms. Lovelace is often cited as the first computer programmer for this reason.

In her notes, Lovelace emphasized the difference between the Analytical Engine and previous calculating machines, putting particular emphasis on its ability to be programmed to solve problems of any complexity. She realized that the potential of the device extended far beyond mere number crunching. This analysis was a conceptual leap from previous ideas about the capabilities of computing devices, and it foreshadowed the capabilities and implications of the modern computer. The Analytical Engine is now recognized as an early model for a computer, and Ada's notes are recognized as a rough description of a computer and software.

Think about it. Commercial computers or higher-level programming languages didn't exist until the 1950s—more than one hundred years later. When you consider technology, you typically think of how fast the industry moves and the speed of innovation as we know it today. The story of Mr. Babbage and Ms. Lovelace is a gentle reminder that innovators are change makers and that sometimes change takes time to take hold.

Inspirational

The final of the five traits we identify at NISC as being make-a-difference traits, is inspirational. When you meet someone or something inspirational, you know it because he or she or it causes you to think and act differently. Inspiration prompts us to be more than we believe we are capable of being. Brian Wolf's credo "go big or go home" is a constant inspiration to NISC employees, reminding us that we have more to give, more to do, more to become. The image of him presenting NISC products before an audience of fifteen hundred, chemotherapy-ravaged and terminally ill but exhibiting every ounce of gusto he'd always exhibited in the past . . . that image is etched in the minds of each of us who had been present in the room that day, because Brian's passion was larger than his cancer. Indeed, it was almost larger than life.

> **"Just thought you might like to let the CEO know he's going to get his butt kicked at the next board meeting."**
> **– Joe Harris**

Inspiration and individuals who make a difference come from every quarter at NISC, and there have been many exceptional and visionary people who have served on NISC's board of directors. I'd like to tell you about one of those individuals now. He's someone who also lives by the "go big or go home" philosophy.

The onetime CEO of Kay Electric Cooperative in Blackwell, Oklahoma, Joe Harris was admitted to the Oklahoma Association of Electric Cooperative's Hall of Fame in 2014 for his exceptional service to electric cooperatives, and he served on the NISC Board of Directors from 1997 to 2010. Joe is blessed with one of those larger-than-life personas and can be intimidating to the uninitiated with his booming voice, imposing size and penetrating stare. When he speaks, he has your full attention.

Joe served as chair of the NISC board in 2002-2003, and as his gift to the board at the end of his term he presented NISC with a chair's gavel that was suitable in size for Paul Bunyan. This gavel reminds me of Teddy Roosevelt's foreign policy approach: "speak softly and carry a big stick." While Joe didn't speak softly, the oversized gavel reiterated the importance of our board's work and the role the board chairman played in leading those efforts. On occasion, Joe would use his chair's seat as a bully pulpit for issues of importance, not just to him but to NISC. Joe was the consummate gentleman, and he would give me advance warning sometimes, saying something like, "Just thought you might like to let the CEO at NISC [me] know he's going to get his butt kicked at the next board meeting on [whatever the topic happened to be]." His intention was not to embarrass; when he would say this kind of thing it was because, in his estimation, NISC had done something to go off mission, and he wanted it to be decisively aired and considered. That professional and gentlemanly heads up also allowed me to prepare a reasoned response.

Joe taught everyone about good governance, and through his leadership he pointed the NISC board and the organization as a whole in strategic directions. For example, he demanded that NISC act like a national company. And he wanted more regional managers to be able to visit members consistently when the leadership team was fully focused on software development. Joe knew future sales expansion was contingent upon those business relationships. He understood that those sales relationships were more critical than the latest technical advancements under pursuit.

The real measure of Joe's leadership and the respect he had for his fellow board members was a technique he used as chair to close discussion. At the end of every directors' meeting, Joe would ask each board member to address any company issue he felt should be discussed or reviewed. If no issues were raised, Joe would move on with a request for a critical assessment of the meeting.

Still in practice today, paying this consideration to every board member has resulted in more than a few new directions being proposed and profound insights being shared. It empowers every board member with an opportunity to be heard, and it also has a cleansing and affirming effect on the business conducted. If everything is going well and

> **"Vision is an image of the future we seek to create."**
> **– Peter Senge**

there is nothing controversial happening, the comments shared are an expression of appreciation and every board member leaves with a sense of ownership for the actions of the board. They all know they had the opportunity to place everything on the table, since even second-guessing is allowed until the board adjourns. This is a truly simple board action and an excellent tool that many boards overlook.

Joe's "go big or go home" style, combined with his servant leadership actions, truly inspired the board members with whom he served at NISC and those who had the opportunity to work for him. Author Peter Senge says that vision is "an image of the future we seek to create." Being wired differently, Joe brought forward a compelling vision that has led NISC to consequent actions like those mentioned above.

Making a Difference Wherever You Are

If it is true that most of us are visual learners and comprehend best when we watch someone else do something first, then NISC has had some great models for make-a-difference leadership on our board of directors. I just mentioned the larger-than-life Joe Harris. An equally great model is Harry Barnes, whose recipe for leadership sometimes calls him to jump into unpleasant circumstances.

Harry is the vice chairman of the NISC Board of Directors, and he also serves on the board as a representative of 3 Rivers Communications in Fairfield, Montana. Harry lives on the Blackfeet Indian Reservation, where he has created three successful businesses. In addition to his businesses and his cooperative board positions, Harry has served as chairperson of the Holy Family Mission Board of Directors and as chairman of the school board for De La Salle Blackfeet School. Clearly, the man has made a solid contribution to the community in which he lives and works. But there's more. Harry also understands that sometimes making a difference means jumping right into the thick of things, even difficult things. Let me give you an example.

The Blackfeet Indian Reservation was teetering on the brink of insolvency in early 2014 due to infighting and mismanagement from two opposing political factions. Friends and neighbors encouraged Harry to run for the Blackfeet Tribal Business Council because they believed that he was the commonsense leader needed who could restore trust, confidence and calm to a tumultuous situation while getting the reservation back on its financial feet.

Harry agreed to run and turned out to be the leading vote-getter in the election of Blackfeet Tribal Business Council members. Following the tribal election, council members also elected Harry as Chairman of the council. At that point Harry addressed the tribal council and said the following:

We have either broken or strained every relationship that we, as a tribe, have. This division has split the community, causing anger and accusations. As leaders, we need to go back and fix those relationships, dedicating whatever time and abilities each of us has in order to re-establish and repair those relationships. The single-most important relationship that we have to mend is the one amongst ourselves. We need to re-establish a trust between the tribal members and their chosen leadership. We've got to put the war club down and pick up the hammer to go to work rebuilding our nation.

Harry understands the importance of community involvement and making a difference as a leader. He also recognizes the value of modeling the behaviors that are necessary to instill trust and restore credibility. Being compassionate while at the same time disciplined and competent—these are critical leadership characteristics. Healthy doses of innovation peppered with inspiration, now that's the recipe to make a difference on the Blackfeet Indian Reservation in Montana or wherever you find yourself.

Why Does Making a Difference Matter?

This chapter has been filled with examples of individuals who made a difference in the lives of others. Sometimes it resulted from something they did intentionally, and sometimes it occurred when circumstances presented an opportunity for the individuals to go big or go home. In each case, they acted in a manner that benefitted others. It is both that simple and that complex for each of us to serve others before ourselves. The choice to help others is one that is available to every human being, and it's one we should not take lightly. For those of us fortunate enough to live in developed countries, our opportunities to help others are far more plentiful and extend beyond providing food, shelter and safety— something I experienced firsthand some years ago. Let me share that story with you now.

In the spring of 1982, a friend asked me to pick up a speaker for a community presentation in Bismarck, North Dakota. The speaker was arriving by bus and his name was Father Bonen. Most people called him Father Beans because he worked at the Salesian Mission in Haiti, where he daily helped to feed rice and beans to almost 2,500 children. After dropping him off for his presentation, I decided to stay and listen. As I sat in the back of the crowded room, the kind and thoughtful words that Father Beans shared about the Haitian people touched my heart. That afternoon I decided to travel to the Caribbean and experience Haiti for myself, and I set off that April.

When I stepped off the plane in Port-au-Prince, Haiti, I was the only Caucasian as far as the eye could see, which was a new experience for me. Growing up in North Dakota in the 1970s, my idea of diversity was a few American Indian friends at my high school. Setting off on my new adventure, my backpack was crammed with personal items, including my beloved 35 mm camera and rolls and rolls of film. Because public transportation is virtually nonexistent in Haiti, I walked from the airport toward my destination, Port-au-Prince, watching and learning as I went. As I entered the city, the chaos that is commonplace in Haiti surrounded me. In retrospect, I should have been scared or perhaps even petrified, but I was still naïve enough to view the whole experience as a conquest rather than a threat. I spent the next four hours in the thick of the small river of humanity that moved within the city. I was struck by the Haitians' friendliness. They smiled, waved and shouted to me as I walked by; I returned the kindness.

It had been twelve hours since my last meal and I was famished, so I began looking for a grocery store. I stepped into a store that looked promising and was greeted by a sight that is still vividly etched in my memory, even though it occurred over three decades ago. This store had aisles and aisles of shelves brightly lit by fluorescent lights above. But unlike the bounty you'd find in an American grocery store, the shelves of this Haitian store were completely bare. There was no fruit. No canned goods. Only a few trinkets, a broom or two, and brilliantly colored scarves.

Suddenly my Haitian experience became very real. What would I eat? I wasn't comfortable buying food from the many street vendors who were cooking who-knows-what on their campfires beside the road. But there were mango stands that seemed safe. The fruit was something I could peel, and the flesh hadn't been exposed to the elements. Out of necessity, mangos were joined by rice and beans. These were my staples for the next four weeks.

When I was done eating I found my way to the city's Salesian Mission, where I had made plans to stay. In Port-au-Prince, the Mission also served as a school and an orphanage. The facility was surrounded by a crude concrete-block wall, located only three blocks from where today the National Palace lies in ruins. The staff greeted me warmly. I was escorted to a courtyard of cots where the workers slept. It was a beautiful evening, and the scent of charcoal lingered in the air. This would be my home for the next month.

My first Haitian morning, I awoke before dawn to the sounds and activity of people moving about with a sense of urgency and purpose. I walked to an open-air kitchen where there were large metal kettles fired by propane, each holding what looked to be about a hundred pounds of rice or beans. The workers moved like a well-coordinated team, feverishly preparing food for the more than two thousand students who would soon arrive at the school. The food was the motivating force that brought children to the Salesian school. For most of them, this meal of rice and beans would be their only meal of the day.

After twenty-four hours of on-the-job training, I was contributing to the kitchen team. The work was hard and hot, but it felt good, as did witnessing the joyful smiles of the children when we loaded their plates with rice and beans. At the end of the day, we handed out small bags of uncooked rice and beans for the children to take home. Their parents would anxiously anticipate these meager portions. Frankly, this connection with others and the sense of contribution that this experience gave me was more valuable than any paycheck I had ever received.

My days in the kitchen were followed by evenings in the orphanage. The other workers and I spent time with the children and tried desperately to fill the lonely void in their lives. Days passed quickly and each night I returned to my cot exhausted. On weekends, I would hitchhike to neighboring cities. Like Haitians, I rode on the back of trucks with other travelers who were heading home with their treasured bags of rice, live pigs or live chickens.

Throughout my travels, I experienced the goodness of the Haitian people. Although they lived in absolute poverty, they were people of joy who were quick with a smile and always willing to help out a confused traveler like me. One of their favorite sayings was, "You Americans have the fancy watches, but we in Haiti have the time!" And it was true: the Haitians always had time to share with me. They reminded me that Americans have so much wealth, comparatively speaking, yet still we fill our days with worries about our next mortgage payment, what colleges will accept our sons and daughters or if our retirement savings are sufficient, and we never seem to have enough time. Joy for life obviously does not come from fancy watches!

When I returned home to Bismarck four weeks later, I was twenty pounds lighter and full of the realization that my Haitian experience had forever changed my life.

You might think that I'm sharing this story because I'm proud of my contribution to the Haitian people. Or perhaps you think I'm making a plea for the less fortunate on our planet. While both are valid, neither represents my motive here. You see, the Haitian people taught me how to make a difference through their genuine compassion toward others, even outsiders like me. The Haitian people I worked with were disciplined and competent, even though they had so few resources with which to work. They were true innovators when it came to meeting the needs of the children they served at the Salesian school, and their selfless giving was inspiration at its finest.

Compassion, discipline, competence, innovation, inspiration. I have learned about these make-a-difference traits through observing many great leaders and, simply, great people. Some, like Brian Wolf, have been obvious, and we at NISC are forever grateful to have had his contribution to the strength of our organization for nearly four years. Others, like the people of Haiti, were a surprise to me. In truth, I went to Haiti to make a difference, but it was the Haitian people who made an incredible difference—in me.

KEY POINTS TO CONSIDER IN THIS CHAPTER

1. Imagine the potential our organizations can have when there is a mindset to make a difference and a culture that expects it to happen. I speak from experience: **one individual with a make-a-difference mindset sets the course for amazing things to occur!**

2. The five make-a-difference traits call us to **be compassionate, disciplined, competent, innovative and inspirational.**

3. **To have compassion is to feel or show empathy and concern for others.** Put yourself in another person's shoes and see the world from their view.

4. When we are disciplined, we show a controlled form of behavior or way of working. A disciplined person is one who has established a goal and is willing to make personal sacrifices to achieve that goal. **In its simplest terms, being disciplined means you will do what you say you will do.**

5. A person who wants to make a difference must be able to innovate: he or she needs to be willing to **make changes in something established, usually by introducing new methods, ideas or concepts.**

6. When you meet someone inspirational, you know it because he or she or it causes you to think or act differently. **Inspiration prompts us to be more than we believe we are capable of being.**

7. Brian Wolf had the necessary ability, knowledge and skill to do many things successfully. He was a gifted teacher, coach and mentor. He went big when it came to sharing his knowledge and information, be it formally or informally. Brian was **constantly raising the bar within our organization because he modeled a level of competence and compassion others want to emulate.**

PART II

VALUES IN ACTION

Most organizations have held the strategic planning session in which a leadership group develops mission and vision statements. Then, in round two of the exercise, the team identifies a series of values, sometimes out of necessity and other times out of desire, that outline how they hope employees will bring the mission and vision to life. On paper or PowerPoint, these items look good. Unfortunately, it is a rare occasion to see these values in action among the very individuals they were designed to influence. Today, putting values in action is precisely what organizations need to do in order to engage employees, inspire customers and spark better results.

Chapter 5

Actions Speak Louder than Anything Else

To be truly satisfied is to do what you believe is great work.
And the only way to do great work is to love what you do.
— Steve Jobs

Every leader wants to believe that the glossy values statement, typically written with little input from across the company, is being actively demonstrated by everyone in the organization, from the highest levels of management to the shop room floor. At NISC, because our employees worked together to write our shared values, the implementation and practice of those values have taken a unique twist.

No matter what your role is at NISC, there is someone on your left or your right who knows the shared values and is willing to hold you accountable to them. In fact, employees set the bar high when it comes to our shared values because they know that our members are also aware of them and so those members are watching to see if the shared values we espouse are actually practiced in the interactions they have with us.

This chapter provides an insider's perspective on organizational shared values, specifically, our shared values at NISC: integrity, relationships, innovation, teamwork, empowerment and personal development. What follows are personal stories from NISC employees and board members. In their own words, each shares their experiences relating to a particular shared value. The actions they've taken or observed speak louder than anything I could say about NISC's culture.

Shared Value: INTEGRITY

We hold ourselves to the highest professional, moral and ethical standards. We are committed to doing the right thing, always.

NISC Board Member: Reginal Rudolph, General Manager, San Isabel Electric Association, Pueblo West, Colorado

The Way NISC Operates

Serving on NISC's board of directors has been one of the greatest privileges of my career. When contemplating the decision to run for the board in 2012, NISC's reputation for quality and integrity made my decision to serve easy. I'm proud to associate myself with an organization that sets the highest standards of integrity.

There are very few words in our vocabulary that carry such weight and responsibility as the word integrity—NISC's first shared value. Do the right thing, always! *Always* means every time, without wavering principles. Upholding that value isn't as simple as just telling everyone to be fair, to be honest and to do the right thing. If it were, we wouldn't see so many high-profile CEOs escorted in handcuffs from the organizations they had been leading. If integrity is truly to be a shared value, it must be ingrained in the way the organization operates; it must be embedded in its culture.

I was raised in the rural electric cooperative family. My father retired as a general manager after twenty-five years in the rural electric industry, and my own career started when I was in the seventh grade, washing cars and service trucks for Mor-Gran-Sou Electric (one of NISC's early members) in Flasher, North Dakota. During those early years, it became clear to me what a rural electric cooperative was: a self-help organization formed to serve your family, friends and neighbors. Coming from a small town of less than three hundred people as I did, serving your family, friends and neighbors is an easy concept to grasp because you generally know those you serve. But whether your organization is large or small, the concept is the same. Your service is based on accountability and integrity. The last thing you want to do is disappoint the membership (customers) you serve, so you complete every task to the highest level of your ability. You want to deliver on the promise of service based on cooperative principles and integrity.

A Reputation for Integrity

NISC's shared values are cultural, ingrained in the daily activities of the organization. Without a commitment to integrity and the ongoing integrity of its employees' actions, NISC couldn't maintain the reputation it holds in the industry. NISC employees are known for being helpful, excited to work with the members and keenly aware of the importance of getting a response back to the user who has a problem. As NISC members, we are the beneficiaries of the organization's commitment to integrity.

NISC's reputation for integrity predates the organization itself, which I can personally attest to. Back in 2000, I was the general manager of McLean Electric in Garrison, North Dakota, a member cooperative of North Central Data Cooperative (NCDC), one of the two data cooperatives that would go on to merge and create NISC. When I initially received information about a proposed consolidation of NCDC with a company in St. Louis, Missouri, called Central Area Data Processing (CADP), I was concerned because I wasn't yet familiar with CADP. I was afraid McLean Electric would be forgotten in North Dakota if NCDC joined forces with them. The deadline for members to vote on the consolidation was approaching, and I was undecided.

Keith Horntvedt at NCDC called me prior to the vote. I remember asking him one question, "Will you promise me you won't abandon North Dakota or any of the small cooperatives that created NCDC?" Keith had no problem making that promise, and McLean Electric voted to support NCDC's consolidation with CADP.

That decision wasn't based solely on one persuasive conversation with an NCDC employee. It was based on years of experience with the organization and its people. It was based on the integrity of every transaction and relationship created since the day I started working for electric cooperatives. Not only is Keith an employee of our IT supplier, he is a friend I've gone hunting and fishing with, a guy whose family I know personally. And so I trusted his opinion, knowing his recommendation wasn't a sales pitch he was directed to give. His personal integrity is stronger than a set of talking points to accomplish an end result. To this day, NISC values the relationship with every member, large and small.

Integrity Starts at the Top

The author C.S. Lewis once said, "Integrity is doing the right thing, even when no one is watching." I agree with this and believe it goes even further with regard to cooperative organizations. We should be motivated to maintain the highest ethical and moral standards because our members have entrusted us with the responsibility to deliver on the promise of serving them.

I believe that the culture of integrity starts at the top of the organization. It is the CEO's responsibility to lead by example and instill within every employee and member a desire to do the right thing, always. In my mind, NISC's CEO Vern Dosch epitomizes integrity as a person and leader. During my career I have witnessed him progress through the ranks at NCDC and then, subsequently, at NISC. I have known him personally as a community servant, biker, runner and an earnest (but mediocre) fisherman. In every situation, Vern maintains the highest professional, moral and ethical standards as a person, not just when acting as the CEO of NISC or when someone is watching.

When the leader of the organization sets such a high standard for himself or herself, it becomes the benchmark others seek to attain. Employees at NISC respect Vern for his integrity and the personal way in which he connects with them. He engages with them and is genuinely concerned about their workload and how they are being taken care of. Vern feels a sense of responsibility not to disappoint the membership or the employees, and he holds himself accountable to deliver on NISC's shared values.

As a board, we entrust Vern with great responsibility: keeping one thousand employees fully engaged in improving the lives of our end-use consumers; managing professional relationships throughout the electric and telecommunications industries; and keeping our technology company at the leading edge while being economically successful. His level of commitment is much appreciated and well respected.

The world is changing rapidly and our technology is evolving at an exponential rate. But integrity is a timeless value. I have been blessed to have a long and positive relationship with NISC. The time I'm given to serve on the board of directors is a privilege, and my motivation will always be to further NISC's positive reputation.

Shared Value: RELATIONSHIPS

We believe people are the heart of our organization. We are committed to building, nurturing, and preserving lasting relationships with our member/owners, customers, partners, our families and friends and one another.

We are passionate about the service we provide and demonstrate that by being responsive to the needs of our customers and constantly striving to exceed their expectations.

We believe in engaging in honest communication, showing respect for others, and treating all people with the dignity they deserve. Because we understand the importance of all our relationships, we support a healthy balance between work and family.

Employee: Deb Burke, NISC Professional Services and Programming Manager

More than a Software Company

I grew up the daughter of an Air Force officer. The military life gave me valuable lessons about relationships at a young age. Our family lived in eight different places, and I quickly learned that people come and go. Several times, I was the new person, feeling awkward and not connected. These experiences taught me how to develop relationships; I learned to be as genuine as my insecurities allowed at the time. The importance of connecting with others and seeking help when needed was a valuable life lesson that serves me well as an NISC employee.

Our business is to create, sell, implement and support software. I often ask myself if that's a true statement or if our line of business is the venue to touch lives, to enrich, influence, encourage, inspire and nurture others. And to let others do the same for us. Every day, these small amounts of effort occur through the people of NISC. By proclaiming relationships as one of our shared values, we intentionally anticipate making a difference, acting with purpose, and adding value to our own life, and to the lives of others. We are more than a software company.

When I welcome a new employee, I explain that he or she will develop an unbelievable amount of care and concern for customer service, for our members and for each other. The importance of shared values and, in particular, the value of relationships courses through our veins. NISC employees often morph into people committed to our shared values, or they may flounder and be uncomfortable with the NISC culture. Over time, if an employee chooses not to commit to, much less practice, the shared values it can be a glass ceiling for their career growth.

In Jennifer Kennedy Dean's book, *The Power of Small: Think Small to Live Large,* she shares her belief that "every moment counts, every decision matters, every act has consequences." With each communication and contact, we have an opportunity to encourage, inspire and enrich another person's life. *The Power of Small* speaks directly to NISC's shared value of relationships. Let me give you some examples.

Relationships in Action

Brawna Sells is an office manager for New Enterprise Rural Electric Cooperative, Inc. (NEREC), one of NISC's member co-ops located in a small rural town in Pennsylvania. Several years ago, Brawna asked NISC to set up live integration between the cooperative's billing and accounting system. To meet this request, I spent a week at NEREC's office setting up the system, training staff and validating the integration. The job was complete, but the relationship was just starting.

A few months later, Brawna called me with a heavy heart. Not because of a system error or a program malfunction. She had just found out that her teenage daughter had a rare and life-threatening health issue affecting her brain. Brawna just needed to talk. For several months, she would call with updates and share her fear and worry with me. After many conversations and prayers, her daughter underwent the needed surgery and came through it without complications.

Brawna's daughter is an adult now and on her own, but Brawna and I still continue to connect and share our joys and pain with one another. NISC employees did their job to advance NEREC's billing and accounting system, and while doing my part of that job, I created and continue to nurture a special relationship that goes well beyond customer and supplier; I consider Brawna a friend.

Here's another example. In 1994, NISC hired a new implementer, a young man named Channon Lowman who didn't look old enough to rent a car on his own. I was Channon's mentor/trainer, and within a few months he introduced me to his girlfriend who lived about a hundred miles away. Shortly thereafter, Joelean became his fiancée and Channon asked me if I would be open to the idea of Joelean living in my two-bedroom apartment until they got married. I said yes, and she stayed with me while she finished her college degree and worked nights. We grew close and when the wedding came, I was Joelean's bridal attendant.

Over the years, I've met Channon's parents and sister and he's met my parents. In March 1997, Channon's family attended my wedding and Joelean was my bridal attendant. We shared in the joy when their three children were born, and they even asked me to care for the children one week while both of them needed to be out of town for work.

Channon was just a new employee learning software when I met him. Who knew that the new business relationship would turn into us sharing major life events together like weddings and the birth of children, and everyday things like dinners, volleyball games, softball games, and so on? But it did! This is because relationships are nurtured at NISC.

Another example: One of our programmers, Shoni Mortenson, worked into the weekend and wee hours of the morning to get data converted for a new member. What did the implementer, Mathew Krogen, do while he was waiting for the conversion to get done? He stayed by her side, even bringing her dinner.

And another: An NISC team worked on a Saturday to meet a deadline, and their team manager, Keith Horntvedt, showed up with a plate of delicious, fresh and still warm chocolate chip cookies for them.

Everywhere you look at NISC, between our employees and with our members and our customers, people embrace the importance of relationships. We understand the difference it makes, and we know that when we value relationships, our organization becomes more than just a software company and our lives are better off for having richer interactions with others.

Shared Value: INNOVATION

We promote the spirit of creativity and champion new ideas. We believe a passion for quality and the desire to constantly improve what we do is critical to our success. We challenge each other to continually strive for excellence and define new ways to build our future.

Employee: Brad Molander, Technology Evangelist and Manager of Innovations

Tuned to Promote Innovation and Collaboration

Innovation is not a concept that can be taught or forced. It is the product of a collaborative environment that fosters trust and respect among team members. Ideas need to be able to be freely expressed and discussed with others, regardless of their position within the organization. Whether the goal is to create a new product feature or simply to resolve an issue, it's critical that the environment is consistently tuned to promote innovation and collaboration. Some of the most innovative people I know at NISC are the same people who inspire, facilitate and actively promote such environments. They are selfless and patient, yet committed and driven.

I have had the privilege to be involved with several challenging projects at NISC, and some of our most innovative ideas were the result of informal conversations in the lunchroom or right after official meetings. One person would suggest an interesting idea, others would build on it, adding and subtracting pieces along the way, until critical mass was reached. This simple yet agile process has allowed us to solve countless challenges over the years, and to do so quickly.

NISC's commitment to employees allows us to attract industry-leading talent in every division. As we grow and add new people, we also add new ideas to an already rich and open atmosphere. Still, one of our best assets when it comes to innovative thinking is our members.

Innovative Approaches to Problem Solving

Several years ago when we started working on our Meter Data Management System (MDMS), we felt that we had a pretty good idea of what the product needed to accomplish, but we didn't know how to get it there. Not a single person in the organization at the time was equipped to lead the charge. What should this platform that would provide energy information to end users look like? What technologies should we use? Could our existing platform scale to meet the needs of a product intended to store billions of measurements?

To help us assess the needs of our customers, we enlisted the help of one our members—Ryan Hentges of Minnesota Valley Electric Cooperative (MVEC). Ryan's humble leadership style allowed our developers to understand fully how we could make his job a lot easier, and how we could provide real and unparalleled value to our entire membership. Whether he was on a call or onsite talking directly with us, Ryan helped us drill down to what MVEC needed and how that might relate to other members as well.

During the project development of MDMS, elite developers such as Mike Friesen, Jeremy Ford and Nicholas Iffrig began creating the most advanced software system I have ever been a part of: the Cooperative Cloud. Early on, we began to see what the technologies behind the MDMS could mean to our entire enterprise. The raw horsepower and the redundancy that the technologies offered would elevate our traditional applications to do things they could never do before.

This new platform stretched the technical limits of anything we had previously worked on, and not everything went to plan. There were a few late pizza deliveries to the office, and even some donuts as we watched the sun come up. No one complained, and non-essential staff stayed with us, just to make sure everyone had what they needed. This level of commitment is unbelievably humbling and goes even beyond our shared value of innovation; it reaches across to teamwork and relationships in a big way.

What is amazing to me is that my personal experiences at NISC are not uncommon. Every meeting I attend, regardless of the context or the people involved, has the same creative passion. All over our organization, projects and challenges are solved daily using the same simple yet innovative methods.

Sometimes great ideas came from the most unlikely sources, from people who were not all that close to the problem we were trying to solve. The example I'll use is of Rob Rabenberg and Andrew Cooper, who manage and monitor our cloud infrastructure. Oftentimes they offer remarkable ideas for application features and data modeling for the MDMS and for another software NISC offers called Messenger, even though this isn't their area of focus. It is supposed to be the developers' role, but sometimes we are too close or too wrapped up in the details to think clearly about what needs to be done. Rob and Andrew are able to see the bigger picture. They understand our goals and they choose to take personal responsibility to ensure the success of the project by actively suggesting innovative ways to get better use out of our hardware.

Fully understanding NISC's purpose and long-term vision at every step of a project is critical to delivering innovative products. This mentality is not just the ideal at NISC, it is required to compete in our industry and it guarantees our future. Best of all, innovation is a shared value among NISC employees. We share the value, and we innovate together.

Shared Value: TEAMWORK

We exemplify the cooperative spirit by working together with respect for one another's ideas and contributions. We believe in using our individual and collective knowledge and skills to improve our organization and agree to show support of all decisions once they are made. We know the combination of our talents allows us to accomplish great things because there is greater potential for success when we share our diverse experiences.

Employee: Don Mastel, NISC Telecom Regional Business Manager

Counting on Each Other to Do the Job Well

I learned a little something about teamwork growing up on a farm near Zeeland, North Dakota. It took a team to get everything accomplished on the farm. Dad was just one person, and he needed the help of all of us doing our share, whether that was working in the fields combining and swathing grain or fixing machinery during harvest. Now, as a business professional at NISC, I find myself a member of a larger team, and the same principles of everyone doing his or her share are equally as important.

It is a privilege to work directly with our member/customers as one of their main points of contact. As a regional business manager and a former NISC programmer, I have a pretty solid understanding of what it takes for our team to deliver the products and services that our members need to support their business goals and future requirements.

But my role as a relationship manager only starts after a member has first worked with various other NISC team members. This includes the NISC sales team members who open the door for our demonstration team to show the software's functions and answer questions on how the NISC enterprise suite can improve a member's business processes. If we get a nod of approval, our sales support staff develops a proposal, selects the hardware that will be needed and maps the timeline for an installation. Our legal staff formalizes the proposal into an agreement, and then the ball is handed off to the implementation team who will then go onsite to carry out the implementation schedule.

As the regional business manager in charge of customer relationships, this is where I get to enter the picture. I introduce my teammates on the implementation team and thereafter keep my fingers on the new member's pulse. The installation will involve our experts from the software billing department, including the software accounting staff, the engineering and operations team, the e-commerce team to provide for credit card billing, and the automated mail room staff who will customize the new member's bills for rendering and mailing.

It's realistic for a new member to work with fifty or more NISC employees during the process of becoming fully integrated with our NISC systems. And this is just getting a member set up on our system. There are many more NISC team members who engage with our co-op members to support them and answer any questions they have.

There's no question, then, that bringing a new member onboard for services at NISC is a team effort. No one person or department, no matter how talented, can do all that needs to be done to support a telecom or utility member. With so many moving parts, it is important to have each other's back to ensure that all assignment hand-offs go smoothly. Trusting our teammates is critical.

I often say I like to walk a mile in my teammates' shoes to understand the demands they have on their time and how I can help them meet the expectations of our members. I believe it is my responsibility to know and understand my teammates because we can all make a positive (or a negative) difference in the success of a project. Each of us needs to remember that everyone else in the process is counting on us to do our job, and to do it well.

The NISC Team Delivers

Over the past twenty-three years, the power of teamwork and the results of working together have been demonstrated to me repeatedly. For example, frequently when I've received calls from members asking for help and I contacted support or programming, the next morning I would see e-mails about the issue sent from Kelley Kunnanz (an NISC programmer) at 2:00 a.m.

Once when I was the manager-on-call, a member had an issue at 6:00 a.m. I followed up by calling Tom Materi's home phone (Tom is an NISC Professional Services Industry Consultant), and his first response was, "I will call them right away." Right away meant right now, while he was at home. I know Tom followed through on his word because I have the privilege of hearing firsthand how much our members appreciate the extra effort NISC employees like Tom provide.

At NISC we are blessed with a board of directors and an executive team who are willing to invest in our organization and lead by example. It takes a well-oiled machine (a team) to do what we do on a daily basis. We need strong role models because NISC is growing every year. It is more important than ever that we get to know each other so we can be better teammates and continue to serve each other as well as our member/customers. Just like Dad used to say: we need all of us doing each of our jobs well to get the work accomplished.

Shared Value: EMPOWERMENT

We believe individuals have the power to make a difference.
We agree to be accountable and responsible in the decisions

we make, use good judgment, and take pride and ownership in our work.

Employee: Brent Roberts, Manager, NISC Technology Solutions Group

An Environment that Makes All the Difference

Shortly after NISC was created, some major decisions had to be made that would shape the future of the company. We needed to bring to market new versions of our products based on current and ever-evolving technology, but would we buy or would we build this next generation of products? And what technology should be used? Answering these questions was made more challenging by the fact that we'd just consolidated two independent and successful organizations with different technology backgrounds. We were not only facing pivotal decisions that would determine NISC's direction for product development, the decision-making process would be a key exercise in determining how employees of the new organization would work together to reach a difficult decision.

Dozens of individuals were involved in the discussions, and many meetings were held over the twelve-month preliminary survey period. There were a number of varying views, and people were spirited and passionate about our next steps. We took our due diligence seriously.

An Exciting and Scary Time

What does this have to do with empowerment? We didn't know where we were headed, but we were empowered to get there. I remember vividly the long hours my colleagues and I worked together to prototype possible technology solutions, and the amount of time we spent evaluating products and researching companies who could possibly meet our needs.

It was an exciting and scary time, as our ultimate decision would set the direction for how NISC developed and delivered its products for years to come. Being able to build upon a viable technology for the longest possible timeframe significantly reduces the amount of developer training. It allows our products to mature gracefully, and the technology can be enhanced to remain competitive (instead of having to rewrite with another technology). This decision was crucial to our immediate and our long-term success.

There were close to twenty-five of us who were empowered to re-search and provide input to help determine NISC's final technology solution. Each of the varying inputs and ideas were seriously consid-ered and debated. In the end, we chose Java technology as our main development platform, and it continues to propel us into the future.

I believe working for a company like NISC with a management team that fosters an empowering environment makes all of the differ-ence in how we feel about our efforts and the products we develop. I see it every day in the Research, Development and Quality Division (RDQ). We are given tasks and, while we are expected to work with-in certain guidelines, we use our skills to the fullest. This includes researching new ideas and collaborating with others to find the best solution. Encouraging collaboration allows us to create products we all take pride in and feel a sense of ownership of. It develops greater ac-countability and empowers all of the individuals involved.

My personal experience has been that the more responsibility you desire, and you make it known, the more likely you will be allowed to work on the things that interest you. I think this is a key component of empowerment that can be overlooked. Sometimes employees expect management to provide the opportunities; however, it is up to employ-ees to recognize an opportunity and seek it out. NISC's management allows for, even encourages, this from its employees. We are required to follow through and take responsibility to complete the task we sought out, but there is always help and advice close by. Realizing that the task is your own responsibility is important, and knowing you can get help and insight from fellow employees is powerful. The ability to capitalize on opportunities and work on issues that interest you within this type of supportive environment keeps motivation high and creates greater accountability in the finished product by all involved.

One of the aspects of my experience at NISC that I have valued the most is the ethical nature of its culture. It is what allows employees to have honest and open discussions that keep the focus on making the best decisions and creating the best products. I believe this to be a criti-cal requirement for employee empowerment. Knowing that we can be up-front with our thoughts and opinions is encouraging. That, coupled with treating each other respectfully and professionally, is how great things happen in our workplace.

Shared Value: PERSONAL DEVELOPMENT

We believe the free exchange of knowledge and information is absolutely necessary to the success of each individual and the organization. We agree to work every day to learn new things and are committed to sharing our ideas with one another. We support education and learning and are dedicated to providing opportunities for every individual to grow in their abilities.

Employee: Pat Shafer, NISC Chief Learning Officer

A Journey of Lifelong Learning

American author and motivational speaker Karen Kaiser Clark says, "Life is change. Growth is optional. Choose wisely." This is so true for all of us. Change is inevitable, and while the pace may sometimes amaze us (and even intimidate us), our ability to adapt to change determines the quality of our lives. Based on my experience, I believe that learning is the antidote, the best way to adapt and thrive in the face of change.

My journey with NISC began in 2006 with a phone call from a former grad school colleague of mine, Brian Wolf. He was the chief operating officer for NISC at the time, and he was searching for someone to lead a new enterprise project. He was familiar with my background and offered me the position, saying, "This would be a great fit, for both of us."

Brian's vision for how the role of learning would fuel NISC's growth and success was intriguing to me, so I accepted his invitation to lead NISC's learning initiative. Actually, everyone at NISC is on a journey of lifelong learning, given our shared value and commitment to personal development.

When I joined the team, NISC was nearing the end of its conversion from legacy software to its new iVUE® platform, and so member users had to be trained on the new products and processes. Our Lake St. Louis, Missouri, location, which included three state-of-the-art classrooms, became the home for NISC's National IT Learning Center. A small team of professionals was assembled to deliver the training, which would be based on the certification curriculum that was created.

Classrooms were filling with members who were anxious to become proficient iVUE® users.

Cindy Holm, an employee of Flathead Electric Cooperative in Montana, was a student in the original certification course and one of the first members to complete the 208 credit hours needed to earn the professional level of certification. Cindy's office in Kalispell, Montana, is a twelve-hour drive to St. Louis, a trip she made many times while participating in iVUE® certification classes. Obviously her personal commitment to learning and development was enormous.

"I was intimidated at first," Cindy says now about the certification experience. "I thought I was too old to learn, but the NISC staff were encouraging and patient from the start. After the first class, I began to believe it was possible, and I even brought some colleagues with me the next time. Even in challenging classes, we had the most patient and supportive teachers. I especially remember John Alls, he was incredible."

I believe human beings want to make a difference, and learning prepares us to do that. At NISC, I've met many colleagues like Cindy who appreciate the value of learning and the opportunities we have. One such person is Robin Castle.

While working for Central Electric Cooperative, Inc. in Bend, Oregon, Robin always wanted to work at NISC. "I would attend the member information conference and sit in awe of the subject matter experts from NISC as they shared their vast knowledge of iVUE®," she says. "I knew I had the potential to be more and I wanted to achieve the professional certification in iVUE®. But unfortunately, my co-op couldn't afford to send me."

In pursuit of her dream, Robin applied for a support position at NISC and was subsequently hired. She moved from Oregon to work at our Lake St. Louis office, where she achieved her goal of attaining the professional level of iVUE® certification. She also became a peer mentor to new NISC teammates, and she taught member classes and was herself a presenter at the member information conference.

"I was so fortunate to be a learner, a teacher and a mentor," she says today of her experience. "I saw firsthand how learning makes a huge difference in people's lives, and I was helping to make that possible. I loved my five years at NISC!" She adds that working at NISC created exciting new career options for her. "I know that the learning opportunities changed my life, including my current position as project manager and data process coordinator at Lane Electric Cooperative in Eugene, Oregon."

Personal Development Requires Adaptability

In response to the continuing need for iVUE® training, we transitioned from offering classroom training to also offering online learning events as well. In just five months, Craig Dahle and the Learning Center team had forty online modules created and posted in our learning management system. This made it possible for us to complete training in advance of the "go live" date for software and to triple the number of implementations possible in a year. At the heart of this personal development initiatve were two other NISC shared values—innovation and empowerment—to deliver a better solution!

Educating members to master the various functions of our software remains a significant part of the Learning Center; however, our directive has always been to create a learning organization that supports our employees. NISC needs to be a place where knowledge is acquired and innovation is fast enough to survive and thrive in a rapidly changing world. This focus on developing and supporting colleagues in their quest for a successful career at NISC was the most intriguing part of Brian Wolf's invitation to me, and it has been a rewarding part of my journey with NISC.

The book *Good to Great* by Jim Collins is a constant reference at NISC, and we know that becoming a great organization is only possible if our people are continuously learning, improving, and thriving on contributions that provide the best possible service and solutions. Under Brian's leadership, a strategic plan was developed in 2007, and it remains our compass today. His vision speaks to every employee's significant value, their role, and their contributions that will ensure a future for NISC and its employees. It explains why we need to strengthen our personal commitment to learning and improved performance, and it promises a commitment by NISC to provide resources and opportunities to ensure everyone's success. The plan provides the framework for a partnership in which opportunity is given and responsibility for self-development is an individual choice.

The successful implementation of this plan is reliant upon executive support, and our CEO, Vern, has always been an advocate for the learning vision, ensuring there was a champion at the executive level even after Brian's death in 2008. Our progress at NISC, which has been significant, depends on continued encouragement and investment in the vision, the infrastructure, the expectations, and the talent that drive a learning organization. We are still evolving toward the ultimate goal of being "great." We aren't yet there; however, we celebrate our small successes along the way.

Our Actions Speak Louder than Our Words

As CEO, I'm passionate about all that NISC stands for, and this definitely includes our shared values. Regardless of a person's role in life, we each need to be true to our values in the actions we take, whether they be the shared values of our employer, the values of a particular organization, or the values we hold dear in our personal or family lives. We must remember that our actions truly do speak louder than our words.

KEY POINTS TO CONSIDER IN THIS CHAPTER

1. **The culture of integrity starts at the top of the organization.** It becomes the CEO's responsibility to lead by example and ingrain in every employee and member a desire to do the right thing, always.

2. By proclaiming relationships as one of our shared values, **we intentionally anticipate making a difference, acting with purpose and adding value to our own life and that of others.**

3. Whether we are creating a new product feature or simply trying to resolve an issue, **we need to ensure that the environment around us is consistently tuned to promote innovation and collaboration.**

4. We all can make a positive (or negative) difference in the success of a project. **Each of us needs to remember that everyone else in the process is counting on us to do our job, and to do it well.**

5. **The ability to capitalize on opportunities and work on issues that are of interest to employees keeps motivation high and creates greater accountability** in the finished product by all involved.

6. We know **becoming a great organization is only possible when you have people who are continuously learning, improving and thriving** on contributions that provide the best possible service and solutions.

Chapter 6

Do the Right Thing, Always

If you have integrity, nothing else matters. If you don't have integrity, nothing else matters.

— Alan Simpson

According to *Merriam-Webster's Collegiate Dictionary*, Eleventh Edition, integrity is "the quality of being honest and fair; firm adherence to a code of especially moral or artistic values." Instead of saying that NISC employees must have integrity and leaving it at that, when exploring and developing the shared values, our employee committee took it further, stating: "We hold ourselves to the highest professional, moral and ethical standards. We are committed to doing the right thing, always."

Holding a company to shared values is challenging and sometimes painful, but it's necessary if we at NISC intend to build a trusted culture that claims integrity as its trademark. Integrity is really a personal statement, and when companies uphold integrity as a value, they make a personal statement that captures both the employees' and the customers' attention. (See chapter 12 for the bottom-line effect that integrity in action can have on organizational results.)

A well-known quote by Ralph Waldo Emerson is, "A man is usually more careful of his money than he is of his principles." As it relates to companies and their employees, this is the value challenge when it comes to the question of how actions or decisions may affect the bottom line or an employee's take-home income. Value statements make for great public relations until they come with a price tag. How will the company executive respond to a value challenge that could mean losing a critical sale necessary to meet a budget or advance the executive's career?

Emergis Technologies versus Flathead Electric

NISC faced just such a dramatic challenge when one of our member co-ops, Flathead Electric Cooperative in Kalispell, Montana, received a letter from a prestigious Chicago law firm in October 2005. The letter advised Flathead Electric that the firm represented Emergis Technologies Inc. (a Canadian e-business company that supplies technology solutions to the transaction-intensive financial services market) and that Emergis was offering U.S. Patent No. 6,044,362. "The '362 Patent," as it's more commonly referred to in legal articles and within NISC, related to Electronic Invoice Presentment and Payment (EIPP), which is a process companies use to collect payments electronically. Essentially, this was a patent to allow automated electronic bill presentment and payment from a personal computer to the retailer offering products or services. The letter said that if Flathead Electric was going to take payments from customers over the Internet, the cooperative needed to pay for a license from Emergis for the privilege to conduct such transactions.

After three or four pages of commentary about the '362 Patent, the law firm revealed the financial terms of licensing this intellectual property. The least expensive price on an annual basis was $250,000 for smaller-sized companies (like Flathead), graduating upward according to the size of the company's revenue. In short, this was a highly expensive proposition for any organization.

The letter suggested that Emergis would be willing to reasonably negotiate on the terms of payment; however, if the license approach wasn't accepted, then a more expensive calculation of damages would become part of a costly lawsuit that would be filed shortly thereafter. So basically the cooperative was being told, purchase the license or be sued!

Ken Sugden was the general manager for Flathead Electric at the time. He reviewed the contract with his company attorney and they contacted NISC, as it was NISC that was providing the current electronic payment solution. In that contract, there was a specific disclaimer absolving NISC of any potential liabilities, and there were no warranties protecting Flathead against patent, trade secrets or copyright infringement.

The standard boilerplate protections in the software industry were very much in favor of the software providers in 2005–2006. A legal nuance that soon became well-known to all the software customers involved was that the software provider whose product design may have allegedly infringed on the design of the '362 Patent was not technically the infringer on the patent. It is the user of the allegedly infringing software who gets charged with infringement, as it is the party actually committing the infringing acts in commerce. Representatives at Flathead Electric found themselves legally in the "buyer beware" category.

In forty years of software development, NISC had never been accused of patent infringement, so the issue before us and our member cooperative was novel. We contacted our outside patent law firm for advice. We wanted to know what was unique or innovative about paying bills electronically over a Website portal and how the design and functionality of NISC's bill payment software was infringing on the '362 Patent. We requested an infringement opinion from our patent attorney, and we received about a hundred pages of complex and expensive explanation.

At the conclusion of the review, our patent counsel issued an opinion of non-infringement for NISC's software product. In every legal sense, it seemed that NISC was protected by our contract with Flathead Electric and that NISC's technology had not violated the patent in question.

In the meantime, five other NISC member cooperatives received similar, heavy-handed letters from Emergis' law firm requesting that they license the same patent. There were over 150 more NISC members using the same e-business software that Flathead was at the time. Our research showed that Emergis had made good on threats to bring companies to court. By January of 2006 the law firm had filed at least eight federal court actions. Shortly thereafter, Emergis sued Flathead Electric for alleged patent infringement. Emergis ultimately filed nineteen such actions by our count, including six with NISC members.

In discussion with our outside legal counsel, we asked for an estimated trial budget if NISC were to assist in the Flathead defense. We were told the defense would cost between $500,000 and $1 million if we completed discovery and went to trial. The discovery phase alone was estimated at $300,000 in legal fees. Legal journal articles suggested that the cost of defense in a typical patent infringement case was about $5 million. We were quickly learning that patent litigation is the legal equivalent of neurosurgery.

When looking at the potential for a bad outcome, we also considered the annual $250,000 base license fee for the use of the patented technology and took into consideration the fact that the royalty for the transaction fees for the '362 Patent were much greater at the time than the cost of a full suite of NISC's billing, accounting and engineering software products. This assessment didn't even begin to address the possibility of past infringement damages that could be brought into question if the infringement action proved successful. That amount would be much higher

We quickly learned that patent litigation is the legal equivalent of neurosurgery.

still. The shocking reality was that this legal action had the potential to literally put NISC out of business. The threat was real, and it provided for many sleepless nights.

NISC operates on modest margins (profits), and in the two years preceding 2006, our margins were $1.6 million annually. We didn't have insurance for patent infringement, as such insurance wasn't readily available on the market; even if we could negotiate a policy, the premium would be too high to be reasonably affordable. This was one of the reasons such liability was disclaimed in our contracts.

Our license agreement with members had expressly excluded any right for the member/customer to sue NISC for defense or indemnification on any allegations of patent or intellectual property infringement, therefore, legally, we had no obligations. To get involved with this situation would mean spending money that NISC didn't have and effectively putting us in the place of an insurance company, managing the risk without any premium dollars to support it. We were off the hook. Or so you would think.

What Is The Right Thing to Do?

If NISC were like most organizations, being contractually in the clear would have meant sending a sympathetic response to our members and expressing our concern about the situation, but letting them know that we had no legal obligation to do anything about the matter and therefore would be doing nothing to help. End of story. For us though, it was only the beginning.

Legal responsibility aside, our senior leadership team had a much bigger issue to address: what was the right thing to do? Should NISC get in front of this situation for our members? After all, it was the use of our product that had presented the "opportunity" for Emergis to enter the picture.

We brought the matter to the NISC Board of Directors at its January 2006 meeting. The senior leadership team asked the same question of the board: What is the right thing to do?

One idea that was tossed around was that we quit providing electronic billing software, although clearly that would be taking a step backward in an area that was quickly advancing. It might make the lawsuits go away, but our members are all about providing the best possible service to the end consumer, so removing the ability for online bill payment would have a negative impact. This option was discarded. The balance of the discussion was lengthy and heated. The letter of the law was evident and easy to follow, but too many of the members in the room weren't convinced that opting for the easy way was what was best or right. Ultimately, the fourteen-member board decided to take a rather unusual step.

The members unanimously decided to provide indemnity and legal defense for NISC members and customers in this case and in all future matters of infringement challenging the intellectual property involved in NISC's software. Let me say that again. The board of directors, without reservation, voted to support the entire membership through the provision of legal and indemnity defense—and they took it a step further. They went on record to say they would do the same for any and all members or customers in all future infringement challenges involving NISC's intellectual property. Now *that's* being wired differently.

This was not the outcome that Ralph Waldo Emerson would have predicted; it certainly put principles ahead of money. All indications were that this was going to be an expensive fight. NISC would be immediately involved in one federal action, with five more being threatened. In effect, the board had stepped in front of the members to serve as a shield. Why, you ask? The board members and the senior management team had determined that NISC was better suited to wage battle with the patent holders than was each individual member. Our software designers understood the technology, and we worked with patent attorneys on a monthly basis. We would likely be legally involved anyway, brought in as experts in the defense of each case that went to trial. Why should NISC members each hire their own patent attorneys to defend themselves, thereby recreating the wheel in each case?

Months later, NISC's general counsel spoke at a legal seminar in Virginia before an audience of corporate counsels and patent attorneys. In his presentation entitled, "Patent Trolls: The Corporate Response to Their Toll Bridge," he discussed the Emergis case and the decision that the NISC board had made. Audience members were critical of the board's decision and challenged our general counsel for the role he had played in it. What immediately became apparent was the difference in perspective of the audience members, who worked within the corporate business model, and the perspective of the NISC board who had made the decision. The latter, of course, came from the cooperative business model, where the owners were the customers and would therefore benefit from such a decision. Under a corporate business model, the investors would not have wanted to incur the risk or expense that NISC had by making its decision. Of the audience members at the seminar, only an attorney representing a number of credit unions in Texas fully understood the position that NISC had taken, and he thought the actions were commendable. (This further underscores the business model difference, as credit unions are also cooperatives.)

The NISC board's decision was clearly not a road that the corporate counsels in the room would have chosen, and many were clear in voicing opinions that our general counsel had opened up his company to risk and expense for liabilities that technically and legally were not NISC's. Technically and legally, these corporate counsels were right. But that doesn't change the fact that there are other equally important, non-monetary issues all businesses should consider—issues that that a cooperative *must* consider. In this instance, the NISC shared values of integrity, relationships and teamwork were of greater importance than what was technically or legally right.

Was the Right Thing to Do Really the Right Thing to Do?

By the time the NISC board made the decision to provide legal and indemnity defense to any member cooperative named in a lawsuit with Emergis, Emergis had already won one major court battle and obtained a number of highly publicized, although confidential, settlements—effectively winning several of the nineteen pending cases around the country and establishing an expensive precedent in the process. Shortly after taking over the defense of the Flathead Electric case, NISC joined a number of other companies that were either in lawsuits with Emergis or had been threatened with potential legal actions. This group split the costs to hire industry experts to review specific aspects in the case. They also began to monitor all of the cases that Emergis was pursuing in the federal courts, following the defenses and rulings in each of the cases.

The legal preparation for the Flathead case required daily involvement from NISC legal staff for preliminary motions, expert selection and patent examinations, and our case was at least a year away from going to court. NISC was writing checks monthly for legal and related fees in the tens of thousands of dollars; nine months into the legal work, the bills were in the hundreds of thousands dollars. It became apparent we would likely burn through the low end of the proposed legal budget ($500,000) just in the discovery phase of this case.

Even though we were gaining confidence in the potential for success with our defense against the claims of Emergis, we felt it prudent to consider a settlement with Emergis for two reasons:

1. We wanted to put a tourniquet on the future legal spending in front of us, and

2. We wanted a resolution that would protect not only Flathead Electric but the entire NISC membership.

Fighting this battle one member at a time would not be helpful, as any company's lone confidential settlement was not going to take our remaining members out of harm's way.

Finding Resolution

Fifteen months and $750,000 after the first letter from Emergis' law firm had been received by Flathead Electric, a settlement was reached.

On Monday, January 8, 2007, NISC announced that we had finalized a confidential agreement with Emergis Technologies to maintain the ongoing and perpetual use of NISC's e-bill solution by any present or future NISC member or customer. Any of our products and technology related to billing are guaranteed with this settlement.

With all claims of infringement resolved, the license agreement also resulted in the dismissal of the lawsuit filed against Flathead Electric. CEO Ken Sugden said at the time, "This is an example of the culture of NISC and how they defend the rights of their member/owners to leverage advances in technology that allow them to better meet the needs of their members. Although they weren't contractually bound to do this, NISC went to bat for us and for all NISC member/owners."

The cooperative business model and NISC's shared value of integrity allowed us to do the right thing and make the long-term decision. If NISC was a publicly traded company, it's quite possible the board of directors would have made a different decision. At a minimum, the need to maximize shareholder wealth would have been at odds with the challenge to do the right thing.

In the short term, the expense of defending and settling this claim was devastating to NISC's bottom line. In the long term, it was key in establishing NISC's reputation in the industry as an organization willing to put its actions behind its shared values. There is no question that the successes NISC has had in the years following this unfortunate event have been fueled by the goodwill generated from our actions. (Cooperative members have very long memories when NISC falls short; their memories are also very long when we defend their best interests.)

"This is an example of the culture of NISC and how they defend the rights of their member/owners . . ."
– Ken Sugden

The expenses we incurred were a result of representing one NISC member. Had we not settled with Emergis, our expenses would have substantially increased if we had gone to trial and won (or lost) our case, before having to then move on and represent the next member. Are the expenses we incurred greater than those we would have realized if we had dismissed Flathead Electric and the NISC board had decided not to represent any members in their lawsuits with Emergis?

(Although in this case we would have still realized internal expenses for each member's lawsuit and their need of NISC staff as experts.) The answer to that is yes. The short-term, hard costs of jumping to the defense of our members was higher, much higher, than if we had left them to their own defense. But because the NISC board stands solidly behind our shared values, we could not allow the long-term negative costs that would have been incurred if we'd taken care of NISC first and our member/owners second.

That is not our nature, nor is it the right answer for NISC. A co-operative is more like an extended family than it is a typical business with customers and investors who come and go. As a matter of fact, in the cooperative industry, we often refer to each other as being in the "cooperative family." We know our members; we care about them; and we want what's best for them . . . like we do for our own families. Do you do things for family you might not do for others? Yes. Do you take risks or make decisions to get in front of potential problems for family members even when you don't need to? Yes. Why? Because it's the right thing to do.

Had NISC's board and senior management chosen to take a hands-off approach to the inquiry from Flathead Electric, we would have been well within our rights to do so. Flathead knew it, and so did we. If we behaved like every other company, why would we deserve a member's second look? We wouldn't. We have to earn that privilege and, at NISC, we believe we earn the privilege to get a second (and a third and a fourth) look because we do the right things.

Shared values can do a lot more than just provide a moral compass for your organization that will enable it to do the right thing (although that is benefit enough). Ideally, shared values also bond employees together, and the consistent practice of shared values builds trust and confidence. As John Mackey and Raj Sisodia write in *Conscious Capitalism: Liberating the Heroic Spirit of Business,* the very best businesses, from Amazon.com to Whole Foods Market, serve a higher purpose that is driven by their shared values.

Speaking of Whole Foods, there is a great story that was re-told by George Gombossy in the *Hartford Courant.* On December 13, 2007, the store located at Bishops Corner in West Hartford was jammed with shoppers anxious to get home for dinner, as a major snowstorm was howling outside. The computer system crashed suddenly, and none of the cash registers could function. Ted Donoghue, the assistant manager running the store that day, consulted his associates and made a quick decision: all customers passing through the registers would get their food for free until the computers were working again. Free! There was no storewide announcement of the problem or its consequence. Customers were simply told at the checkout that there was a computer glitch, then the cashiers bagged their groceries and wished them a happy holiday and a safe drive, sending them on their way.

In support of Ted's decision, Manager Kimberly Hall is quoted in the article as saying, "It was clearly a snafu on our end, and it didn't seem right to punish the customers by making them wait." Hall estimated that up to $4,000 in groceries was given away before the computers began working again. She said

> **"They just totally trust us to do what is right for our customers."**
> **– Kimberly Hall**

Donoghue did not consult headquarters before making his decision, and she said she had no negative feedback from the top brass. "They just totally trust us to do what is right for our customers," she said.

When I hear stories of people or organizations doing the right thing, I want to support them. I re-tell their story and put my personal stamp of approval on it. More importantly, I want to do business with and work for organizations that do the right thing. NISC's employees, customers and members want the same.

The High Cost of Low Trust

There are hard costs associated with low trust. Even though they aren't always realized in the short term, the costs exist. According to Stephen M.R. Covey in *The Speed of Trust: The One Thing that Changes* Everything, when trust is low, the speed with which we work goes down, and the cost goes up. (Thankfully, the converse is also true: when trust is high, the speed with which we work goes up, and the cost goes down.) I cannot discuss the terms of the confidential settlement with Emergis, but as I've made reference to already, our financial statements show that the costs expended for legal defense fees, travel and settlement costs for the case were over $750,000. In a lawsuit, trust reaches all-time lows, and costs skyrocket.

As I also mentioned earlier, our members have long memories when we defend their best interests. During the six years following the Emergis lawsuit and settlement (2007–2013), NISC welcomed 144 new members to our cooperative family. This was nearly three times as many as we'd welcomed in the previous six years (during which time, membership grew from 448 members in 2001 to 500 members in 2007). The 144 new members represent a growth rate of nearly 30 percent or an annual average growth rate of 5 percent, which is the targeted member growth rate our board of directors has set for us.

In 2013 alone, we welcomed 79 new members to the NISC family. Clearly, each new member had its own reasons for leaving a competitor and joining NISC. If we dug deeper into those reasons, I'm certain trust would have been a factor. The trust levels between the new members and their previous providers must have reached a low enough point to cause them to look elsewhere, thereby making NISC a possible solution. Combine this openness to seeking other solutions with the long-term memories of our members, and you have a formula for success that continues to reap benefits for NISC today.

The best marketing is a personal referral, and you can be sure that our board of directors and our members who were aware of NISC's role in the Emergis case all gladly share the story, to NISC's continued benefit today. Members often recount the example of "their" technology provider who did the unthinkable—bearing the burden of a lawsuit when it didn't need to; indeed, when the contract said it had no responsibility to do so. Our $750,000 decision to do the right thing has turned into an unexpected windfall for business.

Interestingly, NISC has been able to bring our increasing numbers of new members on board at nearly the same speed and with the same levels of professionalism and accuracy as we did in the past with fewer new members. How? Thanks to another example of high trust. Our employees generally have high levels of trust in one another, both in their competence to get the job done well and in the character they model in working with members and each other. The higher the trust level, the faster the work can be completed and the easier it is to manage the associated costs.

NISC leadership has confidence in our teams and their ability to produce, implement, convert and support a quality product. Members frequently recommend our products and tout our level of service to others. Above all, our desire to do the right thing, always, means that we continually strive to follow through on our commitments, right any wrongs we have made along the way and work hard to earn the trust, daily, that we have been given.

Integrity and trust are challenging goals in today's environment. Building these shared values into our software products is an everyday pursuit at NISC, just as we strive each day to live these values so we can earn and improve the trust of our fellow employees, our members and our customers.

KEY POINTS TO CONSIDER IN THIS CHAPTER

1. At NISC, instead of only saying we will have integrity, our employee committee that explored and developed the company's shared values went further to state: "We hold ourselves to the highest professional, moral and ethical standards. **We are committed to doing the right thing, always."**

2. **The cooperative business model and NISC's shared value of integrity allowed us to do the right thing and make the long-term decision in a difficult legal situation.** If NISC was a publicly traded company, it's quite possible the board of directors would have made a different decision.

3. Ideally, **shared values bond employees together**, and the practice of shared values builds trust and confidence.

4. **I want to do business with and work for organizations that do the right thing. Our employees, customers and members want the same.**

5. There are hard costs associated with low trust, and even though they aren't always realized in the short term, they exist. **When trust is low, the speed with which we work goes down and the cost goes up**, according to Stephen M.R. Covey in his book *The Speed of Trust*. Thankfully, the converse is also true: **when trust is high, the speed with which we work goes up and the cost goes down.**

Chapter 7

Ethics Lived Out Loud

Ethics is knowing the difference between what you have a right to do and what is right to do.

— Potter Stewart

One of the most difficult but rewarding jobs in a software company is demonstrating your product. All the work and the millions of dollars invested come down to that moment when a prospective member/customer sees the software for the first time. You feel anxious in those first moments, waiting to see if they like it, if they're impressed.

During these product demos, the prospective member/customer will typically ask us many questions. When a question is asked and you aren't sure of the answer or you have to respond in the negative, you can feel the tension in the room—it's the "gotcha" moment. The knot in your stomach tightens with each "no" or "I don't know" response you give. Although it's really hard to respond with "No, the software does not meet that need or request," at NISC we must be honest with our members and potential customers about our capabilities, above all else. We are selling something more important than our software; we are also demonstrating the integrity and ethics of our organization.

We had one of those gut-wrenching "no" moments a while back, and the outcome was a perfect learning moment. One of our regional business managers shares the story like this:

> *We were invited to spend the day at one of our competitor's largest accounts, an electric cooperative in the southeastern*

United States. Four of us comprised the onsite demonstration team and, as you would expect, our desire to please and impress this prospective member/customer with our products and our company was high.

Their IT director asked us an integration question that was one of probably twenty questions he had for us throughout the day. It dealt with how well our product integrates with their third-party vendor's software. We responded that although we have an outstanding relationship with this vendor and a significant amount of integration in place, we weren't familiar with the particular product he was asking about. We wrote down his question to follow up later.

That evening, our team was invited to dinner with the IT director. During the meal, he shared with us that the integration he had asked us about was not yet through beta-testing, meaning there was virtually no way NISC would be aware of this software, much less have any integration. It was a "baited" question to see how we would respond. He made it clear that if we had responded with "Oh yeah, we've got integration in place," NISC's opportunity with this prospect would have been closed forever.

This experience made me very proud to be part of NISC. We took a team of our employees into the office of one of our competitor's largest accounts and, when tested, we proved that far above our desire to sell software is our commitment to adhere to our shared values—the first one being integrity.

In the end, we won this business and earned the right to serve this member. But what pleases me most as CEO is the ownership that the NISC employees had in doing the right thing while working with a prospective member/customer. Honesty was more important than demonstrating software with just the right flair; more valuable than an actual sale of our services. Long after I am gone, the ethical culture at NISC will be demonstrated through the actions of employees like these.

One of the greatest contributions NISC's current leadership team is making is due to each team member's ability to communicate with unwavering clarity the values on which the organization has been built. It is a daily challenge for each of us to hold true to our shared values and to strive to live them in thought and deed, but it is unquestionably worthwhile.

Ethics and Reverence for Life

Albert Schweitzer was born in 1875 in the mountain villages of Alsace-Lorraine, France. He is perhaps best known as a Nobel Peace Prize winner, although he showed no sign of early talent except for having an impassioned curiosity in many areas. He tried writing, became a noted organist, and was a church pastor and the principal of a theological seminary. He was also a university professor with a doctorate in philosophy. Still, Schweitzer wasn't satisfied. He decided to become a medical doctor, and at the age of 37, Dr. Schweitzer and his wife, a nurse, opened a hospital in French Equatorial Africa. There, in the midst of one of the worst climates in the world, he devoted his life to providing health care for the people of the area, and it was where he finally answered a question that had bothered him for years.

Schweitzer had been searching for a deeper understanding of ethics when the phrase "reverence for life" came to him. This phrase became the basis of a personal belief that he developed further and put into practice. Essentially, his Reverence for Life philosophy is based on the notion that the only thing we're really sure of is that we live and want to go on living. And we share this inherent need with everything else that lives, from animals grazing in the African interior to farmers preparing to harvest their wheat fields in the midwestern United States.

Reverence for Life is a concept that may appear incongruent with today's marketplace. I think not. As business leaders, when we have reverence for our employees, we acknowledge the critical role they play in the success of our organization. When we have reverence for our competitors in the marketplace, we recognize their strengths, and we look to better ourselves in proportion, rather than finding ways to tear them down. In our organizations, reverence for life means that we will lead, mentor, listen and coach from an ethical position that is respectful of others.

A Conscious Choice to Be an Ethical Workplace

Once the course is charted, maintaining the right ethical tone in our organizations is a daily challenge. The opportunities to reinforce strong ethical behavior abound; so, too, do the opportunities to stumble. In his book *Ethical Leadership: Creating and Sustaining an Ethical Business Culture,* Andrew Leigh provides some of the common myths he has identified as having the potential to become traps for organizations striving to build and maintain an ethically strong company culture.

For example, many people assume that it's easy to exercise good ethics when, in reality, that's rarely the case. In fact, sometimes we don't even realize when we are facing an ethical choice, or we don't sense that our moral compass is off. According to Leigh, an ethically strong culture provides a foundation to resolve the inevitable conflicts that follow when ethical choices arise or we discover, too late, that our moral compass has been misguided. An ethically strong culture also fosters an environment where organizational values are put into action more frequently and are consistently reinforced between the organization and its employees.

Business ethics is a discipline that everyone in an organization should practice daily. An established code of ethics for your organization will hold no more importance than a plaque with shared values on it if the code is merely posted on a wall or the company intranet. Ethics and shared values need to be lived out loud. Indeed, shared values and your code of ethics work together to indicate desired behaviors and let employees know what is expected of them.

It's important to keep in mind that perfectly legal actions can still be unethical. As discussed in chapter 6, NISC was not legally bound to assume any risk for its member cooperatives in the pending Emergis lawsuits; but for ethical reasons, NISC's board of directors voted to engage in the legal dispute, ultimately negotiating a favorable resolution for all NISC members whether they were involved in the lawsuit or not.

Company ethics are a prime example of an area in which we get only one chance for a great first impression, and if we lose it, it's a long, expensive road to recovery. NISC created an Integrity & Trust Guide that every existing employee has and all new employees receive when they join the organization. It provides an overview of NISC, with a focus on our shared values, and it provides information on the company resources we have in place to help foster a culture of integrity and ethical behavior. (We discuss this guide further in chapter 11.)

Every business, new or old, needs to remember that an ethical culture, or lack of it, shows in the actual behavior and attitudes of all team members, not just in policy documents and executive presentations. A successful business is the result of more than a good product and a good business model—for a business to achieve success it must also develop a culture of ethics that every employee brings to life in their work and the products they make. This kind of culture exudes trust and honesty, allowing for products of quality to be made. It is the kind of place where people want to say they work, and it is the kind of business that people want to refer to their friends.

A Place Where People Want to Work

A technology career spanning four decades is a success in today's world, and it is also a tremendously valuable asset. We are fortunate enough to have that experience with Larry Estal, NISC's national sales manager. Larry has transcended many traditional milestones in the IT arena. His career began before cell phones existed and before computers were on every desk. In January 2015, he celebrated his forty-seventh year with NISC.

Looking at Larry's example, it's easy to see how hard work, dedication and values contribute to a long, fulfilling career. A lifelong learner, Larry strives to bring value to each relationship he forms with NISC members and customers, as well as his fellow employees. His dedication is obvious, not only by his years of service, but also by his willingness to help, to be accessible and to model ethical behavior.

Larry attributes his longevity with NISC to having a career he believes truly makes a difference in people's lives. "The opportunity to work in rural America is a special one, and to work at NISC is very special," Larry says. "This is about having a good life, getting to do great work and being with the best people. It's not often you get to work for a company that fosters change and is committed to doing the right things to keep us number one. With our members, we get to work with the very best, genuine people."

We are truly blessed as an organization to have an individual like Larry committed to NISC for so many years. In fact, we have 125 employees—12.5 percent of our total employee numbers—who have been with NISC for twenty years or longer. Some organizational consultants believe that employees who stay at the same place for more than ten years do so because they are unmotivated or "stuck in a rut." The employees at NISC for over twenty years are anything but stuck in a rut, they are the models for our future. They understand and live our values. They embrace ethical business behavior because it is in alignment with who they are as individuals in our communities.

Let me be clear: NISC doesn't have all of the answers to workplace ethics, and we struggle to get it right more often than we care to admit. We have had incidents of credit card abuse, when certain employees felt it would be all right to use NISC's credit card for their personal purchases, perhaps rationalizing that they would repay the card charges at a later date. We have also had a select few employees treat themselves to meals or beverages beyond the reasonable limits allowed for business purposes. On rare occasions, employees have stayed at more expensive conference hotels when our policies encourage employees to seek reasonably priced and safe alternatives where readily available. Others have added personal travel to their business trips without fully identifying the personal additions.

Fortunately though, such people are the unusual exceptions to the vast majority of our trustworthy employees who respect NISC property and policies as if they were their own. NISC's system of checks and balances, whereby a supervisor and the accounting department review each employee expense, has successfully uncovered nearly every irregularity.

Everyone at NISC is a steward of our members' investments in NISC, and we must treat the dollars we spend in the service of those members as if they were part of a bank savings account. We are on a mission to win the hearts and minds of all our employees. We are not there yet, but we are continually striving to get better aiming to build and maintain a solid, ethical foundation of unimpeachable trust.

Ethics When You Lose

It's been a bit awkward at our Missouri campus to have our electric service provided by a cooperative that isn't an NISC member. When we purchased the land in 2003, we specifically looked for property that was on cooperative lines. We installed a 100 percent electric facility to support the industry we serve, and we hoped some day we could count our power supplier among the ranks of our member/owners. We were thrilled in 2011 when we were notified that the cooperative was going to evaluate IT providers and that NISC would be given a shot.

NISC pays about $250,000 a year to this cooperative for electricity, and close to two hundred NISC employees receive their residential electric service from the same provider. In addition, five of the neighboring cooperatives had recently (at that time) gone through IT evaluations and selected NISC. We knew we needed to earn the business, and we felt we had a strong and compelling position.

Early in the process though, there were warning signs. Our sales and marketing teams were concerned. Representatives from the cooperative weren't returning calls, and they weren't allowing us to come in and work through a business process analysis. They also refused to call references—even those who were former customers of our lead competitor and had chosen NISC as their service provider.

The cooperative ended up choosing one of our competitors as their IT provider. Our Missouri staff and all of those who worked so diligently on winning this business were understandably upset; they truly felt betrayed. Draft letters to the cooperative's management and board of directors were prepared from NISC employees who were members and customers of the cooperative. Some employees wanted to write letters to the editor of the newspaper, and others suggested that, as a key account of the cooperative, NISC should demand a slot on the cooperative's board agenda to voice our displeasure personally. Still others considered running for a board position with the sole purpose of making the individuals responsible for this decision miserable.

It is at times like these when the NISC culture is tested. It's easy to hold on to values and ethics when you win. It takes true maturity, confidence and commitment to keep your composure and remain professional when you lose. It is difficult to lead an organization at a time like this, when so many individuals who give so much of themselves to the work they do were taking the cooperative's decision so personally. Retaliation would have felt so good . . . or would it?

It was the CEO of the electric cooperative who was ultimately responsible for the decision that had been made, and more than two hundred upset NISC employees could have made his life difficult and his board meetings miserable. It doesn't matter whether you are the CEO of a cooperative or the CEO of a corporation—it's the worst position to be in when your membership or your shareholders are angry and disappointed.

It was a hard conversation for me to have with the CEO of that cooperative, letting him know that we had asked NISC employees to "stand down" and not take their frustration with a business decision into their own hands. While the disappointment and heartache was deep, we asked employees to keep their eyes on the long-term strategy and to operate with the highest degree of ethics in this situation. NISC will not allow or condone any retaliation on the part of our employees. End of story.

Honesty and Ethics in the Workplace

In November 2012, the Gallup Organization conducted its annual Honesty/Ethics in Professions poll, rating how those in different professions are perceived in terms of their honesty and ethical standards. In the survey of 1,015 Americans from all fifty states and the District of Columbia, of the twenty-two professions listed in the survey, nurses rated the highest and car salespeople ranked the lowest, preceded closely by members of Congress.

Survey respondents rated each of the professions on a five-point honesty and ethical scale ranging from "very high" to "very low." Americans' views of the twenty-two professions in the poll varied widely, with 85 percent of respondents rating nurses' ethics and honesty as very high or high, to a low of 8 percent rating car salespeople the same.

Members of Congress have never fared well in the thirty-six years of these ratings. The high point for congressmen and congresswomen came in November 2001, after the 9/11 terrorist attacks, when 25 percent of Americans rated their honesty and ethical standards as very high or high. The 2011 survey, which resulted in a 7 percent honesty rating for members of Congress, is the lowest on record at the time this poll was taken. Business executives have never scored particularly high in this poll either, with ratings ranging from 25 percent in 2001 to 12 percent in 2008 and 2009.

Professions with high honesty ratings (whereby over 50 percent of respondents rated the honesty and ethical standards of people in those professions as very high or high) include pharmacists, medical doctors, engineers, dentists, police officers, college teachers and the clergy. Far less than half of Americans feel positively about the honesty of journalists, lawyers, insurance salespeople, HMO (health maintenance organization) managers, stockbrokers and advertising practitioners—all of which have honesty ratings below 25 percent. These latter results are disappointing and prompt the question, why? There is certainly a place for ethics as Albert Schweitzer saw it, reverence for life, at home and at work.

Research from the Ethics Resource Center in Arlington, Virginia, reveals that in 2012-2013, 45 percent of U.S. employees observed a violation of the law or of company ethical standards at their places of employment. Reports of this wrongdoing were at an all-time high—65 percent, or two out of three respondents, who observed a violation reported it. Also high was the rate of retaliation against employees who blew the whistle: more than one in five survey respondents who reported misconduct experienced some form of retaliation in return.

Think about this. Nearly half of the employees in organizations in the United States who responded to this survey say they have observed wrongdoing in the workplace or witnessed, maybe even were asked to participate in, a breach of ethics. Aside from the legal and perhaps financial implications of inappropriate workplace behavior, there's the stress and inner turmoil that employees experience when the ethics and morals they value at their place of work are violated, and which arises from the knowledge that retaliation is a serious possibility for those who bring to light the wrongdoing. How awful it must be for employees who don't feel they can trust their leaders or co-workers to do the right things, or that there will even be support for those who do the right thing.

For our part, NISC began conducting employee engagement surveys on an annual basis in 2008, and we moved to quarterly surveys in 2010. This transition to more frequent surveying allows us to keep a pulse on our employees' well-being, and it allows us to identify quickly any action items we need to pursue. While not scientific, we believe there is a definite correlation between the shared values we claim, the ethics we model and the level of employee engagement we see.

Servants Who Lead the Organization

In the late 1980s, we had a member who served on our board of directors. Every time I was getting ready to make a recommendation to the board on a capital acquisition (and these were the days of million-dollar mainframes), he would stop me and ask, "If this were your company, what would you do?" It was a test, and to this day, we still use that phrase to gauge the validity of our recommendations.

Prior to this, those of us on the management team had viewed our roles as the leaders of the organization, but at a distance. We felt we were good stewards of the resources; we believed we gave our best effort to the work we performed; and yet, we were making decisions for others—for the board, for our members, for the employees. We weren't making decisions and leading the organization like it was ours because we had no financial skin in the game. We grasped the role of serving our members; we were just beginning to understand our role as servants who also lead the organization.

If this were your company, what would you do?

Perhaps we felt it would be wrong to claim ownership of NISC. I'm not sure. What I can tell you is that once we made the small but significant shift from thinking of ourselves as leaders of someone else's organization to feeling we were the leaders of our own organization whose goal was to serve others, that is when we brought our values and our ethics to the table, and that is when it became critical to ask, "What would we do if this was our business?"

And this was only the beginning. To build a truly ethical organization that lives and breathes integrity, we recognized that as leaders we must continually model the behavior we want repeated by NISC's supervisors and team leaders, and NISC's supervisors and team leaders must do the same for front-line employees. If we want our members and customers to believe they are working with an ethical organization that serves them, they must see it in every interaction they have with us. They must know, without question, that every member from our team has their best interests in mind. To this end, we no longer have a Human Resources department at NISC. Today we call it People Services. Kari Reichert leads this team and is a member of our vice presidents group. Kari is a great model to the rest of us for why we shifted our focus from "resources as humans" to "services for people." We value the individual and each person's contribution at NISC.

The Result of Employees Doing the Right Thing

When NISC employee Mike Weber tuned in to the Weather Channel on the morning of August 19, 2007, he was told that a freakish seventeen inches of rain had fallen in Rushford, Minnesota, over the previous twenty-four hours. Mike was familiar with the Rushford area and knew that the town was situated in a valley with a river running through the middle of it, very near Tri-County Electric Cooperative Inc., one of NISC's member/customers.

It being a Sunday, he checked with the on-call team at NISC and, as he had suspected, they had numerous reports of outages among Tri-County's customer base. Next, Mike called Doug Remboldt, the head of his division (now the vice president of Utility & Shared Services). Doug related a call that he'd received from Kaye Bernard at Tri-County, who had told him that the basement of the cooperative building was totally flooded and the main floor was under four feet of water, completely out of service, and all of their systems were in peril.

Mike and Doug decided to do something. Early that afternoon, they met at the NISC office in Mandan, North Dakota, and began to assemble a server and ten computers, along with other network equipment. The details of their plan were developing as they went, but their intention was to build a replacement network for the cooperative, travel to Rushford to install it and get the cooperative back online. They spent all day Sunday getting the equipment together and left first thing Monday morning for Rushford, a little over eight hours away. They hoped that when they got to Tri-County the cooperative's back-up tape could be used to restore the records.

When Mike and Doug arrived in Rushford, they found that many of the Tri-County employees were dealing with their own personal crises. Their homes were flooded and filled with mud, yet at work they were doing whatever they could with whatever they had available to restore power to the community and their customers. Mike and Doug were directed to an old trailer located at the airport on the hill above the flooded valley. It was the best, driest option available. The trailer was dirty, dusty and full of dog hair, but it would work as a site for the replacement network. By Monday evening, the two men had a computer system with current records up and running.

Kaye had secured lodging for them in a nearby town twenty miles away, but with everyone so busy, they overlooked the fact that there would be no after-hours security to protect all of the equipment they had worked so hard to install. How did Mike and Doug respond to this? They slept in the trailer overnight; one of them on the couch and the other on the floor with a pillow and blanket, keeping watch over the system. The next morning when Mike got up, he jumped in the shower to start the day. He came out of the bathroom at 7:30 a.m. and was greeted by ten Tri-County employees already at the computers, responding to customer needs.

Interestingly, neither Mike nor Doug question their decision when they talk about their Sunday afternoon choice to pack up $100,000 worth of NISC equipment without the formal authority to do so. Nor do they second-guess their decision to drive over 550 miles toward a natural disaster and set up valuable equipment that would likely never return to NISC and for which no payment had yet been discussed. Both men view their role as a small piece of the recovery process for Tri-County Electric, viewing the employees of the cooperative as the ones who made the greatest sacrifice. From my vantage point, I couldn't be prouder of their choices.

As Potter Stewart's quote at the beginning of this chapter says, "Ethics is knowing the difference between what you have a right to do

"Out of crisis like this you see how important a relationship of service becomes."
– Brian Krambeer

and what is right to do." According to policy, Doug and Mike didn't have the proper authority to take $100,000 worth of NISC equipment, but according to NISC's ethical standards they did the right thing by taking the equipment to Rushford and helping one of our members become whole again. And at NISC, ethics trump policy.

A few months after the ordeal, I visited with Tri-County's president and CEO, Brian Krambeer, and he shared with me his thoughts on Mike and Doug's actions. "I used to look at the sum of money we paid to NISC each month and wonder what we were really getting for that expense," he said. "I know NISC has been a good company, but after the flood I really know what kind of company it is and how it stands behind us. I will never again wonder about that expense, and I now gratefully pay it each month. Sometimes it takes a crisis to know who really stands behind you, but out of a crisis like this you see how important a relationship of service becomes."

KEY POINTS TO CONSIDER IN THIS CHAPTER

1. It is a daily challenge for each of us to **hold true to our shared values in thought and deed.**

2. When we have **reverence for our competitors in the marketplace, we recognize their strengths and we look to better ourselves in proportion,** rather than find ways to tear them down.

3. A successful business is far more than a good product and a good business model—**a successful business also has a culture of ethics** that every employee brings to life in their work and their work product. This kind of culture exudes trust and honesty; it is the kind of place where people want to say they work, and it is the kind of business people want to refer to their friends.

4. **To build a truly ethical organization that lives and breathes integrity,** the leadership team must continually model the behavior they want repeated by supervisors and team leaders. And supervisors and team leaders must continually model the behavior they want repeated by front-line employees.

Chapter 8

Failure Is Not an Option

The price of success is hard work, dedication to the job at hand, and the determination that whether we win or lose, we have applied the best of ourselves to the task at hand.

— Vince Lombardi

It was late one Friday night in August of 1998. It was the end of an exhausting week marked by a battle to keep a long-time member. At issue was the functionality of our software. The member had raised concerns about our software system at the time, Horizon, and they had good reason. It was a hodgepodge of old mainframe code, fourth-generation software called Progress, and thirty-year-old business software language known as COBOL. In its time, Horizon had been state-of-the-art. But over the years it had been revised, patched, added to, updated, migrated and practically held together with duct tape. In an industry where the shelf life of software is equal to that of a banana, its day of reckoning was close-at-hand.

That Friday night, the better part of two hours had been spent debating the merits of Horizon with our sales team. It was a discussion we'd had many times, and it came down to this: our growth was pathetic. The sales team had a goal they couldn't meet and the problem, they said, was the product we'd given them to sell. In my heart, I knew this was true. Our sales were being hamstrung by the constraints of old technology.

Outside the office walls, competition was beyond tough—it was downright brutal. New competitors were entering our market. Their products were fresh; they didn't have customers running on old software. Fueled by venture capital funds, they focused on product development. Their technology's sizzle, features and functionality were attracting the industry's attention. They were nipping at our heels. To use a metaphor, the competition was in a swift sports car and we were driving a delivery truck loaded with the obligation to maintain and support a legacy software platform at several hundred sites. Our members were loyal, but we were in a battle to grow our customer base and to keep the business we had. This was, without question, a turning point in NCDC's history. It was time to rewrite Horizon. We'd put the decision off long enough.

Seventy Percent of Rewrites Fail

When I took the job in 1990 as CEO of North Central Data Cooperative, which was one of NISC's two predecessor co-ops (more on that in a moment), retiring CEO Ray Clouse told me on his last day, "Dosch, this is a damn lonely job." I nodded as if to say I understood. But my inner voice said, "It may have been for you, Mr. Clouse, but it will not be for me." Eight years later on that Friday night, I sat alone in a dark office building and all I could hear was Mr. Clouse's voice in my mind. I remember thinking to myself, "He was right, it is a lonely job."

> **"Dosch, this is a damn lonely job."**
> **– Ray Clouse**

That weekend, I immersed myself in my unread issues of trade publications. One article caught my attention. It was entitled, "70% of All Large-Scale Software Development Projects Fail." It added insult to injury, offering little hope that a rewrite of our software would succeed. A copy of that article remained on the corner of my desk for the next ten years. It was a constant reminder of the challenges we faced.

While the challenge was clear, the answers and the plan were not. The obstacles were many: Moving to a new platform meant workforce retraining and retooling. Employees would have to learn a new programming language and new operating systems. We would have to rewrite almost six million lines of antiquated code. In doing so, we would have to translate more than thirty-five years of utility and telecommunications subject matter expertise into a new product.

If we took this challenge, we'd also have to keep our existing product suite running until the last customer moved to the new product.

It would be like changing tires while traveling seventy miles per hour. In retrospect, we were just naïve enough to think we could pull it off. Failure was not an option.

Our Trump Card

There were many things to consider before we forged ahead. High on the list was our competitors' response. We knew that when they heard about the rewrite, there would be a feeding frenzy. It would be our most vulnerable time.

True to form, competitors began to sow doubt and fear when we announced the rewrite. They spread the word that our rewrite may not be successful. They told members and prospects that our plan would be very expensive and may put us out of business. They suggested that member support would be dramatically reduced. Although the alarm bells they were sounding for customers were based on opinion rather than fact (not to mention skewed in our competitors' favor), they were damaging nonetheless.

We worked long hours to shore up the confidence of, and support for, our existing customer base. One or two member defections could trigger a tsunami of customer concern and cause others to sever their relationship, which, in turn, would undermine our rewrite plans and certainly lead to a slow and painful demise.

We presumed that our new revenue streams would dry up as loyal members would, understandably, stop investing in the old product and wait for the new offering. With less than $500,000 dollars in the bank, a big capital investment plan on the drawing board, and new revenue no more than a dream, you didn't have to be an accountant to understand that the numbers fell short. Our Achilles heel was capitalization. We didn't have the firm financial foundation we needed. After thirty-five years of service, our equity level stood at a meager 15 percent. Cash came in, cash went out. We were a cash sieve.

The cooperative business model allocates all of its accumulated equity to its members and regularly repays a portion of that equity back to members in the form of capital credits. However, it is never a preferred situation for a cooperative to operate under a 35-40 percent equity level. At this level an organization has the cash on hand to successfully manage day-to-day operations or commercially borrow money if needed. You have probably heard the phrase "operating on a shoe-string budget." Many of NCDC's first thirty years were spent just getting by between development costs, salaries and slow sales. It was a chronic problem. To make matters worse, NCDC was $600,000 in debt after its first two years of operation.

Essentially, embarking on our plan to rewrite software when our equity was so low would be like starting to build your dream home without making a down payment, instead borrowing all of the money necessary. Once your home is complete and you begin making payments, the best you can do is pay the interest without ever getting a toehold on reducing the principle. You can just never catch up.

Further adding to our financial predicament was that we did not have access to outside or venture capital. In our cooperative environment, there is no opportunity to issue public stocks or bonds. And even if there was, no investor or banker would use a software development plan as collateral for a loan.

Despite these daunting realities, we held a trump card. We were a cooperative, and our member/owners had a vested interest in making sure we were successful. Since our humble beginnings, we served at the center of our members' organizations. Our billing, accounting and engineering software was the quiet heartbeat of their operations. Members were dependent on our ability to provide and support the technology that was integral to the smooth day-to-day operations of their local business.

The business articles and industry observers may have been saying at the time that rewrites had a 70 percent probability of failure, but we believed our situation was different. Our business model gave us the confidence we needed to prove the skeptics wrong. We believed in our members, and they had trust in our resolve and the power and resilience of the cooperative business model.

NISC Is Born

A few weeks before we at NCDC made our rewrite public, I attended an electric co-op meeting in Springfield, Illinois. At that meeting I met Gary Hobson, the CEO of our fiercest competitor, the St. Louis area–based Central Area Data Processing (CADP). CADP was also a cooperative and operated under the same business structure as we did at NCDC.

I considered Mr. Hobson to be my nemesis even though we'd never met. As NCDC staff worked to expand our membership base, so did CADP. There was a growing competitive tension as we battled for new business. Therefore, I approached him with caution, thinking he was not to be trusted. Our introductory meeting was superficial. Weather and industry developments marked the discussion, as both of us carefully avoided talking about our business and competitive postures.

During the meeting, I received a message that my flight had been canceled. There was no alternative flight scheduled to leave Springfield that day. I was stuck there. In the course of our conversation, I mentioned my dilemma to Mr. Hobson. Without hesitation he said, "How about if I give you a ride to St. Louis, where there are sure to be options that will get you home today?" I was reluctant to admit my vulnerability to a competitor; however, I saw no other option and so I accepted his offer. Am I ever glad I did.

Gary and I talked non-stop during the three-and-a-half-hour drive. We compared notes on the challenges of leading a technology cooperative. The conversation was open and comfortable, and I slowly lowered my defenses. Then, out of nowhere, Gary delivered the bomb. "CADP is getting ready to do a complete software rewrite," he said. I was stunned. Did he really say what I thought he just said? Did he really share that key, competitively sensitive piece of information? I was taken aback by his willingness to trust the CEO of a fierce competitor and someone who, just a few hours earlier, had been a stranger.

I had a decision to make. The voice in my head was screaming, "Don't say it! Don't tell him we're also planning our own rewrite!" But a door had been opened. After some fast consideration, I walked through it and told Gary that NCDC was also planning a software rewrite.

With our corporate secrets out, there was an awkward lapse in our conversation. I turned to Gary and said, "Let me get this right. Both of our organizations are going to invest millions of dollars to write competing products that arguably will have the exact same functionality. And after we make these painful and duplicate investments, we will each take the new products to market and spend the next ten years vigorously competing with each other." I finished with the question, "Would this really be doing the right thing for our members and for the industries we serve?"

We looked at each other without saying a word. The silence was deafening as the obvious became apparent to us both. We were in the same boat: NCDC's and CADP's software products were at the end of their useful life and so was the regional business model under which both organizations had been operating; we were now competing on a national level. Gary and I each came to the conclusion that we needed to trade in our competitive swords for plowshares, combine our human and financial resources, and write one product that would be shared by our respective memberships and others across the nation.

On July 1, 2000, after months of discussions, National Information Solutions Cooperative (NISC) was formed, consolidating the assets, membership and staff of both NCDC and CADP, giving the new organization the resources it needed to move away from the original regional business scope and become a national cooperative provider. The board approved a simple but inspiring mission statement to guide our efforts:

To deliver information technology solutions and services that are member and customer focused, quality driven and value priced.

The consolidation of CADP and NCDC reminds me of how new mothers talk about having a baby. Many say that if they'd known how difficult it was going to be, they might have thought twice about their decision. Likewise, birthing NISC was difficult. It took longer than we ever anticipated. But NISC's birth through consolidation gave us a new purpose. Its formation made us stronger; it energized our mission; and it gave us the new resources we needed to confront the challenges we and our members would face.

Tackling a Software Rewrite

With the NISC consolidation behind us, our newly formed senior management team met to get on with the business of executing the rewrite. We'd all spent considerable time planning it, and we each brought that experience and energy to the table. We immersed ourselves in discussions and debates about strategy, technology transition plans, development timelines, business issues and forecasts focused on staffing and capital requirements. There was little doubt that the road ahead would involve a lot of work, especially as we now had multiple legacy software systems to support. Although we squared our jaws and talked with optimism about our ability to tackle the software rewrite, we walked around with a constant case of butterflies. It was a time that tested our ability to come together as a team; it tested our leadership skills, our resolve and our confidence.

I believe no other board of directors would have unanimously endorsed this rewrite project. But ours did.

Over the next year, we put together a detailed development and business plan, and in early 2001, we presented it to our board of directors. The plan received unanimous board approval! In retrospect, I believe no other board of directors would have unanimously endorsed this rewrite project, given the project's size, complexity and projected cost. But ours did, and there was good reason for them to do so. The NISC board had just successfully weathered the consolidation of two IT co-ops; they were invigorated by the potential of the young NISC; and they were firmly committed to the plan. They believed in our organization, our leadership, our employees and the cooperative business model. They also believed NISC could do what others said could not be done.

It is worth pausing here to note the selfless nature of the board members. Through the consolidation, twenty-eight board positions became fourteen, meaning one-half of the individuals who had committed their time, energy and talent to leading an IT cooperative had to give up their position. The board vote was unanimous to make this change to its membership, and the transition occurred with relative ease. There was no visible backbiting or inside politics involved.

From an historical perspective, the board's enthusiasm for NISC's development plan was rooted in the examples of how inspired people could make life-changing differences in rural America. From the formation of the Rural Electrification Administration in 1935 and the first electric co-op to the establishment of finance, supply and IT cooperatives, there was plenty of evidence that when people come together, good things can happen.

The board's unanimous support encouraged NISC's staff. Their message was clear: use the co-op business model to do something great; work cooperatively; tap into the power of collaboration and the co-op network; and make a difference for our members.

Our next task was to assign a project leader for the software rewrite. All of us understood that the project's outcome would define not only the chosen leader's career but also the future of NISC. It didn't take long to identify our first choice. Dan Wilbanks had spent twenty years working for CADP. He was well respected by his peers and was a recognized leader who had demonstrated an ability to guide large and complex projects to successful conclusions. When we approached Dan, he agreed to lead the project if he could assemble his own project leadership team. So it was that Dan along with Jim Rapp, Brent Roberts and John Lewis took the first steps on the long iVUE® journey. To say this was an NISC milestone would be an understatement.

Dan and his team were soon joined by almost one hundred other project members. Together they defied the odds, proved the skeptics wrong, and delivered a commercial-grade software system called iVUE®, which became the foundation of NISC's next era of success. Almost twelve years later, Dan is now NISC's chief operating officer and vice president of Research, Development and Quality. He and his original development team—Jim, Brent and John—are still together guiding the evolution of iVUE®.

An important component of the iVUE® project was that we used our own employees and were not lured by the low cost of outsourcing the work to India or China. NISC's core products (Customer Care and Billing, Accounting and Business Solutions, and Engineering and Operations) are living, breathing products. As our industries' requirements and needs change, so does our software. Three times a year, we release a major version upgrade. The dynamic nature of our products would not be served well by the constraints that would come from development occurring eleven time zones away.

Our philosophy is simple: we hire driven, intelligent employees who have an aptitude to learn. We invest in them and build their skills and abilities, one employee at a time. We grow our own employee base with people who want to make careers at NISC, not just those looking for short-term jobs.

Even with employee recruitment, our cooperative business model gives us the option to make long-term decisions like growing our own employee base, and in retrospect, these types of decisions were a key factor in the success of the iVUE® project. In the corporate world, the quarterly analyst call requires often unrealistic, short-term account-ability; still it is how performance is measured in a publicly traded company. In that world, it's difficult to make decisions that require patience and will have short-term negative impacts on financial state-ments when your stock holders question your every move and will not tolerate a sudden reduction in profitability.

When our board cast the unanimous vote to proceed with our re-write, they did so knowing that the project would deplete NISC's cash, negatively affect its revenue stream and place it in a tenuous financial position. The board's view was long-term and looked beyond the short-term financial pain to a next-generation technology product that would be critical to the efficient operation and success of our organization for years to come. The way they saw it, it was a gamble worth taking, and in the end, this gamble paid big dividends in financial stability, growth and progress for NISC and our member/owners.

The One Unanswered Question

There was one rather significant question left to answer. How would we fund the initial rewrite project, which carried an estimated $20 million price tag?

We traveled the country, pitching the NISC software business plan to our member cooperatives. We discussed the benefits, the features and the costs of the project with them. We explained our strategies and shared our vision. With hat in hand, we humbly asked for their financial participation through member loans to help fund a project that, under hard return-on-investment scrutiny, was high risk. There were skeptics to be sure, but we raised the money required to start the project within six weeks. Along the way, we received a huge vote of support and commitment from one particular entity in the coopera-tive family.

That organization is the National Rural Utilities Cooperative Finance Corporation (CFC). As a national lender to electric cooperatives, CFC was familiar with the important role that NISC played in the industry. When we arrived at their offices during our fundraising journey, CFC staff reviewed our proposal and approved a line of credit for the devel-opment capital we needed. Sheldon Petersen, CEO of CFC, explained it this way, "This was an easy decision for CFC because we understand the critical role NISC's software plays in the financial stability and strength of our borrowers."

NISC never ended up having to use CFC's line of credit, but it was worth its weight in gold. CFC's vote of confidence gave our project the credibility we needed to open other doors. It lowered members' concerns about making an investment. The view was, if CFC approved an NISC loan, then our project must be a wise investment.

Once again, the co-op trump card we held proved its worth. Were we a corporation, our business plan would have been basically non-bankable. Had our rewrite project plan been evaluated on traditional return-on-investment criteria, it would not have measured up or been approved by the typically risk-averse investors who purchase the stocks and bonds of publicly traded companies.

An important message emerged. The CFC loan commitment and each member investment told us that our plan was credible. Industry leaders believed in us, and they believed in our success. That message was not lost on NISC's board nor its staff. With human and financial resources in hand, we were ready to move ahead.

All through the planning, the traveling and the member meetings, there was a growing sense that we would be successful, but one defining moment in particular stands out for me. It happened at an all-hands employee meeting when we announced the news that funding was in place and we would begin our software rewrite, all six million lines of code. I looked at the audience of my fellow employees. There were people who had devoted their entire adult life to NISC. For some, it was the only job they'd ever had. I saw in their faces an excitement and an eagerness to move forward. The employee group was fully invested in the organization. They believed in our mission. Our message to them that day was simple: "Our board of directors and our membership have given us a vote of confidence. Failure is not an option. We will not let them down. Let's get going, we have a job to do." With that, the eager NISC employees set to work on building our future.

The Birth of iVUE®

As with most software development projects, delivery of our new product took longer than planned, and it was more expensive and more painful, initially, for all involved. Although there were long days, stolen weekends, speed bumps and potholes, the development team never gave up. They were cheered on and encouraged by the employees who were making sure our legacy systems were still getting the job done as the new product was to taking shape. Some eighteen months after we started the project, we delivered the new product, called iVUE®, to our initial beta test site. It was one of the most memorable moments of many of our employees' careers.

In the next several years, we marched through over six hundred implementations of iVUE®, moving members one at a time, often with some pain, off of the old legacy platform. Also one by one, we decommissioned NCDC's and CADP's five legacy platforms, focusing our members, our employees and our company resources on the single iVUE® platform. There is no finish line in the software business, but there are milestones. In 2010, we celebrated the decommissioning of our final legacy platform when a Michigan electric co-op converted to iVUE®. We were done with the old and fully invested in the new.

There is no finish line in the software business, but there are milestones.

This milestone was a long time coming and unlike any we had seen in NISC's history. I couldn't help but be emotional about what we'd achieved. It had taken a herculean effort involving so much doubt, struggle, hope, disappointment, support, courage, work, resolve, resilience and grit, over a ten-year span, to prove the skeptics wrong and beat the overwhelming odds. We had done it!

The story of iVUE® is intertwined with the formation of NISC. There were clear gains made through the economies of scale, the improved speed to market of new or improved software and expected operational efficiencies. At the time of consolidation, we put together a business plan that detailed projected savings, but our projections turned out to be not even close. The actual savings were much greater, improved with many unanticipated synergies. There is no way we could have anticipated all of the many member benefits realized through the merger of CADP and NCDC. Here are just some of them:

1. Speed to market was increased with a larger development team.

2. We were able to focus on a single product rather than five.

3. We gained technical diversity and filled many of the gaps that each of the two organizations previously had.

4. We expanded our recruiting capabilities.

5. We increased our administration efficiencies.

6. Disaster recovery became much easier with two locations to back one another up.

Hindsight is 20/20. Fifteen years later, we see with clarity the conviction and confidence of NISC's board of directors during the time of transition. They acted decisively to consolidate NCDC and CADP, and then they approved the business plan for building iVUE®. Their actions were truly courageous and extraordinary, and we have them to thank for laying a solid foundation that has made possible NISC's continued success and existence today.

When iVUE® was developed, NISC had to select one of several possible platform approaches. Thankfully our management and development teams picked the right approach (Java), on which we've built a robust and fully integrated suite of applications that includes everything from accounting to smart grid to broadband. We were tempted to take short-cuts rather than endure the pain to rewrite these products. We could have purchased components and bolted disparate technologies together to get to market quicker. But we resisted that temptation and developed products line by line, creating software that would endure the test of time.

When we consolidated to become NISC, we never imagined the organization would grow to be the professional home for as many as one thousand highly skilled employees, nor did we imagine it would have a member and customer population of more than seven hundred electric and telephone cooperatives, municipal utilities and independent telecoms. We had projected modest growth in our customer and employee base, but we never expected that both would double during the timeframe they did. In 1998, it would have taken one powerful crystal ball to predict smartphones, tablets, the growth of broadband, web sites, social media, analytics, and the dramatic increase in the adoption of technology by utilities and telecom organizations. iVUE®'s adaptability underscores the wisdom, vision and insight of our early development team.

Financially, the growth in products, product demands and innovation has taken NISC's 1998 equity level of 15 percent up to more than 51 percent. Our cash position has improved significantly with a cash balance of $19 million in 2014, well beyond the $500,000 in the late 1990s. And while we traditionally returned 21 percent of our margins (profits) to our members annually, based on their use of NISC products, in 2014 this amount was increased to 30 percent.

It is gratifying to see the financial strength of NISC improve year after year. At one point in time, we were a struggling, cash-strapped, low-equity technology firm living hand to mouth. In 2015, we are in a position to pay for all of our capital expenditures, research and development, and asset purchases with internally generated funds. It's ironic that as our nation's economy struggled through 2007–2010, NISC charted our best-ever financial performance.

It's good to be always mindful of your purpose and ensure that you keep that purpose at the center of your work. NISC's founding board of directors provided guidance in the form of a simple mission statement. Have we done our best to stay focused on members and customers by providing them with quality products that are value priced? While we've had a fifteen-year roller coaster ride that daily brings unanticipated benefits and challenges, yes, we've stayed true to the mission of service to our markets. Being wired differently has served our organization and its members well.

The Next Generation

Time passes quickly and you forget the details, issues and things of little consequence. But you never forget the important things. I will always remember that we accomplished what many said could not be done. Looking back, it makes the stress, the extra hours and the frantic discussions all worthwhile. The pride of accomplishment blots out the numerous trips, the discussions with dissatisfied early-adopting members, and their questions and doubts about our ability to deliver iVUE®.

During that time of development and uncertainty, our employees "grew up" professionally. Being a part of such a massive and important undertaking built their confidence and caused them to reach deeper than they ever thought possible. The achievement of consolidation and iVUE® development laid the foundation for NISC to tackle new technical challenges with an attitude of confidence that simply did not exist before.

In my final assessment, I believe that it's our cooperative business model, shared values and servant leadership culture that differentiate us in the marketplace. They are what puts the member/customer and employee in the center of everything we do, guiding our decisions about, and commitment to, customer service and employee development. The cooperative business model gives us the freedom to plan long term and see beyond the technical, organizational, competitive and financial challenges that always loom ahead. The cooperative advantage was our trump card as we worked through the consolidation and the iVUE® rewrite. It gave us the confidence to actually "will" the success of each major endeavor.

There are countless examples of publicly traded technology companies whose stories are legendary. Consider Apple's rise from beginning in Steve Job's garage to becoming the most valuable brand and corporation on the planet. Look at the billionaire status of Facebook's founder Mark Zuckerberg or Google's Larry Page. In each story, there are individuals (innovators) who took huge personal risk and personally profited. This is free-market capitalism at its best. To a large extent, it is how America has become the world's economic powerhouse.

In the case of NISC's iVUE® project, the trappings of success are not as visible or tangible. It produced no solitary millionaires, but one thousand employees have benefited from continuous employment, competitive wages, comprehensive benefit and retirement plans, and the belief that they are part of something truly extraordinary. Additionally, there are seven hundred member systems and about fourteen million end users who benefit from the use of our products each and every day. Our efforts have contributed to the quality of life in rural America, and NISC is an integral part of bridging the technical divide between citizens living in rural America and their cousins living in the city.

It is impossible to adequately express my appreciation and admiration to NISC's employees who were there in the very beginning, many of whom are still with us, delivering on the iVUE® promise. I will be forever grateful to the members and cooperative friends who believed in us, provided funding or rolled up their sleeves and helped us design, test and build NISC into what it is today.

There is still much work to do, and there will be many challenges ahead. But today, NISC stands on a strong foundation built by people and organizations that believed in its future and in doing something great for the greater good. The past fifteen years have set the stage for the next generation of believers and innovators. I can't wait to see what's in store.

KEY POINTS TO CONSIDER IN THIS CHAPTER

1. It was clear our software was at the end of its useful life, and so was the regional distribution model under which CADP and NCDC had both been operating. Independently, **we came to the conclusion that we needed to beat our competitive swords into plowshares, combine our human and financial resources, and write one product** that would be shared by our respective memberships and others across the nation.

2. Business articles and industry observers claimed that software rewrites had a 70 percent probability of failure; we believed our situation was different. **We believed in our members and the power and resilience of the cooperative business model.**

3. **It's always good to be mindful of your purpose.** NISC's founding board of directors provided us guidance in the form of a simple mission statement.

PART III

COLLABORATIVE CULTURE IN PRACTICE

A collaborative culture follows as a result of values being put into action; it's the next logical step. First, employees need to understand with crystal clarity where the organization is headed—that's your mission statement. Next, leaders in the organization must model the behaviors they want repeated by all employees, and this is done most effectively through service to others. Once employees see the big picture and have leaders ready to serve them, they will want to give their best. They will put organizational values into action. With these critical elements in place, a culture of collaboration becomes everyday practice. It's the natural outcome and it generates a level of synergy and passion among employees, encouraging them to exceed expectations. It continually amazes me, and it will amaze you, too.

Chapter 9

Employee Engagement and Satisfaction Are Key

Successful people are always looking for opportunities to help others. Unsuccessful people are always asking, "What's in it for me?"
— Brian Tracy

We've all been through the drill of calling a cab company for an early morning trip to the airport. The cab experience is typically a predictable and necessary evil. Each town has a thousand cab drivers capable of getting the job done. The cab business is highly regulated, so they can't differentiate themselves on price. The vehicles are also very standard; 80 percent of the time the cab will be a Crown Victoria, dark in color. All in all, the cab business is quite ordinary, in my experience anyway. That is, until a cab driver named Mike made one of my trips to the airport extraordinary.

I was in full-on travel mode that morning, standing outside my hotel, backpack swung across my shoulder and roller bag in tow as the cab pulled into the driveway. The interior of cabs is generally a bit grimy, resulting from the numerous passengers they carry each day. As I tossed my bag in the trunk and slid into this cab though, there was a surprise: the interior was absolutely spotless and even had a hint of evergreen scent.

The cab driver turned around to face me, extended his hand and said, "Good morning, Mr. Dosch. My name is Mike."

When you reserve a cab, you give the dispatcher your name. Mike had evidently made it a point to learn and remember mine. I was impressed. This had never happened to me before. "To the airport, please. Delta Airlines," I said.

"Yes, Mr. Dosch," Mike responded. "According to my GPS, I'm estimating it'll take about thirty-two minutes and cost about $43." What a great bit of information, I thought to myself, again surprised. Setting the customer's expectations.

As we pulled out of the hotel driveway, Mike said, "Would you like any particular music, Mr. Dosch?"

My choice of music? Really? It was early morning, but it had to be five o'clock somewhere. "How about a little Jimmy Buffett?" I asked.

"Excellent," Mike said and switched his satellite radio to a station playing "Margaritaville." A smile was growing on my face.

"Would you like to read the paper, Mr. Dosch? I have the *Wall Street Journal* and *USA Today*."

"Yes, please," I replied. "I'll take the *Journal*."

"Excellent," Mike said. "Would you like some water? It's cold."

"Sure, why not?" was my response. Mike's attitude toward customer service was unlike anything I had experienced in the taxi cab arena. I felt compelled to ask him, "Mike, I've had a thousand cab rides, but this is extraordinary. What's your philosophy?"

"It's really simple. Each morning, I stop by the store, purchase a case of water and a couple of newspapers, which costs me about $7. I figure this investment and providing the extra service to my clients increases my tips from an average of $70 to about $160 a day. Pretty good investment, don't you think, Mr. Dosch?"

"A $7 investment to make another $90 a day? That's not bad, not bad at all," I replied.

Mike went on, "I own this cab and lease it to the Yellow Cab Company. So, welcome to my office. This is my own business, and I take pride in being better than my competitors. My take-home pay is almost twice the average cab driver's. About 65 percent of my business is repeat, and many of my customers are big tippers," he said with a smile.

With just a little extra effort and investment, Mike had turned an ordinary and routine cab ride into a lucrative entrepreneurial business, creating a bright spot in every customer's day in the process. I was impressed.

Each day, anyone who works in the world of business is faced with a crowded field of competitors just like Mike is faced with a long line of competing cabs at the airport. Regardless of your industry or your affiliation, some competitors will be better than others, maybe even better than you; some will do well, and others not so well. For most organizations, the number one marketing challenge is standing out from the crowd. We focus a lot of time, effort and money on perfecting and advancing our products, as well we should. But are we like Mike? Do we do more than is expected and provide those "wow" moments for our customers?

After that experience with Mike the cab driver, I would find myself asking if NISC provides extraordinary customer service. It's always the little things that make the biggest difference: extra care, courtesy, promptness, doing what we say we will do and treating every single contact with enthusiasm and focus as if it is the most important thing we will do that day.

As we rode along, I was struck by another extraordinary thing about Mike: he was taking a potentially mundane job and making it a sheer joy. He enjoyed his work each day, and to him every customer wasn't just a few more dollars in his pocket. Each interaction with a customer was an adventure, a learning experience and a challenge. What an inspiration!

When we arrived at the airport, Mike jumped out of the cab and opened my door before I could even gather my things. He handed me my bag, gave me a firm handshake, looked me right in the eyes and said, "It's been a pleasure Mr. Dosch."

"Thanks, Mike." I replied, adding, "I admire the way you're running your business."

His eyes lit up and a sheepish smile crossed his face. I placed a generous tip in his hand. Mike's business philosophy had, once again, proved very successful.

Each of us wants to work for an organization that stands out from the crowd; an organization we can be proud of. Much like the father who puffs his chest when he says "That's *my* boy who just caught the ball in the end zone," that's how every leader hopes his or her employees feel about their organization; that they stand a little taller when they declare where they work . . . rather than shrinking away or avoiding the opportunity altogether.

More than Money

"When we think about how people work, the naïve intuition we have is people are like rats in a maze," says behavioral economist Dan Ariely in his best-selling *Predictably Irrational: The Hidden Forces that Shape Our Decisions*. "We really have this incredibly simplistic view of why people work and what the labor market looks like," he says.

Mr. Ariely has long been fascinated with how emotional states, moral codes and peer pressure affect our ability to make rational and often extremely important decisions in our daily lives—across a spectrum of interests, from economic choices (how should I invest?) to personal ones (whom should I marry?). When you look carefully at the way people work, Ariely says, you find out there's a lot more at play—and a lot more at stake—than money. He provides evidence that we are driven also by meaningful work, by others' acknowledgement and by the amount of effort we've put in: the harder the task is, the prouder we are.

> "We really have this incredibly simplistic view of why people work and what the labor market looks like."
> – Dan Ariely

I am convinced that a good work ethic can be taught by example, but there is nothing quite as effective as a solid work ethic being instilled at a young age. I was fortunate for that to have been my case. When I was growing up, my family had one car, one television, one radio, one newspaper. My siblings and I each had our assigned tasks, whether it was mowing the lawn or hauling bales on our uncle's farm. We weren't given an allowance to do these things, and we didn't receive a trophy for every accomplishment. It was just our job as members of the family. We grew up happy and healthy, despite what some would consider a deprived childhood. A strong work ethic and a desire to contribute in a meaningful way were ingrained in all of us.

With the Internet and all of the technological distractions that exist in the twenty-first century, I believe it is now much more challenging to instill strong values in children. Road trips used to be times of conversation, stories and games, which served as opportunities for parents to model behaviors to and instill values in their children. Today, each kid with an iPad and headphones is living much of the time in his or her own world. They are growing up with others, but they are largely alone. The same challenges arise in the workplace, where it can be difficult to connect with employees who are surrounded by the same technological distractions.

As parents and as managers, we need to make an effort to resist the technology addiction that is prevalent in society. We must model for our children and our employees the importance of being a member of an engaged, vibrant family or team and show how this can be one of life's most rewarding experiences. We need to provide opportunities for meaningful work and, as leaders in our homes or our companies, we must remember the enormous value of recognizing the contributions of others.

From time to time, I receive notes from NISC employees who want to share their concerns, present an idea or express an opinion. One of these notes came from an employee at the end of his thirty-one-year career, and it speaks volumes about the value of meaningful work and the importance of recognition:

I'm not sure how to put this on paper, but I will try. Just saying thanks to a great organization doesn't really do it justice.

I remember back when I first entered the working world, green and right out of college. I never really had a serious job before, only a couple of summer jobs. Walking in to my first day of employment at [then] CADP was very intimidating. Everyone knew everything except me! And there was no book to read or study to catch on. Thinking about a retirement date seemed incomprehensible. Who stays at one job for thirty-one years? Who even works that long? There were so many questions from an immature newbie!

Looking back, where did the time go? If you would have told me that thirty-one years after walking in to my first job I would be getting this amount of money for retirement, I would have never believed you. And, I also got paid for every day of those years. And I got other benefits like medical insurance, life insurance, paid time away from work and the list goes on. Not possible.

Add to all of that the fact I got to make many lifelong friends. It's all too good to be true. I will admit many times during my career, I read articles about unhappy, dissatisfied employees (sometimes even got to see them face-to-face). A part of me doesn't really understand their unhappiness, the other part is so grateful for what I found at NISC. This organization, this environment is truly one of a kind, in a world of companies very different than we are. I have had many discussions with co-workers at NISC covering many topics and many times our conversations ended with, "How lucky can you be?"

This has been such a wild and fun ride I am at a loss for words. My gratitude to this organization cannot be measured, and as you can tell, is very hard for me to put into words. NISC has seen me through births, school, sports, family emergencies and everything in between. The highs and the lows. No matter how much NISC grows, this will always be family to me.

Let me close by saying thanks for absolutely everything. I am and always will be a crusader for NISC!

In this instance and for this NISC employee, meaningful work plus healthy doses of recognition for a job well done equaled a thirty-one-year career. It might sound like an anomaly, but a long term of employment isn't unusual in the cooperative world. Just like in the Industrial Age, when our parents and grandparents often worked diligently to keep the same job for their entire career, many employees who work at cooperatives find an alignment between their personal values and those held by the organization.

Mastery, Purpose and Autonomy
When your organization is able to infuse motivating qualities into the work you offer your employees, you have a recipe to decrease employee

turnover and increase employee engagement. Daniel Pink, the author of *Drive: The Surprising Truth about What Motivates Us*, suggests that there are three things equally as important as salary in our careers: mastery, purpose and autonomy.

According to Mr. Pink, when careers consist of rudimentary tasks or repetitive jobs requiring little thought or creativity, money is the motivation for working. These are positions in which employees aren't asked to add their own personal value to the process; they are just expected to complete the same task in the same way with the same level of quality, time and again. In positions that require problem solving, innovation and imagination, typically individuals are also motivated by mastery, purpose and autonomy.

Pink explains that mastery is our desire to master what we do. It could be playing a guitar, running a marathon, developing a new piece of software, closing a deal, solving a business problem or mentoring a new colleague. We've all experienced a sense of victory or mastery when we successfully accomplish a task or project. It's a wonderful feeling.

Purpose is another important motivator, according to Pink's theory. Of course, we all want to earn a comfortable living, but true satisfaction comes from contributing to a higher purpose: making our industry, community, town or nation a better place; helping someone in need; being part of building a business; making an organization more efficient or effective. Purpose is what we mean when we say we want to make a difference. The notion of purpose as a motivating factor reminds me of a quote I read many years ago: "Being successful at something that doesn't matter is our worst nightmare." What a tragedy it would be to retire and feel like you had wasted your time.

Autonomy, the third motivating factor, refers to having a career that gives a person his or her own space. When we were kids, it was frustrating to have parents or teachers always looking over our shoulder. It felt like they watched our every move and tried to control our every action or decision. In the work world, having autonomy means that, although we may be assigned a task, project or problem to solve, how we tackle it is up to us. It requires the use of our imagination, experience and intellect to creatively bring the assignment to a successful conclusion. And when we do, there's a great sense of accomplishment. With each challenge met and problem solved, our confidence and self-worth grows, and the value we bring to the organization increases.

A perfect example of the power of autonomy is Todd Eisenhauer, our vice president of Engineering and Operations. Todd joined NISC straight out of college after getting his electrical engineering degree. He is smart and loves a challenge. Over the years he's sought out additional growth opportunities, which is what advanced him to being in the position he is today, leading one of NISC's most critical areas, and NISC is all the better for it.

This is why, beyond providing a decent compensation package to our employees, we also have a responsibility to sustain a culture that enables them to fulfill their needs for mastery, purpose and autonomy. We must build a learning organization and encourage a collaborative culture that motivates employees to excel, develop, and share new skills and abilities. Our cooperative business model and leadership-through-service approach allows NISC to create this kind of environment, and we believe that doing so is critical. It is why we make a commitment to our employees that we will provide a professional environment that gives them the opportunity to experience the satisfaction and sense of accomplishment each of them deserves. And our shared values of innovation, empowerment and personal development directly reflect this.

What Matters Most in Employee Engagement?

The report entitled *State of the Global Workplace: Employee Engagement Insights for Business Leaders Worldwide* highlights findings from Gallup's ongoing study of workplaces in more than 140 countries from 2011-2012. The report provides insights into what leaders can do to improve employee engagement and performance in their companies.

According to the report, there are two keys to doubling employee engagement:

1. Hiring and developing great managers, and

2. Building up and leveraging the strengths of every employee.

Another great insight from the report is this: How employees feel about their jobs starts and ends with their direct supervisor. This is similar to how we feel at NISC. We believe employees don't leave organizations, they leave their supervisor. We have found that if employees feel that their supervisor takes a real interest in their development, or offers frequent praise and recognition, they are more likely to be engaged in their job and less likely to want to find work elsewhere.

Hiring the right managers is absolutely essential to building an engaged workforce, according to Jim Clifton, Gallup Chairman and CEO. As Mr. Clifton says in the *State of the Global Workplace* report:

> *Trying to get employees to fix their weaknesses doesn't work. Weaknesses can't be developed much at all—but employees' strengths can be developed infinitely. The problem is, too many companies focus on fixing weaknesses, and this only breeds non-engagement or, worse, active disengagement.*
>
> *Great managers build development plans around every employee's strengths. When employees work from strengths, nothing motivates them to achieve more—not money, not love, not vacations, not good benefits, not company volleyball games, not motivational speakers. And employees working from their strengths win new customers.*

With this in mind, it makes sense for an organization to survey and measure employee engagement. Things can always be improved, and more is always better when it comes to compensation. At NISC, we have come to understand that it is equally important to know whether we have a happy and engaged workforce as it is to have a profitable bottom line. As such, we conduct quarterly employee surveys to keep a pulse on the engagement of our employees. This allows us to quickly identify action items we need to pursue, and it demonstrates to employees our commitment to ensuring their engagement.

That is key to employee engagement: the knowledge that management is genuinely committed to improve and enhance the work environment for their employees' benefit. As leaders in our organizations, it's our responsibility to

"Weaknesses can't be developed much at all—but employees' strengths can be developed infinitely."
– Jim Clifton

carefully consider all survey feedback and, most importantly, let employees know what we are or are not going to do about it. The worst thing we could do is ask for an opinion and not acknowledge its receipt.

One of our inherent challenges as organizational leaders is that we judge ourselves by our intentions, and we judge others (be they our employees or our peers) by their actions. And it also works the other way: our employees and our peers judge us by our actions, not by our (usually) unstated but well-meant intentions.

Understanding that employees will judge us by our actions and not by our intentions is invaluable when it comes to motivating them, especially if we are striving to build a workplace culture that is focused on collaboration and leadership through service to others. In short, words of affirmation for a job well done may make the difference in an employee staying engaged in the organization. The repeated withholding of positive feedback or praise can prompt disengagement or even departure—both of which equate to organizational costs we can't afford to pay too much of in today's competitive marketplace.

According to the Gallup report, only 13 percent of employees across 142 countries worldwide are engaged in their jobs, meaning they are emotionally invested in and focused on creating value for their organizations every day. Gallup's 2009–2010 global study of employee engagement found that actively disengaged workers—that is, those who are negative and potentially hostile to their organizations—outnumbered engaged employees at a ratio of nearly 2:1.

These statistics are downright frightening! A little more than one out of ten employees are emotionally invested in and focused on creating value in the organization? At NISC, we truly cannot afford to have such a low rate of employee engagement, and thank goodness, we don't. Chapter 12 will highlight some of the ways NISC measures organizational success, including employee satisfaction. Let it suffice here to say that our goal is to be in the top 10 percent of all companies in our peer group when it comes to employee engagement, and I'm grateful to say that we are in the top 10 percent in four of seven categories. So while we have made progress, we still have much work to do.

Leaders often say their organization's greatest asset is its people—but in reality, this is only true when those employees are fully engaged in their jobs. Engaged workers stand apart from their not-engaged and actively disengaged counterparts because of the discretionary effort they consistently bring to their roles day after day. These employees willingly go the extra mile because of their strong emotional connection to their organization.

It's easy to throw up your hands and say, "Well, you can't please everyone all of the time." Or here's another good one: "We know 10 percent of any target market won't like what we do, so why should we make decisions to please the 10 percent?" While these are valid points, they are also excuses to keep us from doing the right thing for our employees. We can never fall short of the mark when it comes to recruiting, hiring, maintaining and growing our workforce. Our employees are who make our organization's success a reality.

A Role for Benevolence in Employee Engagement

Great organizations win more than their employees' minds, they win their hearts as well. That's the real challenge. There is a quiet movement afoot that can offer insight to businesses wanting to achieve that level of greatness. It does not propose a set of beliefs or require membership dues. At its core, it calls us to simple acts of kindness. Nothing more and no less.

One of my all-time favorite musicals is *Les Misérables*, based on the book by Victor Hugo. My wife and I have seen *Les Misérables* at our local theatre several times, and we love it a little more after each viewing. *Les Mis*, as it is affectionately called, is the longest-running musical in the world, according to www.lesmis.com. It offers a vivid example of the difference each of us can make in the life of another if we are willing to engage in simple acts of kindness.

The story starts in 1815 in southeastern France, where the convict Jean Valjean is released from a French prison after serving nineteen years for stealing a loaf of bread and for subsequent attempts to escape from prison. When Valjean arrives at the town of Digne, no one is willing to give him shelter because he is an ex-convict. Desperate, Valjean knocks on the door of Monseigneur Bienvenu (or Myriel), the warm-hearted bishop of Digne. Myriel treats Valjean with kindness, and Valjean repays the bishop by stealing his silverware. When the police arrest Valjean, Myriel covers for him, claiming the silverware was a gift. The authorities release Valjean, and Myriel makes him promise to become an honest man.

Because of the bishop's kindness, generosity and advice, Valjean changes his life to become the benevolent man the audience sees from this point forward. Valjean finds himself in a constant struggle between doing the right thing and the lure of choosing the easy way out. *Les Mis* is masterfully written in such a way that, at every turn, you feel Valjean's fear, love, pain and his desire to forgive as well as be forgiven. The essence of *Les Mis* is the incredible change of heart that can occur when we show another human being simple kindness and understanding.

On the NISC Community (our internal version of Facebook that connects our employees and members), we have a section called Employee Recognition. It allows individuals to publicly acknowledge an extraordinary or selfless act of service and post kind words. It is amazing to watch the response from our employees and how they "pile on" with thanks and gratitude when someone's actions are noted. I am especially pleased with how employees use this forum to thank and recognize retiring employees, one response after another speaking words of appreciation and admiration that should not go unspoken. It is so gratifying to the retiring employee, and it's also a great affirmation for the rest of us to observe an admired colleague's exit to retirement.

In the summer of 2014, Tim Emmerich, a telecom sales manager who works remotely for NISC, was traveling on business when a devastating hail storm passed through his residential area in Omaha, Nebraska. Fortunately, Tim's family was unharmed; however, there was extensive damage to their home. As Tim was an offsite employee, we had learned this via an e-mail from his division supervisor, who told us about the situation and asked for our prayers. Less than a week later, we received this update from Tim:

Good morning everyone,

I wanted to send an update on our situation here, but first I must say thank you. When I brought in the mail last night, there was a card from NISC. Inside the card were more cards, including gift cards for Home Depot and three restaurants. As I stood there reading the card to my wife, I was reminded of how glad and fortunate I am to be a part of the NISC family. When I stopped reading and looked up, my wife was crying.

We have received so much support from so many of you, and we can't begin to say just how much it means to us. The people at NISC are hands down the best in the business, and I am so grateful for the special friendships that have grown out of my ten years as a member of this family. It is with sincere, heartfelt gratitude that we say again, thank you, to all.

Another way we show kindness to and reverence for one another at NISC is through tree planting. When an employee passes away while still employed, we plant a tree to honor his or her service and contribution. As a part of the tree-planting dedication, employees gather around the site and a reflective reading is shared to dedicate the tree in the employee's memory. It is incredibly powerful to observe acts like this when they occur in your organization as a result of employees putting their values into action.

The Benevolence Committee
Wherever they occur, acts of kindness represent benevolence in action. This benevolence can take on many forms. You can send someone a card to congratulate them on their new child, or you can volunteer your time at a local shelter to help feed the hungry. Both are acts of kindness showing benevolence.

At NISC, benevolence has a more formal role as well, albeit a rather quiet one. It comes in the form of the NISC Benevolence Committee. Typically, benevolence committees are a function of religious organizations, designed to support members in times of need, and ours is similar in nature. Formed in 2000, the committee serves all of our office locations, including employees who work remotely, and its purpose is to lend financial and emotional support to NISC families in times of need. As a committee e-mail to all employees states: "We want you to know NISC has you in its thoughts and prayers during emotional events like the death of an immediate family member, hospitalization of you or an immediate family member or the birth/adoption of a child." Eight to twelve committee members are nominated and then voted on by employees. Those elected are evenly represented throughout NISC locations, so it is easy to bring a situation to the attention of a committee member.

An important aspect of the committee and any request brought forward to it is the level of confidentiality with which requests are handled. Again, as the committee puts it: "What is said among the Benevolence Committee, stays with the Benevolence Committee. There is ZERO, NADA, NO compromise on this. After a meeting takes place, all evidence of the discussion is destroyed. The only trail that exists would be in the checkbook (if we administered aid), and only treasurers have access to that register."

On most counts, the NISC Benevolence Committee may sound no different than typical organization employee groups that function to meet common employee needs during times such as the death of a family member, hospitalization, birth or adoption. But one area in which our committee uniquely serves NISC employees is in the category of financial hardship. The Benevolence Committee provides assistance to NISC employees who find themselves faced with an immediate financial crisis. Medical bills, rent, utilities and special needs are just a few examples of the expenses eligible for assistance. Factors considered in the decision to provide assistance include the severity and urgency of the hardship and also the availability of other resources for the employee.

"The high destiny of the individual is to serve rather than rule."
– Albert Einstein

Albert Einstein is quoted as saying, "The high destiny of the individual is to serve rather than to rule." At NISC, our service to employees doesn't end with aiding them only when they experience things such as a death in the family, an extended illness in the hospital or the adoption of a child. Certainly these are stressful life events that impact the contribution an employee can make in the workplace while they journey through them. But as an organization, we want each NISC employee to know and feel that we support them and their family through the good times and through the challenges, and this includes financial hardship, which can be every bit as devastating to a family and an employee's mental well-being. If it is within our power to ease that hardship and it's appropriate to do so, then it is our responsibility to offer that kind of assistance in addition to offering guidance and emotional support.

You may be wondering how the funds to support the Benevolence Committee are generated. Employees have the option to make a one-time contribution, or they can request to have a certain amount withdrawn from their monthly paycheck. Making such a request is completely voluntary, and the contribution amount in either case is up to the individual person. All employee-contributed funds are matched dollar-for-dollar by NISC. In 2013, 80 percent of employees chose to make contributions to the Benevolence Committee. Funds can be distributed to any employee whether they contribute to the Benevolence Committee or not. Once a year, the board of directors receives a report on the Benevolence Committee's financial aid fund. The report simply shows the beginning balance, the total amount contributed by employees, the amount matched by NISC, the amount expended that year and the ending balance.

Without question, the stories we could share of employees who have been helped by the Benevolence Committee would be powerful testimony to others, and there may be some greater value to be gained by telling those stories that we miss by choosing to leave them out. That's okay. Some things are better left in private, and at NISC, we believe that the specifics of our benevolence for one another is one of those things.

A MOMENT OF SILENCE

How many times have you raced to a meeting a few minutes late, tried to sneak in the back with your heart pounding, and then needed several minutes to dis-engage from your previous front-burner project and change your focus to the agenda at hand? In today's crazy-paced workplace, this is more common than it should be, and no doubt more common than is healthy.

One of the things we do at NISC to help ease the transition from one project to the next when we are in a group setting is have a moment of silence. In team meetings, executive meetings, board meetings and even at our annual member information conference, where there's a couple thousand people in attendance, we practice a moment of silence at the start of each setting.

It is nothing fancy or drawn out; however, it is deliberate, and it's an intentional choice from our leadership team. We want to give ourselves, our employees and our members a brief respite, during which time we can all gather our thoughts and quiet our hearts. These few seconds before each meeting, along with a couple of deep breaths, have greatly impacted everyone's ability to focus, and it communicates a simple message: we respect one another enough that we will pause together in silence to better focus on the task in front of us. The practice requires a good deal of trust among participants, as well as trust in NISC's leadership that we are not imposing beliefs on anyone. Rather, we are respecting everyone as equal and inviting them to a higher level of collaboration.

The Rest of the Story

I have the privilege of speaking to a good number of groups around the country on a variety of topics related to NISC: its position in the software industry; its role as a cooperative; our aspiration to be an ethical organization; and the desire we have to model servant leadership in today's business world.

One of my favorite slides in the PowerPoint deck I commonly use in my presentations is the word STORY in bold, black letters, but with some letters appearing not quite right. As illustrated below, the base of the letter "T" has been removed and one arm of the "Y" is missing. The point of the slide is to always make sure you know the rest of the story.

S⁻OR⟍

Stephen R. Covey, renowned author of the classic book *The 7 Habits of Highly Effective People*, would say that the point being made in my slide is related to the fifth habit: seek first to understand, then to be understood. The concept of seeking first to understand involves a commitment on our part to shift from being heard (translation: hearing ourselves) to understanding so clearly that we can repeat back to the speaker what we understand, and they will nod in agreement, confirming that we "get" the rest of their story.

According to Covey, most people do not listen with the intent to understand, they listen with the intent to reply. They are either speaking or preparing to speak. In order for effective communication to take place, we need to listen more deeply: we need to listen for what is said in word, and what is spoken through the tone of the voice and the body language used while conveying the message. If we listen only so we know when we can reply, we've done nothing for the other person or people in the conversation except use them as a means to express ourselves. Most people don't take kindly to being used in any form.

If we actively listen, nodding our head or showing through our body language that we are paying attention but don't acknowledge what others have said, instead using the speaker's words as a springboard to our own ideas, we are controlling and manipulating the conversation to our benefit. Most people don't take kindly to being controlled or manipulated.

When we make a conscious choice to listen in a manner that gets us inside another person's frame of reference, we begin to see the world through their filters, through their emotions. Then, and only then, will we begin to understand how they feel. This is empathic listening . . . listening with empathy.

Albert Mehrabian was an early pioneer in the understanding of human communication, beginning in the 1960s. In his book, *Silent Messages*, Mahrabian shares his findings that only 7 percent of our communication is represented by the words we say, 38 percent is represented by our sounds or the tone we use, and a full 55 percent is represented by our body language, specifically facial expressions. When we listen empathically, we listen with our ears, and more importantly, we listen with our eyes and with our heart. We listen for behavior.

New phrases and responses creep into our vocabulary when we become empathic listeners. Responding in these kinds of ways indicates to the speaker that we have been truly listening:

That experience must have been exhilarating for you. I bet you felt like you were on top of the world!

I can hear the pain in your voice when you talk about the conver-
sation with your supervisor. I'm sorry it was so difficult for you.

Seeking first to understand is a simple, valuable skill that each of us can cultivate, although it takes time to learn and to practice. Within organizations, it requires an investment in the people we say we value most. Perhaps the greatest value in seeking first to understand is in how well it lays the groundwork for the second part in Covey's fifth habit of highly effective people: to be understood.

If seeking to understand requires consideration, then seeking to be understood requires courage, according to Covey. Seeking first to understand is an inside-out approach. It means that we begin first with something within our control: ourselves. We work to understand another, to consider another's views as important as we know our own to be. Once we make the initial investments to understand deeply the people with whom we work, it's important that we also provide context and meaning for our point of view. We must have the courage to share what we see, how we feel and what we value in moving beyond the current situation. When we do this, we find we can get to sticking points in situations more quickly. It becomes easier to confront reality with others. Another ironic thing happens in this process. We become more easily influenced. That might sound uncomfortable, even the opposite of what we really want. The strength in being influenced is this: only when we are willing to be influenced can we influence others.

When we listen, we learn. When we listen empathically, our respect for others grows and our understanding of how they see the world opens. This allows us to present ideas and solutions in a manner others can receive because we are expressing the ideas in their voice.

A quote from a truly wise individual comes to mind. Charlie Brown once said: "Few people are successful unless other people want them to be." I'd say Charlie understands a good deal about what motivates people.

KEY POINTS TO CONSIDER IN THIS CHAPTER

1. **In today's knowledge economy, efficiency is no longer more important than meaning.** We care much more about a product if we've participated in its creation from start to finish rather than if we've produced one item or piece of a whole, repeatedly.

2. **How employees feel about their jobs starts and ends with their direct supervisor.** If employees feel that, among other things, their supervisor takes a real interest in their development or offers frequent praise and recognition, they are very likely to be engaged. Hiring the right managers is absolutely essential to building an engaged workforce.

3. **As leaders in our organizations, it is our responsibility to carefully consider all feedback and, most importantly, let employees know what we are, or aren't, going to do about it.** The worst thing we can do is ask for an opinion and not acknowledge its receipt.

4. Once we make the initial investment to understand deeply the people with whom we work, we find we can get to sticking points in situations more quickly. Another ironic thing happens in this process: we become more easily influenced. That might sound uncomfortable, even the opposite of what we really want. **The strength in being influenced is this: only when we are willing to be influenced can we influence others.**

Chapter 10

Earning Trust through Truthfulness and Transparency

Trust is equal parts character and competence. . . . You can look at any leadership failure, and it's always a failure of one or the other.
— Stephen M.R. Covey

In chapter 9, we talked about Stephen R. Covey's fifth habit: seek first to understand, then to be understood. His eldest son, Stephen M.R. Covey, is also a best-selling author who has prompted positive change at NISC with his book *The Speed of Trust: The One Thing That Changes Everything*. For each of the last several years, our leadership team at NISC reads a book together, discusses it and identifies ways we can assimilate elements of it into our culture. In 2009 we read *The Speed of Trust*.

The Speed of Trust is packed with valuable insights for organizations, and NISC has worked to incorporate several of these into our culture. Why? Because when we trust one another, especially those with whom we work, we demonstrate competence and character in all of our actions. Higher trust levels nurture relationships and create greater collaboration. With that in mind, the insights offered in *The Speed of Trust* have inspired us to do the following at NISC:

1. We talk a great deal about behaviors that build trust;

2. We recognize the value of slowing down when working with people; and

3. We try to approach relationships with a "trust and verify" mindset.

Covey identifies thirteen behaviors of a high-trust leader in his book, and one of them in particular has had great applicability for our company in the last few years. The behavior is the act of creating transparency, which Covey describes in this way:

Tell the truth in a way that can be verified. Transparency is based on principles of honesty, openness, integrity and authenticity. It is based on doing things in the open where all can see. Part of transparency is sharing information. If ever in question, err on the side of disclosure.

Transparency is closely connected to communication. At NISC we're often told by employees via our quarterly pulse surveys that they feel we can improve communication, and this can be in any number of ways. In some instances, they would like to see better communication between teams; in others, they'd like there to be better communication between themselves and their supervisor. The situations vary, but the desire for more transparent communication is evident.

Transparency Can Be Tough

One of my family's favorite programs when I was growing up was *I Love Lucy* (I'm dating myself with this admission). Lucy was always getting into trouble and when she did, her husband, Ricky Ricardo, would say, "Lucy, you got some 'splainin' to do!"

It doesn't matter if you are working on mergers or flipping burgers, we all make mistakes. How we address these errors often defines our individual success, and that of our companies also. Think about it: an organization doesn't make a mistake—someone or some group within the organization does. Society today is unsurpassed in placing blame, pointing fingers and finding fault in others. In my humble opinion, there are far too many of us who "got some 'splainin' to do!"

Living transparently and leading an organization by always doing the right thing isn't easy. Every single day, I'm stretched to determine what "right" really is. Being a CEO feels harder than ever when the level of transparency expected by employees and society continues to climb. The older I get, the more aware I am of my shortcomings, but I've also learned that one thing is certain: the more frequently we practice trust and transparency, the easier it gets to hold each other accountable to it. Let me give you an example.

Each year during employee benefit sessions, NISC leaders talk about the issue of delivering health insurance coverage for all of our employees. To say maintaining coverage has been a challenge for us would be an understatement. Since 2000, we have bucked the national trends and stubbornly refused to back away from what many corporations today feel is a benefit that is no longer afford-able or sustainable. But fortunately, we have been able to maintain our health coverage by aggressively pursuing options and changes to our

The more frequently we practice trust and transparency, the easier it gets to hold each other accountable to it.

plan. In addition to ensuring continued coverage for our employees, our efforts demonstrate to our board of directors that we recognize the negative impact that yearly double-digit increases from our medical insurance provider would have on NISC's bottom line and cost structure.

Since 2010, we've stepped forward with a wellness program, health screening clinics and a proactive attitude toward improving the overall health profile of our employee population. We aligned ourselves with a health insurance provider who developed an impressive offering of programs designed to provide information, enabling employees to adopt healthier lifestyles and detect any medical issues or problems early on so they can be addressed promptly.

The approach NISC has taken is that we don't want to be in a position to only pay for claims when our employees have medical bills. We want to make investments in wellness education and encourage the adoption of healthy lifestyles in order to help prevent our employees from having medical issues. In other words, we want to be part of the solution to our nation's health care crisis rather than contribute to the problem by embracing and funding traditional medical insurance.

In 2010, we introduced a high-deductible/health savings account (HD/HSA) to employees. Our intent was to continue to offer both the deductible and co-pay plans we had used for years, but with the new third HD/HSA option. We used several methods to communicate the upcoming changes to our health care coverage, making clear what the benefits were for the employee and for the organization. During that time, I closed one of my blogs to employees in this manner:

We have been doing a great deal of research on health savings accounts and are comfortable that ours is a viable option for some of our employees, while admittedly not for everyone. The good news is, you have several health insurance options at NISC, and when it comes to the diversity of our employee group, options are always a good thing.

The blog containing that excerpt was posted October 1, 2010, and at the time, I believed NISC had done the right thing in choosing to continue our current coverage and add the high-deductible/health savings account as a third option. But when we began the process of adding the HD/HSA option to our health care coverage plans, as we got deeper into the numbers, they didn't add up.

No matter how we looked at the scenarios, the only way we could continue providing full coverage for our employees was to switch everyone to the high-deductible/health savings account, not just those employees who chose that option, and it would have to happen in a matter of months, not over a three-year period as we had planned. Our great intentions for a gradual transition to a new way of thinking about health care needed to be put into action now.

In an effort to be fully transparent, the team working on the project sent out an all-employee e-mail as soon as we could, letting everyone know about the need to change direction. We thought this kind of information might spread like wildfire if we were to follow a more traditional communications strategy that included sharing information from the top, down, and along organizational chart lines. We told ourselves we were erring on the side of transparency with our actions, but in all honesty, our main concern was that if we didn't explain the situation quickly, someone might unintentionally "slip" and share pieces of information that would undermine the entire process.

One month after my first blog announcing the planned addition of the HD/HSA option, I posted another entry about our health care coverage; one I hadn't planned to write but that quickly became necessary after the all-employee e-mail had been sent. I needed to admit that we had screwed up. Here are excerpts from that follow-up blog (you will recognize the opening):

One of my family's favorite programs when I was growing up was I Love Lucy *(I'm dating myself with this admission). Lucy was always getting into trouble and when she did, her husband, Ricky Ricardo, would say, "Lucy, you got some 'splainin' to do!"*

Based on the responses we received from the e-mail announcing NISC's adoption of a single high-deductible/health savings account for all employees, it appears that I have some 'splainin' to do. In the e-mail, we told you what we are doing with health insurance next year; I'd like to explain why we are making the move.

First, I want to apologize to our managers and team leads for not informing them of our health insurance decision before we sent an "all NISC" e-mail. The last they'd heard, we were still offering health insurance options. While the vice presidents had some information, we did not inform the managers and team leaders in our haste to get this information out. So if you went into their offices with questions and they had that "deer in the headlights" look, it's my fault, not theirs. I hope you will forgive me.

Back in October, I talked about the HD/HSA concept and our desire to offer this new approach to health insurance as an added option to our traditional co-pay and deductible plans. With the goal of developing a three-year plan, we rolled up our sleeves, analyzed our current data, asked hard questions, ran the numbers, reran the numbers . . . and reran the numbers.

There was one piece of data that sent these discussions in a completely different direction. When we began looking at our *current year's claims data by plan (i.e., co-pay and deductible), what we learned was startling. The experience data (the amount of claims paid in a particular plan vs. the premium paid) for the co-pay plan was 114 percent. That means that for every dollar in premium NISC paid in the co-pay plan, our insurance provider paid $1.14 in claims.*

You don't have to be an accountant to know this is an unsustainable trend. Our co-pay plan last year experienced a single premium increase of 16 percent; this year, with the poor experience ratio, that premium would need to go up an additional 64 percent. For the first time we were being forced to consider employees picking up part of the premium cost.

The way to ease the situation was to get all of us into a single plan sooner rather than later. We were disappointed in not being able to provide plan options, but we knew that while this was a difficult choice to have to make today, it was the right thing to do to benefit all of NISC in the long run. This is what prompted our decision to offer only the HD/HSA option in year one. Moving to an HSA is a significant change for NISC, but it is an inevitable change and, frankly, a necessary one.

Please do not draw any conclusions until you have all of the facts. We have much to discuss during our open enrollment sessions, and I will personally be attending each of these sessions.

This entry received one of the all-time highest engagements from our employees. Unfortunately though, in this instance, it was negative engagement: employees weren't happy; they were confused and felt that I had misled them. Some questioned our transparency and our intent because it appeared that we were changing our minds about health benefit options like the wind blows.

Think about it: One month I'm rolling out an upcoming change that impacts every single employee, including me, and I'm introducing it in the typical voice-of-authority way, essentially telling them: "Don't worry, we've got this under control. We've done our homework, and you (our employees) will find that it's the next best thing to sliced bread." Then things changed the very next month (after a whirlwind of research, meetings and heart-wrenching discussion), when our leadership team had to make the decision to move a three-year process forward at Mach speed, cramming the change into several months, due to the new and compelling information we couldn't ignore.

In our hurry after making the decision, we took the shotgun approach that many organizations use to communicate when under a time crunch. We crafted (that's the appropriate verb) an e-mail (how impersonal) to deliver highly personal and important information because we thought it would be the best, most real-time option. It might have been the fastest, most inclusive way to communicate information, but we failed miserably to take into account our basic tenet: do the right thing, always. Organizational change that touches every employee—like health care coverage—is sure to elicit high levels of interest and it should therefore be treated with the greatest allowable transparency if we expect employee trust to remain solid. Many of our employees thought that I had hidden our original agenda. My intentions may have been golden, but what they saw—in my actions—was something very different.

This experience is a powerful reminder that processing change comes slowly for each of us, especially when it's not of our own making. Mr. Covey offers a wonderful statement in *The Speed of Trust* that we should have remembered in this instance: "With people, fast is slow and slow is fast."

How many times have you hurried through a project discussion with a coworker, and then needed to have a follow-up conversation (or two) in order to clarify what you didn't cover originally? All too often, we try to be too efficient in our dealings with people, much like how we seek greater efficiencies with our organizational processes. This is a mistake.

With people, we must always remember that taking the extra time to understand their view and fully clarify our own is well worth the long-term investment. When you move more slowly to build a relationship (or in NISC's case, explain a change in health benefits), you lay the groundwork for greater trust, which will allow you to subsequently move forward with implementation much faster and with reduced costs.

We are now four years into the implementation of NISC's high-deductible/health savings account for employees. Compared with before, we are better, more informed consumers of health care, and NISC employees now retain and control a cumulative total of over $2.6 million in their personal health savings accounts. This money belongs to each individual employee and gone is our previous "use it or lose it" mentality toward medical insurance premiums.

Does Organizational Transparency Really Matter?

According to the 2013 Edelman Trust Barometer, only one-fifth of members of the general population surveyed in twenty-six countries (including the United States) believes that business leaders and government officials will tell the truth when confronted with a difficult issue. This means that four out of five respondents are suspicious of these types of leaders and more than likely expect "spin" instead of substance.

And, interestingly, based on the survey results, it also means that the average individual is now trusted nearly twice as much as is a chief executive or government official. Traditional hierarchies are being replaced by more trusted peer-to-peer relationships and horizontal networks of trust.

According to Richard Edelman, President and CEO of Edelman, the global public relations firm that created the annual Edelman Trust Barometer:

> *Running a profitable business and having top-rated leadership no longer, alone, builds long-term trust. In fact, these operational-based attributes have become an expectation. Today, business builds trust by treating employees well, exhibiting ethical and transparent practices and placing customers ahead of profits, while also delivering quality products and services.*

What can organizations do better if we are, or want to be, one of the transparent few?

Use Simple, Believable Messages

Not so long ago, senior management would prepare and deliver communication down to the employee audience or out to external stakeholders. That was it. Today, this one-way communication method is joined by another, where employees, stakeholders and anyone who wants to engage (including management) can be involved in real-time dialogue about an organization or its products and services. The two-way method of communication can be challenging for some leaders, as it doesn't allow a person to ignore or control the conversation. If you are unwilling to participate in this kind of communication, the conversation, whether positive or negative, will happen without you.

In 2009, NISC welcomed Jeff Almen to the organization as our National Business Relations Manager. Jeff is based in Herndon, Virginia, and has nearly thirty years of knowledge and expertise in the cooperative world. He is "our eyes and our ears" when it comes to the industry and the political conversations that take place within it. Jeff has helped us to discover that one way to increase organizational transparency at NISC is to communicate key messages broadly enough to reach employees multiple times through multiple strategies, and simply enough to be believable. We need to use vertical, one-way communication in addition to participating in the ongoing horizontal conversations. The message we carry forward, regardless of topic or audience, must be transparent enough to pass this single test: does it contain verifiable truth?

> **The message we carry forward . . . must be transparent enough to pass this single test: Does it contain verifiable truth?**

It's easy to see where we fell short in the HD/HSA example. We sent a single e-mail to all employees: one communication from a team within one of our divisions (who were not even senior management) to nearly a thousand employees in four locations on a topic that impacted every individual. We hit the mark with a clear message, but we missed a number of opportunities to leverage ongoing horizontal conversations, which were rampant as soon as we pressed the "send" button. Here are a few communication strategies we typically use at NISC but overlooked in that instance:

- Advance notice to supervisors and team leads of an upcoming change
- Face-to-face meetings with teams
- A virtual CEO conversation with all employees

- A "Lunch and Learn" session at each location
- Employee meetings
- Weekly e-updates to all employees
- Intranet blog post on change when decision is made

As the younger Covey said, with people, fast is slow and slow is fast. We moved far too fast in delivering the information about our decision regarding the high-deductible HSA. We did so believing that employees would understand we had their best interests and those of the organization in mind. But ultimately, moving so fast only prompted a backlash of questions and concerns that slowed everyone in the organization to a standstill until the matter was addressed properly. All of this additional stress occurred because we tried to move fast in our approach with people rather than being as slow and deliberate in our communication as we had been in the decision-making process.

Let's face it: We pride ourselves on how many people are in our company; how many of them we manage; how many people's problems we solve on any given day. We never intend it but we frequently treat people—our employees, coworkers and peers—like the numbers by which we measure our success. We must do better. American leadership expert John C. Maxwell has said: "People don't care how much you know until they know how much you care." We express our care and concern for others best when we slow down and take time for them.

Over the years, one of the most successful and gratifying efforts we launched at NISC is a gathering called "Conversations with Vern." These conversations take place when I join small groups of ten to fifteen employees for lunch or breakfast. There's no agenda, it's just an informal chat, and no question is out-of-bounds.

In the early days following NISC's consolidation, these gatherings tended to be confrontational with a self-appointed spokesperson who had a list of prepared questions, most often complaints. Today these sessions are casual, heartfelt conversations in which the employees take turns sharing their dreams, concerns and aspirations. The visits also provide an opportunity for me to look the employees right in the eyes and speak from my heart.

These kinds of sessions are undeniably the very best communications effort an organization can make. Their casual and intimate nature allows leaders to connect with employees at a level that doesn't happen often enough. The only problem is that, in an organization with hundreds or even thousands of employees, it can literally take years to get through the entire employee population. Nevertheless, taking time and slowing down when it comes to employee communication is, without a doubt, one of the single, fastest ways to establish, enhance or restore trust with your team.

Tell Verifiable Truth

For most people, verifiable truth equates to transparency. When we tell the truth in ways another person can verify, we demonstrate our trustworthiness. Why does this matter? Because we are more likely to stay engaged with an organization we trust; we are more likely to say good things to others about a company we trust; and we are more likely to buy a product we trust.

Consider the results of the 2010 Deloitte *Ethics & Workplace Survey*. One-third of the respondents indicated that they planned to look for a new job when the economy stabilizes. Of those, nearly half (48 percent) cite as a reason for wanting to leave, a loss of trust in their employer as a result of how business and operational decisions were handled over the two years prior to the survey; 46 percent said that a lack of transparent leadership communication is what will drive them to seek new employment opportunities.

Loss of trust and lack of transparency in this survey were the leading reasons for one out of every three respondents to want a new job. Can you imagine one-third of your workforce leaving for another company primarily because they don't trust your organization's leadership and don't perceive that the leadership is being transparent with them? Almost worse is the thought that the 33 percent who say they plan to look for a new job won't leave; they will remain with the organization, possibly non-engaged or, worse yet, actively disengaged, and choose to do nothing about it.

Sharon Allen was Deloitte LLP Chairman at the time of the 2010 survey. Here is what she had to say in the report on the survey results: "Regardless of the economic environment, business leaders should be mindful of the significant impact trust in the workplace and transparent communication can have on talent management and retention strategies.

By establishing a values-based culture, organizations can cultivate the trust necessary to reduce turnover and mitigate unethical behavior."

I appreciate Ms. Allen's perspective because she does more than place value on trust and transparency because they represent the right things to do; she connects them to hard costs for every organization—managing turnover and the skyrocketing costs associated with unethical behavior. We haven't drawn a direct line between NISC's low turnover and the high trust levels we strive for, or connected our ability to contain costs effectively to our ethical business practices. But what you will see in chapter 12 and in our business results is that NISC has turnover rates that are one-half of the software industry average, and we work hard to maintain employee satisfaction levels (often a result of high trust) that hover above 95 percent.

> **"Organizations can cultivate the trust necessary to reduce turnover and mitigate unethical behavior."**
> **– Sharon Allen**

There's no question in my mind that a cooperative business model fosters trust and transparency. By its very nature, the employees and member/owners of a cooperative must find the best ways to cooperate—to provide information and share ideas for the betterment of the products and services they exchange. In addition, this foundation paves the way for a set of shared values that frames the entire structure on which a collaborative culture is built.

A New Level of Transparency

The power of new media is incredible and certainly not for the faint of heart. Every implementation, every e-mail, every phone call, every service instance has the potential to be scrutinized in a public forum. Transparency is a powerful force and one we need to respect given all the opportunities that individuals have to broadcast their experience with our organization in ways and to an audience we never would have imagined a decade ago.

Every person has the opportunity to share their experience in three kinds of ways, and they can choose any one or all of these methods:

1. **Private testimonial:** This kind of information-sharing is usually kept to one's self or with perhaps one or two other individuals.

2. **Semi-public testimonial:** This involves sharing one's positive or negative experiences within small group settings. According to the 2011 American Express® Global Customer Service Barometer, Americans say they tell an average of nine people about good customer service experiences, and they tell nearly twice as many (sixteen people) about poor ones.

3. **Mega-public testimonial:** The audience size for this type of testimonial/referral can be in the hundreds or even thousands, depending on the size of an individual's network and sphere of influence. Social media play a large role here.

We have seen the use of all types of these testimonials at NISC over the years, to varying degrees.

Private Testimonial

The private testimonial is the scenario used in our coaching sessions at NISC. We've moved from having annual performance reviews to regular coaching sessions. It puts the focus on employee behaviors that drive successful performance rather than on the performance itself. This has been beneficial for us as an organization because it allows us to begin the conversation with NISC's shared values and look at the individuals we are coaching in terms of their ability to incorporate the shared values into their work. The session focuses on encouraging an employee's strengths rather than trying to correct or continuously improve weaknesses.

Coaching in this manner is also an effective tool to build trust and engagement with employees. It sends a powerful message to an employee when you ask "May I coach you?" instead of telling them, "Here is what I think you should do." Rather than assuming the employee is waiting with baited breath for our words of wisdom (rarely the case, I'm sure), we ask permission to offer our insights. I should note that these discussions should be (and are) kept private, especially as they can move from intellectual to emotional when specific affirmations for living values fully or suggestions for improvement are offered.

Another example of a private testimonial where information sharing occurs between one or two people at NISC is with our individual development plans. In this setting, supervisors meet with employees to discuss their career aspirations. We want to be sure we do everything we can to provide our employees with the tools and guidance they need to meet their full potential and increase their value to the organization.

Semi-Public Testimonial

When I think of the semi-public type of testimonial, I think of Malcolm Gladwell's discussion of mavens in his book *The Tipping Point: How Little Things Can Make a Big Difference*. Mr. Gladwell portrays a maven as the person who connects others to the marketplace with the best products, services and pricing. What sets mavens apart from the rest of us is that once they figure out how to get a great deal or determine which product will last the longest, they want to tell you about it, too. They find it very difficult to keep their vast information to themselves, and so they tend to share it with small-to-medium-sized groups whenever they can. This is similar to how information is shared in a semi-public testimonial.

In 2012, NISC held a regional member meeting in Cincinnati, Ohio. During the social before the meeting, there was a crowd gathered around an elderly gentleman (clearly a maven) who was proudly using his iPad as a demonstration tool. "I didn't think I would ever want one of these iPads because I don't care much about technology," he said. "But take a look. I can pay my bill, report an outage and, best of all, I can see how much electricity my house is using, by the hour. Isn't this the coolest thing you have ever seen?" He went on, saying, "I remember when we used to read the meter and send the reading in to the cooperative. I don't have a clue how this works, but I think it is just amazing."

This gentleman is a board member from one of our member cooperatives, and he is close to eighty years old. It was clear he was enjoying his role as a technology rock star. He went on to tell the group of a dozen or so individuals that he couldn't wait to get one of NISC's new apps, which would electronically replace the volumes of information board members usually receive in three-ring binders and must review prior to board meetings. He never thought he would say it, but he told them he was ready to "chuck his board book for the iPad."

Mega-Public Testimonial

Mega-public testimonials are increasing with frequency, and this is no less true in the business world, where marketers are clamoring to figure out the best ways to leverage the influence of such testimonials to help promote company products and services. For the majority of cooperatives, however, engagement with the public most frequently occurs at the private and the semi-private level. In fact, we often refer to NISC as a stealth organization because we usually operate under the general public's radar.

This approach aligns well with our humble beginnings, but it does pose some challenges today as we attempt to compete at higher levels and in bigger marketplaces for business and employees. It is a constant balancing act to ensure that NISC has a significant enough presence to be a respected player in future business opportunities and for recruiting employees, but not become too large or grow so quickly that we lose sight of our shared values and the importance of each individual. In that sense, our biggest concern regarding mega-public testimonials is the potential for negative ones involving NISC or our software industry, the kind we don't initiate or desire. This isn't to say that we would ever hide any negative information about NISC; as an organization we must be open to transparency even when it puts us in an unflattering light. But we obviously wouldn't take any part in the propagation of untrue or unfair testimonials.

The audience for mega-public testimonials can include hundreds and thousands of people; they can also have a significant impact on your employees, your member/customers and the communities in which you live and work. For instance, if you visit www.glassdoor. com, you'll find a wealth of information on almost any organization, position or business leader almost anywhere. The name of the site is truly spot-on.

For those not familiar, the way Glassdoor works is that employees—current or former—write public reviews about their organization anonymously. They discuss the pros and cons about the place of business, and they advise senior management on how they can improve. They can rate the CEO right there, out in the open, for anyone who stumbles across the site or, more specifically, any person examining the organization with an eye for employment or future business opportunities. Every company receives a rating on a scale of one to five (five being the best rating, one being the worst) in five different areas: culture and values, work/life balance, senior management, comp and benefits, and career opportunities. In addition, employees indicate an approval rating for the CEO.

I try to visit glassdoor.com with some regularity. To be transparent, I will tell you that the last time I looked, there were only a few handfuls of reviews of NISC in the database. Our overall rating (the average of how we rated in the five categories listed above) is 3.9. Eighty-six percent of the employees reviewing NISC would recommend our organization to a friend, and 88 percent approve of the CEO.

A challenge with mega-public testimonials is that a company often has no way to know who has submitted them, nor do we have a truly accurate way of knowing how many potential recruits or customers visit review sites like glassdoor.com. As a point of comparison, Microsoft is also included in Glassdoor's database, and it has over 8,500 employee reviews. With that many current and former employees voicing their opinions on one social networking site, it's easy to imagine the thousands of conversations underway at any given moment.

Today, many organizations espouse a set of values and promote themselves as having a great corporate culture. And many of them do. Part of the collaborative culture at NISC demands that we practice transparency when it celebrates our successes, and we must also be open to transparency when it shows our failings. To do anything less would make significant withdrawals in the fragile trust accounts we have with our employees, members and customers.

Simple Really Is Better

I pay attention to the businesses that model the behavior I hope NISC emulates. One that has captured my attention is Nordstrom, Inc. For years, Nordstrom's Employee Handbook was a single 5" × 8" gray card containing these seventy-five words:

Welcome to Nordstrom. We're glad to have you with our Company.

Our number one goal is to provide outstanding customer service.
Set both your personal and professional goals high.

We have great confidence in your ability to achieve them.

Nordstrom Rules:
Rule #1: Use best judgment in all situations.
There will be no additional rules.

Please feel free to ask your department manager, store manager or division general manager any question at any time.

During the time that this handbook was in use, Nordstrom had the highest sales per square foot performance in the retail industry—by almost double. You can say a lot about their approach, but what I offer is this: Nordstrom wants their employees to do the right thing, always. And with that employee mindset, the company reaped great rewards.

NISC isn't perfect. We haven't achieved full trust and transparency in our organization, and I'm not sure we ever will. If I had to define our spot on the journey, it would be that we recognize the importance of trust and transparency. Stan Scott, a salesman for our iGEAR division, explains it this way:

Co-ops are like a family; each member of the family has a different role, but when they come together great things are accomplished. Initially, I was a little surprised there is such great trust and loyalty in NISC from our members. Our cooperative clients all know we truly have their best interests in mind. It is clear to me they trust us and like working with another cooperative.

That customer attitude wasn't the same at my previous non-cooperative positions, where your regular customers might buy from your competitor for just a few cents difference in price, no matter how much attention and good service you previously provided. Your relationship was built on the price you could offer today, no matter what you had done yesterday for them.

We try to hold one another accountable to high-trust behaviors at NISC, and we strive to be as transparent as we possibly can. Each day we get a little better, and we are moving in the right direction—a direction that gets us closer to a collaborative culture in practice. Employees who join NISC from organizations where there wasn't this focus are often the best ones to describe it. For example, Nate Boettcher, one of our managers, says it like this:

> When I first started at NISC, I thought it would be a place to work for two or three years, then I would go out and find a "real" job at a "real" company. I've now been with NISC for a decade, and I've come to realize that it is a great organization and one I am proud to work for each and every day. What makes NISC different is the action of doing the right thing, always, for our members.
>
> At other organizations where I worked, the focus was always on quarterly and yearly results. I recall in previous jobs this sense of driving the bottom line, ensuring we had billed for every bit of work that was completed and making sure no source of revenue was left untouched.
>
> The culture at NISC has and will always be focused on the member. It's a very simple premise that allows us to make good business decisions for the co-op each and every time. Now, over ten years later, I appreciate working for this "real company" that has provided so much for me and my family.

It's hard to say it better than that, so I'll let Nate have the last word here.

KEY POINTS TO CONSIDER IN THIS CHAPTER

1. One thing is certain: **the more frequently we practice trust and transparency, the easier it gets to hold one another accountable to being trustworthy and transparent.**

2. An effective way to increase transparency in our organizations is to **communicate key messages broadly enough to reach employees multiple times through multiple strategies, and simply enough to be believable.**

3. **Verifiable truth equates to transparency.** When we tell the truth in ways another person can verify, we demonstrate our trustworthiness. Why does that matter? Because we are more likely to stay engaged with an organization we trust; we are more likely to say good things to others about a company we trust; and we are more likely to buy a product we trust.

4. **Transparency is a great teaching tool.** Today, many organizations espouse a set of values and promote themselves as having a great corporate culture, and many of them do. We believe part of our collaborative culture at NISC demands that we practice transparency when it celebrates our successes, and we must also be open to transparency when it shows our failings.

Chapter 11

Building Blocks for Great Culture

Servant leadership is more than a concept, it is a fact. Any great leader, by which I also mean an ethical leader of any group, will see herself or himself as a servant of that group and will act accordingly.
— M. Scott Peck

In 2009, our Lake St. Louis office hosted Mr. Jim Duncan and Mr. Ted Purser, the CEO and CFO respectively of Sumter Electric Cooperative in Sumterville, Florida. Sumter is one of the nation's largest electric distribution cooperatives, and in 2009 it was NISC's largest utility member. Sumter was on an older legacy NISC platform and had initiated the due diligence process to determine who their technology provider would be for the next generation of software to be implemented in their offices.

We were hopeful that our existing member would choose to stay with NISC and choose our iVUE® product, but our past association didn't guarantee that we would be a shoo-in. Experience has shown us that no member should ever be taken for granted, no matter how deep the relationship goes and no matter how long they have been associated with the organization.

The NISC "A" team was ready and began their pitch after the obligatory introductions. It was impressive the way our team adapted to the questions, changing the direction of the meeting, even modifying our agenda, to make certain we focused on Sumter's highest priorities. Employees passed the baton as they worked their way through the topics, each of them passionate, professional and competent. After eight exhausting hours of intense presentation and discussion, we called it a day and headed for dinner, hoping a more relaxed atmosphere would prompt a discussion that might give an indication as to whether or not we had hit our mark.

Mr. Duncan began the discussion in a careful, measured and reflective manner, saying, "Well, NISC, this has been a very good day. You should be proud of what you have accomplished. In my estimation, you are light years ahead of where you were just a couple of years ago."

There was a collective sigh of relief from all of the NISC employees. We were absolutely elated! Without being overly dramatic, this was the best possible outcome.

Better still, after dinner Mr. Duncan said, "What is so impressive to me is the quality of the NISC people I met today—their passion, their professionalism and their competence. It is clear to me that they love their jobs; they are proud of their products; and they truly care about us as member/owners."

NISC went on to win and keep Sumter as our member/owner, and over the years, Mr. Duncan has become one of NISC's most important references. The respect he has in the industry makes him an influential voice. He has been instrumental in fostering NISC's growth in the southeastern United States. Just as important are Mr. Duncan's words about NISC and what we must continue to develop in each employee and in our culture: passion, professionalism and competence.

Trial and Error

Today NISC is producing some of the best business results in its history, including fostering and improving consumer and employee loyalty. Thanks to plenty of trial and error, we are beginning to understand the common behavior traits, values and leadership principles that help build a sustainable culture. But though our culture is ever evolving and improving, we've yet to fully arrive and we haven't got a proven recipe. Still, we recognize that culture is a key ingredient to the success of every person's experience with NISC, whether they be the CEO of the local cooperative, a member employee with hands-on experience with our products, a Walmart energy manager who uses our Capturis product, an NISC employee or someone who runs across our web site while searching for information solutions.

Socrates once said, "The unexamined life is not worth living." Just like in our personal lives, where we must reflect upon what is worthwhile and significant to us, it is just as important for an organization's leaders to examine the workplace culture, which affects the lives of so many individuals, to determine what is worthwhile and significant. Much like a physician during an examination, a leader always

"The unexamined life is not worth living."
– Socrates

has the fear of finding a serious dysfunction in his or her organization, one that will require the business equivalent of surgery and rehabilitation. However, every organizational examination establishes a baseline and a new measure for accountability. Some of the things we have learned about culture may help others go through a similar process of examination, understanding, practice and feedback. And that's why, as students ourselves, we freely share in *Wired Differently* a number of the resources we study and a few of the methods we have employed to continuously improve our culture.

What Is Culture?

When I became CEO of NISC, I had my reservations about the value of company culture because I thought it was one of those "soft" sciences that would have little bearing on our bottom line, let alone on things like innovative software design or the all-important satisfaction and engagement of our employees and our member/owners. What I came to discover is that culture has everything to do with our bottom line, now and as we move into the future.

In his book *The Soul of an Organization: Understanding the Values that Drive Successful Corporate Cultures*, Richard Gallagher offers one of the best straightforward explanations I've heard in answer to what business culture is. He says, in part:

> In an organizational setting, the meaning of culture extends to the core beliefs, behaviors, and actions behind its daily business life. . . . Much of what forms your business culture is neither good nor bad. It simply defines the context of who you are, and that context then drives your day-to-day actions in the marketplace.

A business culture is your values and beliefs, generally unspoken, your style, the types of people you hire and what behaviors you reward. A business culture is not your products and services, your policies and procedures, your recruiting process and what behaviors you say you want.

Organizations with great cultures seem willing to share the secrets of their success with the outside world, even with their competitors. For example, Disney has made a business of educating others, even competitors, on how to spread the pixie dust that has led the company to be profitable in nearly everything it does. Southwest Airlines openly discusses its team-based methods for achieving rapid turnaround of aircraft, thereby establishing industry lows in the costs of owning and operating aircraft. Why do companies do this?

I believe it's because organizations with strong, adaptive and open cultures that foster employee loyalty and productivity are not concerned that competitors will borrow their policies, methods or processes. They know that the real key to making those policies, methods and processes work is something much more difficult to emulate—culture. When Alfred Lin was COO/CFO and Chairman of Zappos.com, he put it this way, "Our web sites, policies—all can be copied, but not our special culture."

The Cooperative Advantage in Building a Culture

Cooperatives have an advantage when it comes to building strong and effective cultures because most of them have a clear and often compelling mission statement that promises mutual benefit to the community of like-minded people who join the cooperative as members. Typically, the mindset of the member/owners of a cooperative is shared by its employee population because the communication between the two groups is so frequent. It's clear that individuals with similar value systems are attracted to the organization, whether it be as a member or an employee.

Gina Huck is a certified public accountant at NISC who had several career opportunities from which to choose. She shared with me the following thoughts about her experiences:

As I was applying for jobs when I returned to Bismarck-Mandan, NISC had an opening. Even though I grew up in Mandan, I had never heard of the company. I had opportunities at accounting firms around town, but NISC was compelling; there was something different. My interview had a relaxed, comfortable feel. I was thrilled to find out I was offered the position.

I have learned in the following seven years of my career that NISC is a special place where people genuinely care about each other and take care of one other and our members. We are one big family. NISC's cooperative culture and attitude of service toward one another and our members are a few of the many reasons I enjoy working here.

Mark Weishaar, an employee in NISC's technology division, didn't know what a cooperative was when he started with NISC in 2007. He says now:

I didn't choose to work at NISC because I understood cooperatives; I didn't know what they were exactly. Now that I do know what's involved in being a member-owned cooperative, I can't imagine working anywhere besides a cooperative.

Our purpose isn't to sell as many products as we can to make money for a group of stockholders from around the world. We work in the best interests of the members who own NISC and who depend on our products, because without our members, we would not exist. I like having a direct relationship with the member/customers we serve nearly every day. That cooperative philosophy is why I hope to finish out my career at NISC.

When it comes to creating a positive business culture, the cooperative business model has certain advantages because of the fact that each cooperative starts with a defined mission statement that is based on beliefs and core principles that link the employee with the member/owner and the more localized community of interest that is served. I believe cooperatives excel at transforming their mission, vision and values into action. But cooperative or not, maintaining a positive culture isn't always easy, especially following a consolidation.

A Rocky Start to Our Culture

A consolidation is the most difficult method of bringing two organizations together. In a takeover or purchase, there is a dominating entity that brings the money to the table and gets to make most of the decisions. In these scenarios, policies and practices are normally dictated with little regard for the acquired entity. But in a consolidation like that of NISC's two predecessor cooperatives (NCDC and CADP), every policy and every practice needed to be reviewed and created anew. There were many compromises made leading up to the final documents, and as you would expect, there was plenty of scorekeeping going on in Missouri and North Dakota.

Nobody wanted to offend anyone as we joined forces, but it was messy nonetheless. Employees from each company had been fierce competitors, and now they were vying for playing time on the same team. The organizational structure of our consolidated cooperative had more than its fair share of duplication, from two CEOs down to two vice presidents in charge of research, development and quality, not to mention there were five different software platforms.

Gary Hobson guided NISC as the CEO for the first two years of the consolidation, retiring at the end of 2002. A leadership transition ensued when the CEO's job shifted to me. I have to say that when I began my career, never in my wildest imagining did I think I would be a CEO. The day the board appointed me as CEO of NISC was rather surreal. The phrase "the buck stops here" became very real. I am grateful that our board members were patient and gave me the opportunity to build the skills, while on the job, that I needed to effectively lead the organization. I am fortunate to be working with colleagues who are smarter than me and who have the skills and abilities that I don't.

The mission statement that the NISC Board of Directors adopted at the start of the consolidation was the first stake in the ground for bringing the cultures together. It told us that we needed to deliver IT solutions and services (together) that focused on our members and customers. Our services also needed to be quality-driven and value-priced.

The Shared Values Employee Committee

From 2000 to 2002, the former competitive rivalry simmered down and we got to know each other. Slowly we began to gel as a team that did more than just wear the same company logo. One of the healing activities that helped this process was the development of a Shared Values Committee. It comprised six employees from our Missouri campus and six employees from our North Dakota campus. Committee members represented a wide variety of disciplines within NISC, and a vice president acted as facilitator. The committee's assignment was to establish values for a company for which they would be proud to work.

Admittedly, NISC leadership took a significant risk in forming and empowering the Shared Values Committee. We recognized that if our senior leadership team or the board of directors didn't get behind the recommendations from the committee, it would deal a devastating blow to the committee members as well as our entire employee population, in which case, so much for establishing a collaborative culture. But in our minds, it was a risk worth taking. And we needed to extend trust to demonstrate our own trustworthiness.

After several meetings and much discussion, the committee came up with the six shared values I outlined earlier in the book: integrity, relationships, innovation, teamwork, empowerment and personal development. (The complete description of NISC shared values is included in chapter 2.)

Bonnie Haupt, one of the committee members, became fully engaged in the shared values identification process. Once the six had been identified, the group reviewed them before finalizing the document. At the time, the last sentence of the integrity value was, "We are committed to doing the right thing." Bonnie asked if the word "always" could be added to this statement. The group liked the idea, and so the statement became, "We are committed to doing the right thing, always."

The committee brought their proposed shared values to the NISC senior leadership team for consideration. We were impressed and pleasantly surprised with the committee's work. We approved their shared values with only minor changes. The next step was to bring the shared values to the board of directors, who unanimously supported the committee's work.

NISC's new culture was launched the day our shared values were approved. The committee's work was met with enthusiasm and positive feedback from all corners of NISC. The beauty of this solution was twofold:

1. It began with employees and received unanimous support at the highest level; and

2. The employees bought into the core values they themselves created.

These shared values deepen and mature every year they are in practice at NISC. They also enhance our ability to transform values into action right down to the individual level. For example, we are in the process of implementing a comprehensive competency matrix that aligns the shared values with the expected proficiencies for all jobs at all levels of responsibility in the organization, and demonstrates how the two should, ideally, work together. When fully implemented, each employee will know the expected proficiencies for their position and how that proficiency is aligned with and important to living out our shared values.

These shared values deepen and mature every year they are in practice at NISC.

The shared values fully support NISC's adaptability and agility for long-term survival. It is no coincidence that as we mature in our shared values and servant leadership culture we find that our innovations, business results, margins and recruiting have never been better (see chapter 12 for more detail).

Integrity and Trust

The time I value most as CEO is when employees stop by to visit me in my office, to chat about something that's on their mind or a topic that interests them. This gives me a window into our organization that I don't have as often as I'd like. There is something a little daunting about the CEO title that places inevitable distance between the person who fills that role and the other employees within an organization. Establishing a sense of approachability is critical, in my mind, to staying in sync with the passion, vision, concerns and aspirations of NISC's employees. I am reminded of the Zig Ziglar quote "You don't build a business—you build people—and then people build the business."

Most of my visits from employees are invigorating; encouraging reminders that we are headed down the right path. A few visits have been challenging or confrontational. In those cases, it was usually a result of the person having experienced a violation of integrity or trust.

In these situations, I was glad for the employee's willingness to come forward, as I believe that bringing to light and addressing trust and integrity concerns is absolutely critical to enhancing, validating and improving the effectiveness of our culture.

In 2004, NISC established an Integrity & Trust Guide to let employees know that we stand behind the company's mission, vision and shared values. The guide outlines specific conduct standards and policies that are in place for each shared value, and it emphasizes the importance we place on ethical conduct. In addition, we appointed a five-member Integrity and Trust Council, with Kari Reichert, our vice president of People Services, serving as our Integrity and Trust Officer. The group meets on an as-needed basis for any of the following reasons:

- to ensure all employees understand our focus on ethical behavior;
- to create awareness of NISC's cornerstone shared value of integrity;
- to serve as an anonymous point of contact for employees with ethics-related concerns; and
- to provide ongoing employee education related to our shared values and ethical business culture.

NISC also enlists an outside third party, EthicsPoint, in order to provide a confidential hotline and web site for employees to report issues or events of concern to them. A reported issue is sent directly to NISC's legal counsel, our vice president of People Services and the CEO. If the complaint is against the CEO, it is directed to NISC's legal counsel and the board chairperson. I'm happy to report that the Integrity and Trust Council rarely needs to meet to address a concern brought forward by an employee, and the EthicsPoint hotline and web site, while available twenty-four hours a day, has managed only a handful of contacts since we began using it ten years ago.

The cynic would say that employees must fear coming forward or don't believe action will be taken if they do. We've considered this possibility ourselves, and what we found is that over the same time period the guide, council, hotline and web site have been in place, our employee engagement, retention and satisfaction scores have steadily improved across all teams, business units and campus locations. This is contrary to what we would expect if we had an unresolved ethics-related issue. We believe we are on solid ground as we continue our journey to becoming a more ethical organization that provides a safe, collaborative culture for our employees to find their passion and excel.

The Creation of a Learning Organization

A key element of NISC's culture is the strategic plan that was created in 2007 to position NISC as a learning organization. We are relative newcomers to the journey; however, we have hit numerous milestones that were identified in the plan's vision statement and we are building a foundation of support for personal self-development. Some of NISC's key achievements include:

- We acquired a technical infrastructure (called Pathways) and provide employees and members with thousands of learning opportunities via online classes, which are available 24/7 and cover a wide variety of personal and professional development topics.
- We created special organization-wide events dedicated to learning, such as a series of Lunch 'n' Learns, WebEx sessions and face-to-face presentations by our senior management group on NISC's various products, services, and research and development projects. These efforts are made because we believe an engaged workforce wants to have a broad perspective of the company. We have become an organization of narrowly focused specialists, and our responsibility to inform employees has increased substantially as we grow in size and the scope of our products increases.
- We launched the NISC Community, an online tool for sharing knowledge and solutions, which facilitates collaboration between employees and members.
- We introduced quarterly pulse surveys to garner employee feedback and make decisions based on their recommendations.
- We have improved the coaching skills of all supervisors by delivering Ken Blanchard's Situational Leadership II (SLII) training across the entire organization and providing a proven coaching process and tools that ensure increased engagement and productivity. (Note: SLII was selected because

of its strong association to NISC's six shared values and our common conviction to developing people for individual and companywide success. Eighteen months after introducing SLII, employee engagement scores increased by 5 percent, and three years later, they had risen by 13 percent.)

• We offer an annual leadership development forum, which is where we first introduced the lattice concept (described in more detail later in this chapter). The lattice concept is now used to help employees transfer to new positions within NISC. By broadening an employee's industry and product knowledge and providing new learning opportunities, it increases the individual's career progression and the value he or she provides NISC.

• In 2014–2015, we are focusing on creating tailored development plans, transparent career paths and a leadership development program for those who aspire to greater responsibility for helping others succeed.

Bringing Servant Leadership to Our Culture

One of the defining works our senior leadership team studied and which plays a critical role in developing our culture at NISC is the book *Seven Pillars of Servant Leadership: Practicing the Wisdom of Leading by Serving* by James Sipe and Don M. Frick. We use the guiding principles in the book to help us discern if NISC effectively models servant leadership practices, much like *Good to Great* helped us identify the most effective leadership styles for a company that wants to achieve greatness (recall the capabilities of the Level 5 leader, discussed in chapter 3). In chapter 4, we discussed NISC's five leadership characteristics: compassion, discipline, competence, innovation and inspiration. As you will see below, there are many similarities between these NISC leadership characteristics and the seven pillars identified in Mr. Sipe and Mr. Frick's book.

The seven pillars of servant leadership represent a set of concrete, observable competencies that provide structure for incorporating a servant leadership model into your organization. These pillars are the personal characteristics an organization will want to develop in order to create a servant leadership culture, and as such, they can easily serve as a job description. As outlined in Sipe's and Frick's book, the pillars comprise these traits:

1. **Personal character** (makes insightful, ethical and principle-centered decisions)

2. **Puts people first** (shows care and concern)

3. **Skilled communicator** (listens earnestly and speaks effectively)

4. **Compassionate collaborator** (strengthens relationships and creates a sense of belonging)

5. **Has foresight** (takes courageous and decisive action)

6. **Systems thinker** (leads change effectively and balances the whole with the sum of its parts)

7. **Leads with moral authority** (creates a culture of accountability)

Ideally, you want a servant leader with these traits not only as an organization's chief executive, but filling every leadership role in the company. This kind of leader will model servant leadership and thereby make it a reality. That is why it is a gradual and emerging process. In a servant leadership culture we learn by choice or example that if we want to be great, we have to serve others respectfully.

Best Practices

We try regularly to identify the characteristics of the culture that has evolved at NISC so that we can measure the growing evidence of servant leadership because, as I say, it is a gradual process. As I already pointed out, one of the most important and valuable qualities of our culture is that it is highly collaborative. Collaborative practices provide fertile soil for the growth of servant leadership, and some of the following practices have supported our efforts at NISC.

We design software on a daily basis to serve the present and future needs of our members. One of the ways we ensure the software will meet these needs is through face-to-face interactions with member advisory committees (MACs). There are currently twelve MACs that meet quarterly and include over one hundred NISC members. These committees are a built-in focus group, and members take great pride in influencing the direction of the software that will serve them. Taking it one step further, our requests for feedback also encourage members to engage with their respective member/customers so that we are designing software with feedback from the ultimate end user as well as from our direct customers.

Another collaborative practice in use at NISC is its intranet (what we call the NISC Community), which is set up for questions and idea exchanges. Over time this has become a valuable tool for interaction between employees and customers. As of March 2014, this forum has seventeen thousand users and averages nearly three hundred views a day.

In 2014, we introduced a Customer Engagement Index that allows designated NISC staff to assign a score between 1 and 100 to each of our customers. The score is continually updated and reflective of the number and quality of the engagements with each of our customers, including attendance at the annual member information conference and regional meetings; participation on MACs or our board of directors; and the use of NISC training programs. This index is an important tool that helps us identify members who are not engaged and who may require additional attention or additional effort on our part to improve their satisfaction with our products and services.

A few other ways we support a collaborative culture at NISC include:

- The Brian Wolf National IT Learning Center, with its online and classroom instruction, allows us to fully explain the use of our software through interactive exchanges with members.
- Our service centers are available around the clock to respond to any member issue via telephone or e-mail.
- Our management team receives regular feedback from our board of directors, the majority of whom are CEOs of our member/owner organizations.

Each of these practices provides opportunities for two-way communication and increased collaboration.

Sustaining a Servant Leadership Culture

To sustain a servant leadership culture, the leaders must continually encourage the adoption or continuation of a service mindset throughout the organization. Once built, a servant leadership culture requires regular reinforcement because it is a less travelled road. After all, does anyone really want to be a servant? The phrase servant leadership is by nature an oxymoron that challenges the view of leadership dominating today's business culture.

Leadership plays a critical role in every form of business culture. If a servant leadership culture appeals to you, you will need true servant leaders to model the culture by their example. This can happen at any level; however, it will fully permeate the organization only when the president, CEO, general manager, commander or owner is on board as a servant leader. And then it needs to take hold at every other level.

One of NISC's most challenging and important accomplishments over the past fifteen years has been to assemble an effective and efficient vice presidents group. Our goal was to bring together a group of driven, passionate, confident, experienced, diverse individuals, some who were homegrown and others who brought important experiences, expertise and relationships to the VP table from outside of NISC.

> **Servant leadership is by nature an oxymoron that challenges the view of leadership dominating today's business culture.**

I wish I could say we got this right the first time, but we did not. Rather, it took years, first to build the right foundation for a collaborative culture and then to find the right mix of leaders for that culture. You cannot create a culture of servant leadership, trust, engagement and passion if those characteristics are not present at the most senior management level of your organization. It is about doing what you say you will do, not just saying you'll do something. In other words, the senior leaders in our organizations must walk the walk, not just talk the talk. At NISC, our vice presidents group openly expects each other to be servant leaders, and the actions for them that matter most are their commitments to serving others. Modeling the behaviors we want repeated serves to instill trust between individuals at any level, builds confidence in the organization and where it is headed, and inspires great results from employees.

Today, there is no question that the strength of NISC begins with the VP group. You will not find a more committed, competent, supportive, honest and cohesive group. They have become the heartbeat of the organization. Their backgrounds, skills, strengths and weaknesses are very different, and together they form a powerful and effective servant leadership example at NISC. This is where our culture begins.

The Right People on the Bus in the Right Seat

Part of our challenge in getting the best VP group assembled was ensuring that we have the right people in the right seats on the bus. If we were to take only one page from Jim Collins' research, it would be from chapter 3 in *Good to Great*, where this excerpt appears:

> *The good to great leaders understand three simple truths. First, if you begin with "who" rather than "what" you can more easily adapt to a changing world. If people join the bus primarily because of where it is going, what happens if you get 10 miles down the road and you need to change direction? You've got a problem. But if people are on the bus because of who else is on the bus, it is much easier to change direction: "Hey, I got on this bus because of who else is on it; if we need to change direction to be more successful, fine with me."*
>
> *Second, if you have the right people on the bus, the problem of how to motivate and manage people largely goes away. The right people don't need to be tightly managed or fired up; they will be self-motivated by the inner drive to produce the best results and to be part of creating something great. Third, if you have the wrong people, it doesn't matter whether you discover the right direction; you still won't have a great company. Great vision without great people is irrelevant.*

This is simple wisdom, and it is a deeply embedded part of NISC's culture, beginning with our recruiting. We find that this is the best way to ensure a good fit both for the person being recruited and for NISC. We assess an individual's basic character and values, and we seek to understand what the motive is for applying to the job, why he or she is attracted to our organization. We obviously also assess a candidate's talent, skills and desire to meet the high demands of the ever-changing technology world, as well as his or her capacity to learn. However the biggest factor we consider is the likelihood that the person will embrace the core values and mission of NISC. Experience has taught us that if an individual is not really willing to have a servant heart and attitude, NISC will be an uncomfortable fit.

The Benefit of Lattice Moves

Sometimes an organization has the right-minded and talented people on board, but those people find themselves in a position where they want to contribute more (or less), they want to contribute differently, or they are ready for a new challenge. It is the job of respectful leadership to always be watchful for this and to be willing to relocate people to different positions when it's called for.

To support our employees who are ready for a change, for whatever reason, we initiate what we call "lattice" moves to other divisions or teams in the organization. This allows us to find the best fit for employees and continually stimulate growth and engagement for them. The word lattice is an apt term because it reflects a vertical pattern (the stereotypical move within an organization) along with a horizontal pattern. A climbing plant has a better chance of growing healthy and strong if it is supported in both directions; at NISC, we believe the same is true of developing our people. Many of NISC's leaders have kept the same level of duties but have worked in multiple divisions across the organization through lattice movement.

During regular coaching sessions, employees are encouraged to discuss openly their level of challenge and engagement in their current position, and supervisors understand that it is their responsibility to take action whenever low engagement or disengagement is identified.

Our senior leadership team and our supervisors monitor the organization as a whole for individuals who have leadership potential or who show a desire to be a leader. We've found in the IT industry that, all too often, we falsely assume a highly talented engineer or programmer will automatically make a great supervisor. Now, when we're seeking a new supervisor we look for individuals who put NISC's shared values into action and practice servant leadership, regardless of their position in the organization.

A high school student recently visited our Mandan campus to learn more about NISC and explore the idea of a possible career in information technology. We listened to his interests and told him about how NISC likes to "grow our own" and what that means for someone like him. I later learned from the student's mom, who happens to be a friend of mine, that when she asked her son what he liked best about his visit to NISC, he highlighted two things: "They like to grow their own, and that means they would want to help me get better at IT from the beginning—maybe even through an internship. They also have lattice moves, if I was ready for something else or I was bored, they would work with me to find a better fit and help me keep learning." He then added, "I like that *a lot*."

A Great Mentor for Servant Leadership

Servant leadership at NISC has not been accidental nor coincidental. This has a lot do with our close relationship with the University of Mary in Bismarck, North Dakota. Four of our nine senior leadership team members, numerous managers and many employees of NISC have graduated or received advanced degrees from the University of Mary. The campus was founded in 1959 by the Benedictine Sisters of the Annunciation, whose goal for the university was for it "to prepare leaders in the service of truth."

Current president Monsignor James Shea captures the essence of the campus' focus on servant leadership well:

> *In our time there is much talk about leadership, but leadership at the University of Mary has always been understood to be something distinctive. For us, servant leadership in the pursuit of truth is not an academic fashion statement or a marketing gimmick. . . . It is fundamental to our mission, it is why we exist.*

The Benedictine values emphasized at the University of Mary include community, hospitality, moderation, prayer, respect for persons and service. The similarities between the university's values and NISC's shared values are evident. There is no question that the seeds of

NISC's servant leadership culture likely germinated on a hill over-looking the Missouri River, on a campus that prides itself in producing servant leaders.

What's Next after a Great Culture Is Established?

The Lakota, a Native American tribe who are part of the Great Sioux Nation, have a wonderful expression that reflects the connectedness of all beings. The expression is *Mitakuye Oyasin*, which means "All are related." At first glance, this idea might seem contrary to how things are in today's work world, where there is much talk of the generational differences between employees within organizations. On one end of the spectrum, some employees are just grateful to have a job, while many on the other end would seriously consider leaving the company over something like the dress code being too stringent.

Our management team spends a good amount of time discussing the generational differences we see at NISC. We find that the gap is widening and the differences are becoming more evident. The range in age goes from teenagers to seventy-somethings; we have employees who could be grandchildren of other employees. Three generations under one roof. That could be really intense. But it's not in our case, and here's why.

Ask any NISC employee what matters most in our service to customers, and you will hear something along the lines of *do the right thing, always*. I talked about this earlier when discussing the shared values committee and their ownership of our values statement. Universally, NISC employees get it. They might not be able to repeat our mission or vision statements verbatim, but everyone at NISC knows that we all need to dig deep and ask the tough questions so that we do the right thing with our every action.

You may be thinking, so what makes the statement *Mitakuye Oyasin* so special? I'll tell you, because it's in that answer that we find what is next after a great culture is established. Regardless of what generation we belong to, each one of us has an innate need to make a difference during our life. We want to know that our physical presence on this planet means something. We can make a difference through words of encouragement to our spouse and children; it can manifest itself in the time we dedicate to causes we believe in or philanthropy because we've been financially blessed.

Employees of all ages appreciate and thrive in an organization whose culture aligns with their personal values. At NISC our shared values and servant leadership culture have combined with our work to maintain, grow and recruit great employees. This combination has laid the foundation for a truly magnetic culture that crosses traditional boundaries and brings like-minded people together for the same purpose. The work we do at NISC matters because the relationships we build and the needs of those we serve matter. It is true: we are each wonderfully special and unique, but we are all related. *Mitakuye Oyasin*. At NISC, we all make up the same organization with a singular focus to do the right thing. Always.

KEY POINTS TO CONSIDER IN THIS CHAPTER

1. **Culture has everything to do with our bottom line**, now and into the future.

2. **Cooperatives have an advantage when it comes to building culture**, as most have a clear and often compelling mission that promises mutual benefit to the community or association of like-minded people who join the cooperative as members.

3. In a servant leadership culture we learn by choice or example that **if we want to be great, we have to serve others respectfully.**

4. **Leadership plays a critical role in every form of corporate culture.** If a servant leadership culture appeals to you, you will need true servant leaders to model the culture by their example. This can happen at any level; however, it will fully permeate the organization only when the president, CEO, general manager, commander or owner is on board as a servant leader.

5. Employees of all ages appreciate and thrive in an organization whose culture aligns with their personal values. We believe that our shared values and servant leadership culture have combined with our work to maintain, grow and recruit great employees.

This combination has laid the foundation for a truly magnetic culture that crosses traditional boundaries and brings people together for a like-minded purpose. **The work we do at NISC matters because the relationships we build and the needs of those we serve matter.**

Chapter 12

The Power of Culture-Driven Results

Coming together is a beginning; keeping together is progress; working together is success.

— Henry Ford

In 2000, Jim Bausell was the chief operating officer for Touchstone Energy Cooperative, Inc. and he had an idea. What if someone developed a service to manage the numerous utility bills that big companies receive? Jim envisioned that he could promote such a service to electric cooperatives as a way of adding value to their large accounts. He pitched his idea to NISC, and we liked it. We recognized that a product like he was describing would allow us to process and pay multiple utility bills for a single customer in a timely manner. So we moved ahead with developing a utility bill pay product, which we called Capturis.

Capturis allows clients to access information on all of their utility usage data from multiple utilities in one place, and they receive a PDF file of each utility bill on a secure web site. The product also aggregates payment of each utility bill for a company, greatly improving efficiencies for the customer. The customer issues one payment to NISC, and NISC issues payments to each of the individual utilities serving the customer.

NISC's chief financial officer, Tracy Porter, explains the value of Capturis like this: "The consumption data is very powerful for the people who manage facilities and who manage energy in these large companies. Having access to the data allows them to make good, solid decisions on improving energy efficiencies."

Once we had Capturis ready for customers, we partnered with Touchstone Energy® and the National Rural Electric Cooperative Association (NRECA). This opened doors for NISC, through which we were able to demonstrate to potential clients how Capturis would reduce costs, improve efficiencies and lead to smarter decision making with regard to energy efficiency measures. One of the first doors opened was at Walmart.

We sent a two-member team to Bentonville, Arkansas, to meet with more than a dozen Walmart executives and energy managers. It was an intense meeting and the Walmart team asked tough questions. In advance of the meeting, they had requested that as part of our presentation we include general information about NISC, our cooperative business model, and our historical and current business results. We prepared a thorough presentation that highlighted our revenue, growth, margins, debt, R&D investments and more. All of the trend lines showed a conservative and methodical growth pattern, and we felt confident about our story. The feedback we received following our presentation was not what we expected at all.

"I completely understand your strategy and totally disagree with it."
– Walmart executive

"I completely understand your strategy and totally disagree with it," one Walmart executive said. "We are looking for a partner that will grow their business to the point that Walmart is an insignificant part of their total volume."

Wow. One of the most successful retailers in the world had just told us that our business model was underwhelming . . . really underwhelming. The executive wanted us to grow the Capturis side of our business to such an extent that Walmart, as one customer, wouldn't matter to our organization. But that's just not how NISC is wired. In our cooperative business model, every member and every customer matters. To ever think of them as insignificant would be completely contrary to who we are.

We didn't adopt the executive's suggested business model of growth for the sake of growth; however, NISC did go on to win Walmart's business. Today, we have a favorable, enduring relationship with the company. They are one of our more than one hundred Fortune 500 Capturis customers.

It's not surprising that Walmart's idea of corporate growth and diversification doesn't align with our own approach to business, which is based on the cooperative model. Nor is it surprising that our board of directors passed up a blank check and the opportunity to write in whatever number they deemed enough to be compensated for the purchase of our cooperative. As I mentioned in chapter 1, the decision not to sell NISC would be atypical for a corporation, as such an offer would have maximized shareholder investment value, and fiduciary responsibility for the corporate directors would have required a sale.

What may be surprising to learn is that NISC offers many of our products and services to cooperatives at one-fourth the cost offered by our tier-one corporate competitors. This is possible when the two parties involved in a business transaction have a mission to keep costs at the lowest level possible. There are no third-party investors who need to maximize a return on the transactions.

Those of us who have practiced the cooperative business model throughout our careers understand its sustainability. It nurtures a loyal, respectful partnership between the cooperative employees and the customers. It also delivers an exceptional focus on customer service.

It's a Difficult Business

One of my favorite cable channels is CNBC. I love learning more about how the capital markets function and how they are affected by politics and the global economy. I find it interesting to chart stocks and listen to the drama that moves their prices; it's like a high-stakes chess match.

Generally speaking, a free-market capitalist economy has standard measurements that define the success of an organization and its leadership. These measurements include:

- Stock price
- Dividend payments (earnings ratio)
- Market capitalization
- Market share
- Revenue
- Gross and net margins
- Cash balance

There are many more, but these are the most prevalent indicators of success. All of them center on the value created for the shareholder, as well they should. Increased shareholder wealth is the major purpose of any for-profit corporation.

Absent from the measurements of a company's success is any kind of indicator of the corporation's impact on its local community. Similarly, there is no measure of the contributions an organization makes to serve its customers, nor is there any indicator of efforts made to sustain and uphold employees and their families or society as a whole. Corporations, however, are showing more responsibility in these areas (to varying degrees), and more than ever, the general population expects businesses to operate with a conscience. But it is a slow process because corporate conscience, generally speaking, is being driven from the outside in, rather than the other way around. Following is one relatively recent example of elevated corporate conscience that was demonstrated in the wake of a horrific disaster.

The Gulf of Mexico oil spill is recognized as the worst in U.S. history. It began on April 20, 2010, with the explosion and sinking of the Deepwater Horizon oil rig about forty-two miles off of Louisiana's coast. The accident resulted in the deaths of eleven people, and shortly after, underwater cameras revealed that the pipe leading from BP's Macondo exploration well was leaking oil and gas on the ocean floor. The well was capped eighty-seven days later; nearly 4.9 million barrels of oil had leaked into the gulf by that time.

The spill affected many of the industries in the Gulf Coast states, and economic prospects were bleak. At the peak of the spill, fears of contamination caused over one-third of the federal Gulf waters to be closed to fishing. U.S. President Barack Obama's administration enacted a moratorium on offshore drilling that left 8,000–12,000 people temporarily unemployed, even though a district court later reversed the moratorium. The tourism industry plummeted along the Gulf Coast, as few travelers wanted to visit beaches stained with oil. In response to pressure from multiple sources, BP created a $20 billion compensation fund for people affected by the spill. As of December 31, 2013, BP reported that the company had spent more than $14 billion on its response activities.

How do you ever recover from something like this? How do the organization(s) responsible begin to rebuild trust with the communities and region they have so greatly impacted? And how do the communities and regions impacted begin to re-establish a positive reputation with the citizens and visitors they desperately need to rebuild their economies?

Challenging dilemmas are posed for any kind of business in which the bottom line is profit or shareholder wealth. How does the unique value of the employees' contributions play a role? What value do we place on the communities where we live and work? How do we balance a ledger if it includes both margins and meaning—meaningful work that makes a difference in the lives of employees and the lives of the customers they serve?

It must truly be difficult to do any of that using a traditional capitalist model. In all the programs I've watched over the years on CNBC, there has yet to be one that features integrity or corporate responsibility being held up as the highest value regardless of the cost. Regular programs on CNBC include *Shark Tank, The Profit, Money Talks, American Greed, Prosperity and Power, Fast Money, Secret Lives of the Super Rich* and, my personal favorite, *Mad Money*. No mention of servant leadership, shared values or the importance of returning time and talents to our communities and nation in those titles.

> **"I am skeptical of any business today that says it cares about employees and places its focus on profit."**
> **– NISC recruit**

The CNBC network, which many consider to be the epitome of capitalism, has clearly made its focus corporate America's bottom line: profit. Or, as Larry Kudlow, a highly regarded CNBC commentator, would say, "We believe that free market capitalism is the best path to prosperity!"

One of our recent recruits to NISC said something that ties in to this topic: "I am skeptical of any business today that says it cares about employees and places its focus on profit. How can you care about me when everything you do is driven by a desire to make more money?"

When you compare NISC's cooperative business model to corporate measurement standards, the executives from Walmart were right when they said our business results were underwhelming in their for-profit stock world. At NISC we live within our means, and we work hard to ensure that we are good stewards of our members' investments and our employees' contributions. Some will say we are conservatively foolish; others will point to lost opportunities. But we relish our self-sufficiency, stability and service to others. It is not an either-or situation—either the bottom line or social responsibility. We strive to do well by both measures.

NISC by the Numbers: Measures of Business Success

You don't have to work at NISC long to hear the phrase *there's no mission without a margin*, and I've talked a great deal in this book about results and their critical importance to the sustainability of an organization. You will find that business results for a cooperative and a corporation are a bit like sports. In general, all sports teams are focused on winning the game and achieving success, whether the sport be baseball, basketball, football, hockey or soccer. Where sports teams differ is in their scoring, time intervals and rules. Every sport is exciting to the loyal fans who follow the teams and their players. Similarly, corporations and cooperatives play by different rules and are scored differently, but like sports, both have their loyal followers and advocates.

What follows are NISC's business results during the timeframe 2000 to 2014 (the year 2000 being a benchmark, as it was the year of the consolidation that brought NISC into existence). Because several non-traditional business measures are of equal or greater value to us than are financial measures, we've also included them. For example, in the following you will find results in the areas of employee engagement, member/customer satisfaction, member/customer retention, satisfaction with supervisors and ability to contribute to organizational success. Many organizations also measure these or similar areas. We commend them for their efforts and believe that those that strive to improve the metrics associated with employee, customer and supervisor satisfaction, engagement, retention and the ability to contribute have found, like us, that the financial results improve in direct proportion.

Stock Price

NISC isn't a publicly traded company, so we don't have stock to sell or trade.

Dividend Payments

Dividend payments are normally associated with publicly traded companies; however, cooperatives have a similar model whereby we annually return a percentage of margins (also known as patronage or capital credits) to our member/owners based on the amount of software and services each uses. Graph 12.1 depicts NISC's annual member patronage paid as a percentage of NISC's total equity from 2000 to 2014. Our target is 1.25 percent of revenue.

Graph 12.1: Patronage Paid as a Percentage of NISC's Equity

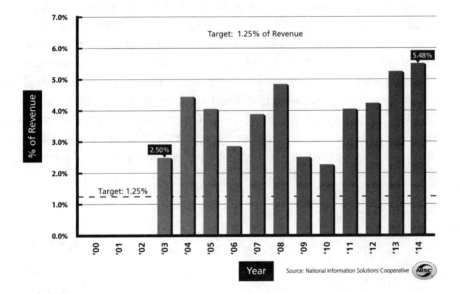

As you can see in the graph, our members received no patronage from 2000 to 2002. This was due to the costs associated with our software rewrite. Since 2003, patronage allocations have been made to members each year, the returns being lower in years when the board approved major expansion projects or acquisitions. In 2014 the patronage allocation (slightly over 5.0 percent) was double what it was ten years earlier (2.5 percent).

Market Capitalization

The way that the investment community typically determines a company's size is by multiplying the company's shares outstanding with the current market price of one share; however, this really doesn't apply for the cooperative business model, as a cooperative doesn't have shares of stock to sell or trade.

Revenue

As a cooperative, we approach revenue from a cost management perspective rather than increasing a product price point to a level we believe the market will bear. Our focus is to deliver our products at cost to our members, thereby allowing them to deliver their products (electricity, phone service, broadband, entertainment) at the lowest possible cost to the end user. In any given year, the margin we build into our pricing model for products and services is 5 percent. Without this small margin, we clearly would not be able to deliver on our mission.

As you can see in Graph 12.2, NISC's revenue trends show consistent growth of 6-10 percent per year from 2001 to 2014. Our target annual revenue growth is 5 percent. We achieved a significant milestone in 2013 when we surpassed the $150 million mark in annual revenues.

Graph 12.2: NISC's Revenue

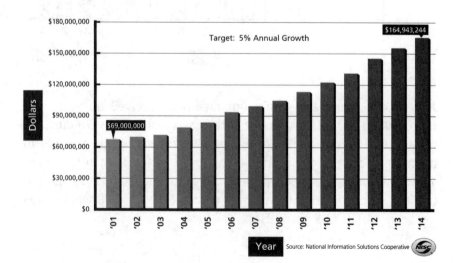

Net Margin

Net margin is an indicator of how much of each dollar a company earns is profit. Net margin ratio can generally be calculated as net profit divided by revenue. The average net margin ratio in the software industry (for corporations) is 25-50 percent. Our board of directors (who are members and, therefore, owners of NISC) set the target for NISC net margins each year. Their target is generally 5 percent, and at that modest level we are able to finance all of our research and development (R&D) and our asset acquisitions, and pay for them in cash.

Protecting our liquidity and avoiding dependence on borrowed funds has been key to NISC's financial stability. We have seen some growth in our net margins over time, which is demonstrative of the difference between a corporate mission that is focused on profit and a cooperative mission that is focused on delivering products at the lowest possible cost. Net margins for most corporations are expected to be closer to 20 percent. Graph 12.3 shows NISC's annual net margin ratio from 2000 to 2014 as a percentage of the total annual revenue.

Graph 12.3: NISC's Net Margin Ratio

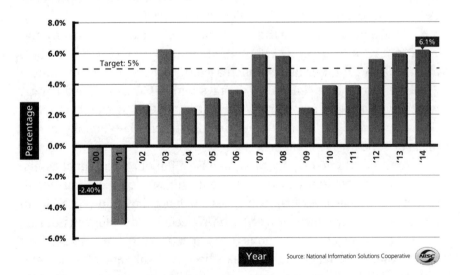

Source: National Information Solutions Cooperative

NISC's negative net margins in 2000 and 2001 are a reflection of the costs incurred during consolidation and our software rewrite. Dips in the annual net margins for 2004 and 2009 reflect substantial R&D investments and asset acquisitions in those years.

Cash Balance

The amount of cash a company typically keeps in reserve at any point in time can be a moving target. Usually the figure strikes a balance between the lost investment opportunities of holding too much cash and the danger of having too little liquidity. Operating in the software industry as a cooperative provides additional challenges. While most companies have bankable assets like manufacturing plants or buildings, equipment, inventory and infrastructure, for software companies, our assets are intellectual property (brain power) and the software itself. Bankers are not generally comfortable using something as intangible, short-lived and volatile as software for collateral to support a loan.

Typically, businesses raise needed capital in one of three ways: through debt (mortgages or bonds); through the issuance of stock (increasing the amount of available stock for sale); or through passive investors or venture capital firms. NISC can't sell bonds, does not issue stock and generally doesn't generate a high enough return on investment to attract venture capitalists. (Venture capitalists usually expect a return on investment of 20 percent or more and, many times, partial or full control of the company in which they invest.)

Of the 5 percent net margin that NISC strives to maintain in any given year, it returns 21 percent of that margin (profit) in cash to members annually. (In 2014, this number increased to 30 percent.) The remaining 79 percent (or 70 percent in 2014) stays with NISC as retained equity, which is basically a member investment in NISC. Our members retain the individual rights to that equity, and as such, they literally own a piece of NISC.

From the retained equity, we purchase all of our operational assets, we fund our research and development and we complete our acquisitions, all in cash. Growing this cash balance has allowed NISC to be self-sufficient, which proved to be especially advantageous during America's financially tumultuous times in 2007–2010. Many technology firms struggled or failed in those years because banks and other sources of funds lost their appetite to provide funding to this sector, whereas NISC (backed with internally generated funds) had the best years yet in its history and was able to complete two mergers and two major expansions.

In the early years following consolidation, NISC was strapped for cash because we didn't have the usual sources of cash available to a start-up (these sources don't exist in the cooperative business model). We had never been adequately capitalized at the beginning, and this is evident in Graph 12.4, which illustrates our cash balance from 2000 to 2014.

Graph 12.4: NISC's Cash Balance

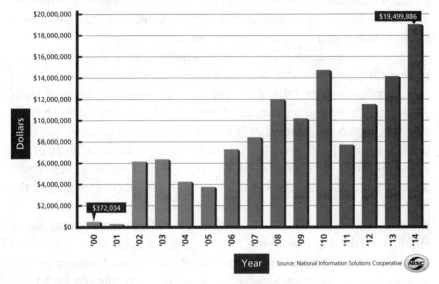

Source: National Information Solutions Cooperative

We've slowly built our cash balance to a place where we are aggressively retiring debt, and today we are making long-term investments in our people, facilities and products without dependence on banks, investors or the volatility of the market. For example, in 2011, we paid cash to acquire Computer Systems LLC and Quintrex Data Systems Corp. As our highly capable CFO would say, "Cash is king!"

Member Satisfaction

In 2007, NISC launched a comprehensive effort to become a learning organization, and we developed a strategic plan to support this focus. One part of the strategic plan calls for us to work with a third-party vendor in order to measure, evaluate and implement actions that will help us improve our scores in the areas of member, employee and supervisor satisfaction; employee and member retention; and our effectiveness at enabling our employees to contribute to the organization's success.

In our quarterly pulse surveys we include several other areas, in addition to member satisfaction, which evaluate NISC's performance against the national norm and the best in class. The national norm is the average score of several thousand companies (from all industry sectors) that participate in quarterly pulse surveys. The best-in-class number represents the top 10 percent of all businesses participating in the same survey. Our vice presidents group, with the support of our board of directors, has determined and stated that our goal is to meet or exceed the best-in-class measure in every area we evaluate. We believe strongly that if you can't measure it, you can't manage it.

Another measurement method we employ is one that's conducted by our third-party vendor, who gathers the contact information of all NISC service centers daily. Each evening the vendor launches a short electronic survey to a percentage of the contacts from that day. The survey asks members to rate NISC's performance in the areas of courtesy, proficiency and timeliness. The trended results are shared with all of our service personnel and are available to them in near real time. Whenever we see an unresolved customer issue, that customer is contacted the next day, at which time we apologize and determine what needs to be done to rectify the situation. In April 2014, Help Desk International (HDI) named NISC one of the Elite Top 50 for customer service. HDI ranks technical service and support centers worldwide based on the highest level of customer satisfaction as indicated by the scores. NISC's Customer Care & Billing support center was ranked number 26 in the top 50.

In the early years after the consolidation, NISC began surveying members to establish an annual satisfaction score. In honesty, those scores were all over the board, and rightly so. We'd just brought two unique and different organizations together; we were building a new software platform that would require change from everyone; and we were not yet entirely united in our new direction. As time went by and we got our feet under ourselves, we instituted the quarterly pulse surveys, and in addition to these, in 2012 we brought back the annual member satisfaction score. Graph 12.5 shows the annual member satisfaction score in December 2012 and November 2013. The scores are humbling to say the least, at 98 and 97 percent respectively. They set the bar high for our organization as we move forward.

Graph 12.5: Overall NISC Member Satisfaction

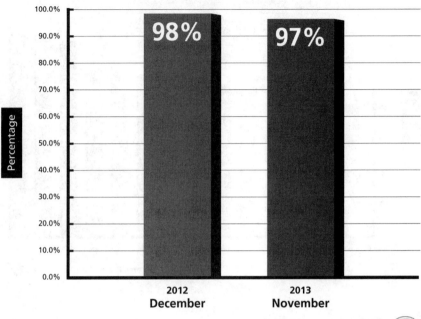

Source: National Information Solutions Cooperative

Member Retention

It is always a wise business strategy to diversify your revenue streams, and this strategy presents an interesting challenge when you must balance diversification with staying true to the organization's mission. It is common among our vice presidents group to hear questions like:

- Is this project the best use of our resources?
- How is this product aligned with our mission?
- Does that expense support our members' best interests?

NISC members are the heart of our organization, and as employees we must understand that without our members, we have nothing. Earning the right to serve a new member and the right to retain the members we have is a daily commitment every NISC employee supports, without exception.

Graph 12.6 shows our member growth from 2001 to 2014. NISC has never experienced more than a 0.5 percent annual loss of members, and we have had many years where we successfully retained 100 percent of our members.

Graph 12.6: NISC's New Member Growth

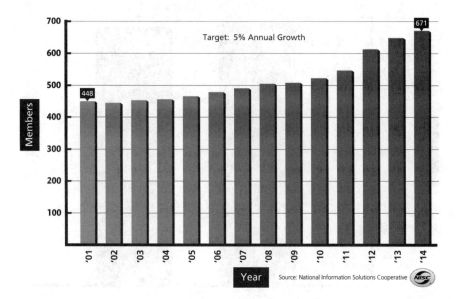

Source: National Information Solutions Cooperative (NISC)

Employee Satisfaction

We began measuring employee engagement in 2008 through surveys that asked about things like communication (is there enough?), compensation (is it adequate?) and effectiveness (is your manager/supervisor effective and fair?). We decided, over time, to shift to indicators that help us identify whether employees love their job; are passionate about serving our members; and have the resources and training they need to excel. We shifted focus because we realized that most people would say they could always use a better salary or benefits package. We also took a cue from several national surveys, which indicated that more important to employees are how well they enjoy their job, how much of an impact they have in their position (including the recognition they receive for a job well done) and whether they have the resources needed to do their job well.

Based on feedback received in 2013, Graph 12.7 shows how NISC employees rated the organization according to their agreement with the statement "My job gives me the opportunity to do the things I do best." NISC is compared with the national norm and best in class for 2013.

Graph 12.7: Job Satisfaction of NISC Employees as Compared to that of the National Norm and of the Best in Class

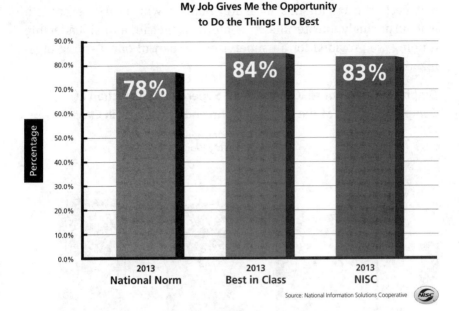

My Job Gives Me the Opportunity
to Do the Things I Do Best

Source: National Information Solutions Cooperative

Satisfaction with Supervisor

At NISC, we are firm believers that employees leave their supervisors, not the organization. We recognize the importance that our supervisors have in modeling NISC's shared values and in coaching their team members for continuous growth and enhanced engagement. We hold supervisors accountable for their role in improving employee satisfaction in these two ways:

1. Peer reviews are conducted for each supervisor, and his or her manager can select any NISC employee to complete the review. The results are discussed in regular coaching sessions.

2. Quarterly employee pulse surveys include questions asking whether or not the supervisor is keeping employees informed and whether the supervisor is taking action based on survey results.

Graph 12.8 shows the level of agreement that NISC's employees had in 2014 with the statement "My supervisor regularly gives me feedback on my work performance." Also shown are the national norm and best in class for this measure, both of which NISC exceeded. Not surprisingly, our results correlate with the situational leadership training we provided for all supervisors as part of our learning organization initiative.

Graph 12.8: Level of NISC Employees' Supervisor Satisfaction as Compared to that of the National Norm and of the Best in Class

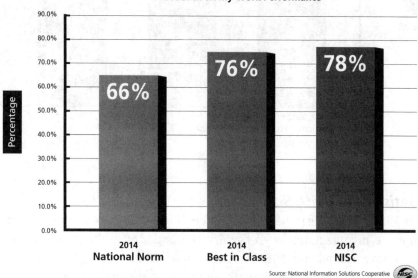

One question we've yet to address at NISC is whether 78 percent is an acceptable level of general employee satisfaction with supervisors. If we truly believe that supervisors are the primary reason employees stay or leave an organization, are we okay knowing that nearly one out of four of our employees say they don't get regular feedback on their work performance from their supervisor? As always, there is room for further discussion and improvement.

Employee Retention

NISC takes pride in having 125 employees out of 1,000 (or 12.5 percent) who have worked for the organization twenty years or more (as of the end of 2014). Several of these employees have chosen NISC as their employer for their entire career. This is quite contrary to the current employment trends and, without question, not typical of the software industry.

According to a 2013 PayScale study of Fortune 500 companies, in those with the highest turnover rates the average tenure for employees was a little over twelve months. In Fortune 500 companies with the lowest turnover rates, the average tenure was ten years. No surprise, the industries with the highest turnover rates were retail and information technology. Fortunately, and humbly, we can say that in 2014 NISC had an average employee tenure of 10.1 years.

At an executive training seminar I attended in 2013, the CEO from a well-known technology start-up discussed how he handles the ramp-up for a new technology launch. He said, in part, "If the product development and launch will take an additional one hundred employees to complete the work, we hire 125. That way, on any given day we will have one hundred at work to complete the project in front of us on time."

His comments addressed employee tenure and absenteeism in the same breath, indicating that a 25 percent absentee rate on any given day is the norm at his company and, apparently, an acceptable one. At NISC we have never tracked absenteeism because we literally don't have it. If employees need a day off for whatever reason, they take it from their Time Off Bank (similar to a combined vacation and sick leave account). Otherwise, they show up for work and are ready to make a difference. Graph 12.9 shows a breakdown of the results that make up NISC's 5 percent average annual turnover rate from 2007 to 2014.

Graph 12.9: NISC's Annual Employee Turnover Rate

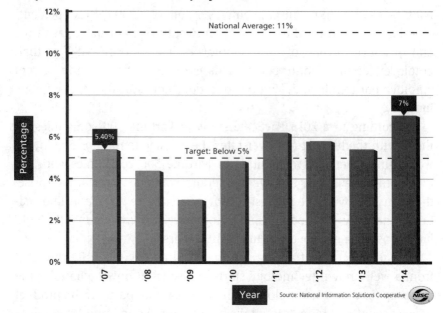

We acknowledge that our location may have some impact on our low turnover, as many of our employees are from the Midwest, where their agricultural roots ingrained in them a strong work ethic. But the fact remains that NISC's average employee turnover rate is less than one-half of the estimated turnover rate for the software or high-tech industry, which was 11 percent according to a 2011-2012 Society for Human Resource Management study.

Employees' Ability to Contribute to Organizational Success

A common theme throughout this book has been NISC's focus on ensuring that employees feel valued and that their contributions matter. We strive to align an employee's skills with the work that needs to be accomplished, and we've incorporated different opportunities to assess when a change would be beneficial for an employee (such as coaching sessions, individual development plans, pulse surveys and lattice moves).

Based on feedback received in 2014, Graph 12.10 shows the level of employee agreement with the statement "This organization makes it possible for employees to directly contribute to its success." The graph shows how NISC's positive response level of 87 percent compares to the national norm (70 percent) and the best in class (83 percent). The year 2013 was the first time this question was asked, and at that time NISC's ranking of 84 percent also exceeded the national norm (71 percent) and the best in class (82 percent).

Graph 12.10: NISC Employees' Level of Satisfaction as Compared to the National Norm and the Best in Class

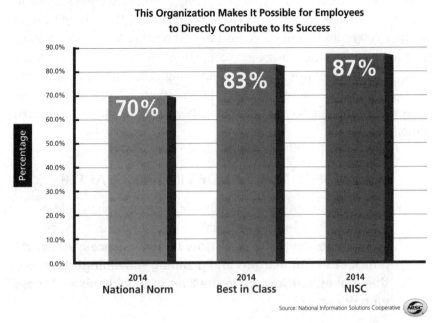

This Organization Makes It Possible for Employees
to Directly Contribute to Its Success

Source: National Information Solutions Cooperative

We will continue to request employee feedback in order to help determine if, over time, NISC's model of shared values, servant leadership and collaborative culture is providing the foundation for employees to contribute to organizational success in ways that are meaningful to them.

Final Thoughts on Measuring Business Success

As successful as NISC has been over its more than forty-five-year history, measuring our success according to the things that are typically valued in the corporate world is a challenge. Our numbers are solid (not wildly impressive); the indicators show us as generally headed in the right direction; and there is something to be said for the foundation on which the numbers stand. It is that foundation that matters most to us at NISC.

Our founding fathers placed great importance on a cooperative business model that has a simple yet clear mission, giving us the framework for Leadership Through Service (Part I of this book) to take hold. Our consolidation provided the opportunity for employees to come together from two different cultures and identify the values they would want their employer to uphold. Today, putting our Values in Action (Part II) guides every decision we make, be it big or small. We have come to understand that a Collaborative Culture in Practice (Part III) really does matter. Power and strength come from embracing values-based decisions, and clarity and consistency come from measuring your decisions with the simple phrase "Do the right thing, always." The indescribable joy of serving our members and each other . . . well, at NISC, we believe these intangible measurements help explain why we are wired differently.

KEY POINTS TO CONSIDER IN THIS CHAPTER

1. If the bottom line for an organization is profit or shareholder wealth, then where does the unique value of our employees' contributions come into play? **How do we balance a ledger if it includes both margins and meaning—meaningful work that makes a difference in the lives of employees and those who we serve?**

2. Fortunately and humbly, we admit that NISC has never tracked absenteeism because we literally don't have it. If employees need a day off, for whatever reason, they take it from their Time Off Bank. Otherwise, **they show up for work and are ready to make a difference.**

3. NISC members are the heart of our organization, and if we miss everything else, as employees we must understand that without our members, we have nothing. **Earning the right to serve a new member and retain the members we have is a daily commitment every NISC employee supports, without exception.**

4. At NISC we live within our means and we work hard to ensure that we are good stewards of our members' investments and our employees' contributions. Some will say we are conservatively foolish; others will point to lost opportunities. We relish our self-sufficiency, stability and service to others. **It is not an "either or" situation—either the bottom line or social responsibility; we strive to do well on both measures.**

Afterword

An Open Letter to NISC Members and Employees

Two days out of college in 1975, I was introduced to a unique business model as an employee of Capital Electric Cooperative in my hometown of Bismarck, North Dakota. In 1979, I moved to another cooperative, Basin Electric Power Cooperative. Seven years later, my co-op career continued when I accepted a job with North Central Data Cooperative (NCDC), a predecessor to NISC. In 1994 I was selected to be the CEO of NCDC, and eight years later, in 2002, the opportunity to be NISC's CEO was presented to me.

Initially, I viewed these employers and their organizations as a place to earn a buck, pay my bills and support my growing family. Time has taught me that the jobs were really the start of a journey; and the journey is one of lifelong learning. When I started working, it was with the mindset of seeing what the company had to offer me; now, I come to the office each day eager to see how I can contribute.

In my years with NISC, many times I felt undeserving of the confidence that NISC's board of directors extended to me, and I am forever grateful to the supportive group of seasoned employees who sustained me in more ways than I probably know. Both groups helped me grow in my knowledge of technology, industry trends and the importance of member and employee relationships. You have been counselors when I needed a friendly face and good advice, my hale and hearty traveling companions on this remarkable journey. Time and again, you show me what we can accomplish with a cooperative business model as our foundation; a mindset to lead others through serving them first; and a set of shared values that we daily put into action.

Although there have been challenging times during the journey, my greatest satisfaction as an NISC employee and its CEO comes from the knowledge that I am part of an organization that truly does make a difference in the lives of the members we serve in rural America and elsewhere. Without the dedication, imagination and innovation of NISC employees, our organization would simply be a collection of buildings and computers. You are remarkable individuals, an unrelenting army, who constantly move forward on the path of continual improvement. I watch you take on challenges day after day and rightfully claim victory. I see you pour your hearts and souls into NISC's projects and member relationships. You never succumb to the constant stress of our always-on service environment. You keep lit the passion that makes NISC's stretch goal, your goal.

Most importantly, you are my friends, my inspiration, and yes, you are NISC's greatest assets. Each of you deserves thanks and recognition, and for that reason in Appendix A of this book you'll find a complete listing of the one thousand inspiring professionals who make up the current NISC family. Please take the time to review the names. In so doing, you will also honor, in a small way, those who came before us.

I cannot speak for all of you on your decision to join, remain and build your careers with NISC. For me, it has been thirty-nine years since I first stepped through the doors as a (then) NCDC member. My wife, Lynne, and I talked about this recently, and we counted our blessings.

Since joining the NISC family in 1986:

- We have never once been without my paycheck.
- My positions have always been challenging and rewarding.
- We have always had a full benefit package.
- I have worked for a company that respects the work/life balance.
- We feel part of a family larger than our own that welcomes and supports us.

When it comes time to retire, we won't have stock options to cash in whenever the market looks optimal. But then, that wasn't our goal, nor do I believe it's the goal for most cooperative employees. If it had been, we all would have found our way to the best corporate ladder and started climbing.

We've talked at length in this book about the unique qualities that the cooperative business model offers as an organizational foundation. It begins with a crystal clear mission statement that directly connects the employee through the products and services we provide to the end user/member/customer. At NISC, our connection to our member/owners is paramount. Not only do we serve them, we also rely on them to teach us how we can do better, improve our products and make their jobs easier. Ours is a symbiotic relationship that I believe is unique compared to most businesses today.

NISC leaders evolve from being people who provide strategic direction and course correction to becoming passionate and caring coaches with the essential role of serving those of you whom they lead. The way that individuals supervise others at NISC reminds me regularly of my father's favorite saying, "The best sermon is a good example." Servant leadership wasn't the originally intended outcome at NISC, but its evolution in our culture is one that I believe we should embrace because the fit is natural and logical. This model will continue to evolve and thrive as we serve each other and our members.

It was a stroke of genius to have had NISC employees envision the kind of organization at which they would be proud to work, and then have them use that vision to create the shared values that now guide our daily actions. NISC's journey to success is due in great part to your faithful living out of these values: integrity, relationships, innovation, teamwork, empowerment and personal development. It doesn't matter which NISC campus I'm on or what team I'm working with, you put our shared values into action. And you are a constant reminder of my role as CEO to do the same.

One of my greatest joys at NISC is the way we thrive on collaboration. Daily I see examples of people helping one another (sometimes without being asked, just because it's the right thing to do) and others showing the courage to ask for help. This demonstrates a level of trust in each other that most organizations can only dream of their employees having. We've slowly found our way to the front steps of a collaborative culture. That place where we recognize we are only as great as the sum of each of our parts working remarkably well together. Preserving that cultural development and the critical elements that have led us to it was one of the prime motivations for this book.

I couldn't be more proud or more humbled by your success. Your work at NISC yields impressive, sustainable results that are worth a second look. And in that second look, you will see the many intangible benefits that arise from NISC's success; benefits that are highly sought after in today's cutthroat marketplace. They are important to employers, and employees like you are growing to expect them. Following are some of the most noteworthy results and benefits:

- NISC has demonstrated nearly five decades of planned growth and stability.
- Business relationships with many of our member/owners span almost fifty years.
- We design, build, deploy and support products and technologies that meet and often exceed member needs, year after year.
- NISC helps bridge the digital divide in rural America and, in the process, helps improve the quality of life and economic viability of the communities that we, and our members, support.
- We share the joy and the sense of accomplishment that comes from building a business from scratch and seeing it prosper.
- Many of you have spent your entire career—from entry-level positions to places of responsibility and authority—at NISC.
- NISC takes an active interest in building our skills and abilities on the job, even footing the bill for employees to complete or extend our education.
- Employees enjoy the blessings of never being without health insurance or a retirement plan.

Corporate financial reports and personal bank statements may not validate these measurements, but the opportunity to serve NISC's member/owners and our fellow employees gives us fulfilling careers, friendships that span a lifetime, amazing stories and hopefully, grateful hearts.

At the end of the day, I believe we work for NISC in a spirit of stewardship, where personal values and priorities complement our career goals. And when we choose to leave here, I hope each of us can say that we spent our time wisely, that we dedicated our talents well and made a contribution to something much larger than ourselves. Indeed, our work here does make a difference. And, yes—at NISC, we are wired differently.

Take good care,
Vern Dosch

Acknowledgments

One of my mentors taught me a valuable lesson: As leaders, we must lead with our head *and* our hearts. If we manage with our head only, we will be rock solid on the analytical side of the business, but we will get into trouble because we will tend to overlook the value of the people who help us achieve success. If we manage with just our heart, we will be wonderfully compassionate and understanding, and we may even be well liked, but we will get into trouble because we'll have a blind spot on the financial side of the operation. (As we have said at NISC for years, "There is no mission without a margin.") To be truly effective leaders, we must lead with both the head and with the heart.

My first two mentors were my parents, and my dad was all about the head part when it came to leading. He was a banker, and in his mind, things needed to be logical. My mom was more about the heart and showing compassion, giving to others. As parents, they were a wonderful combination of using your head and your heart. Together they led our family well, and their influence in my life was huge. I acknowledge that I am the person I am today, first and foremost, because of them.

Embracing the idea of a book about NISC was difficult for me. In my head, lots of people talk about writing books, and sometimes that strikes me as a boastful thing. I prefer to do the job and then let the outcome of the project speak for itself. If others talk positively about it, then that's a good thing. In my heart, I was concerned about missing the mark in any way and possibly diminishing the great reputation NISC has established through the amazing work of its employees.

The idea for a book began in conversations with Wally Goulet, NISC's General Counsel, who has been my friend for many years. Wally and I are both readers and have great appreciation for the role books have in sharing information and insight with people; he and I regularly exchange titles and discuss our most recent learnings with each other.

We are both in a place career-wise where we see our achievements as the culmination of valuable life experiences, and we felt a desire to give back to the organization (NISC) and the business model (cooperative) that have taught and given us so much. We also recognized that as NISC grows, the connection to its foundation and the importance of its culture could be diluted, or even forgotten. Wally's gentle prodding with early suggestions for possible chapter outlines kept me focused on the value of capturing the essence of our culture in a way that could be easily shared with others.

For these reasons, I overcame my reservations about writing a book and *Wired Differently* is now a reality. I've had the luxury of nearly forty years of learning, some of which occurred through the school of hard knocks, and this book tells many of these stories. It is my hope that in reading it NISC employees, members and anybody else who is interested can learn about such things as the cooperative business model, servant leadership and shared values at an accelerated pace—certainly in less than forty years.

In some ways, this book is a formal thank you to the employees, past, present and future, at NISC. And it's a chance to pause and take note: Look at everything you've accomplished! Maybe you will flip through the pages of the book and view NISC through your head (chapter 12 offers a review of our financials) or you might want to listen to NISC with your heart (chapter 5 provides some great employee stories related to our shared values). Either way, *Wired Differently* is yours. It talks about the organization that is built by its employees, and I am humbled and privileged to walk with you on that adventure. For a current listing of NISC employees, all of whom are important and valued people, please see Appendix A.

The NISC Board trusts our employees; indeed, the level of trust they have shown is almost unbelievable. We are indebted to the board members for the support they give us as an organization and for their support of this book project. When I talked to them about the need to preserve our culture, the specific conversation about a book was perhaps three sentences. They are behind the project and have given us their full support. To them I say thank you for this vote of confidence.

To be sure, the skills and abilities required to manage a complex IT business are daunting. I have the good fortune of working with the finest, most dedicated and competent group of senior executives, bar none. NISC's vice presidents group includes Dan Wilbanks, Tracy Porter, Doug Remboldt, Ed Wolff, Wally Goulet, Todd Eisenhauer, David Bonnett, Kari Reichert and Jeff Almen. They routinely accomplish the impossible with remarkable skill. While they are a diverse group, each is passionate about our work. They understand NISC's mission and, without exception, have each other's back. It is a privilege to work with them. I have been richly blessed to benefit from the experience, talent and friendship of these professionals.

There are numerous amazing leaders in the electric and telecom industries who, over the years, have directly contributed to NISC's success and provided me with valuable insight. I humbly acknowledge Martin Lowery, Executive Vice President for Member and Association Relations at the National Rural Electric Cooperative Association; Sheldon Petersen, CEO of the National Rural Utilities Cooperative Finance Corporation; Andy Brown, Vice President of Industry and Client Relations for ANPI; Steve Collier, Director of Smart Grid Strategies with Milsoft Utility Solutions; Mark Glaess, former CEO at the Minnesota Rural Electric Association; Ron Harper, former CEO of Basin Electric Power Cooperative; Paul Sukut, current CEO of Basin Electric Power Cooperative; Shirley Bloomfield, CEO of NTCA—The Rural Broadband Association; and so many others who have been wonderful examples of selfless, visionary leadership in the industries we serve. I am forever grateful for their guidance and mentorship.

I am grateful to the individuals within each of our seven hundred member systems. Their loyalty and their willingness to work with us to help move NISC from being just a good organization to a great one—this is the magic of NISC. The wants and needs of our end users are our prime consideration, and our relationship with our members is critical in defining who we are. I can't name the number of times one of our retiring employees has said that one of the things they will miss most is dealing with the members. It's true; the relationship with our members is that important.

In addition to Wally for his early encouragement and his own contribution to shaping the book's content, I owe a debt of gratitude to many others for its completion. I've been a member of many teams throughout my life, and the team assembled to complete this book project is more than a good one, they are a great team. Please accept my humble thanks. Without your contribution, *Wired Differently* would be merely a book, rather than a sincere representation of a truly unique organization.

To you, the readers of *Wired Differently*: thank you for your time. Here at NISC we are mostly technicians, and at this point in my life I wish I would have paid more attention in Sister Hugo's composition class, but we've had some good help along the way. If there are any errors or omissions, I take full responsibility for these. We never set out to write a book when we started our careers at NISC. If we had, we would have done a better job of taking notes and capturing the milestones that have shaped us. Perhaps in a small way we can contribute to the success of others as our predecessors have contributed to our journey. Sandpaper our stories and best practices as needed.

My deep appreciation goes to the reviewers who provided the first round of feedback to the original chapter concepts for *Wired Differently*. They include: Colleen Stoxen, John Stoxen, Al Anderson, Mike Mabin, Rod Backman, Sister Thomas Welder, Sister Kathleen Atkinson, Mary Miller, Kayla Effertz, Sandy McMerty, Wes Engbrecht, Linda Donlin and Jane Greer. Similar thanks go to the first group of individuals who provided insight on book titles and subtitles: Connie Sprynczynatyk, Dave Skalicky, Mike Eggl, Dan Waind, Mary Jo Van Horn, Pamela Schmidt and Pam Thompson. We also received great feedback from individuals willing to read early versions of the book, even before it was named. I am grateful to Pat Shafer, Larry Spears and Dave Pearce.

Once we decided to move forward with the project, Wally and I invited Tracy Finneman to join our team as an outside writing consultant who could look at NISC with objectivity. She brought a level of enthusiasm for and confidence in the project that we welcomed. Tracy has a gift to see the end game, and she is a methodical project manager. She kept us on task, reminded us to celebrate the small successes along the way, and helped us achieve a goal that, hopefully, will benefit NISC for years to come. (She also makes exceptional granola, which sustained us through many an early morning meeting when we molded the dream into reality.)

The team of editors and designers was wonderful to work with, and their expertise improved the caliber and the quality of *Wired Differently* beyond what I had hoped. My sincere thanks to Todd Moore, Jason DeKock, Karen Milner, Lindsay Humphreys and Adrian So.

To John Doggett, you are far more than a business consultant. You have become a friend and a confidant, inspiring me to be a better leader than I ever thought I could be. Thank you for taking the time to set the stage for *Wired Differently* with the thought-provoking insight and context you offer in the Foreword.

No one achieves anything in a vacuum. Any progress I have made is due, in large measure, to others. At a personal level, NISC has provided me with more opportunities and satisfaction than I could have ever imagined, and for that I am grateful, but being a husband and dad is, without doubt, more important and rewarding. As NISC's CEO, I've traveled more than two million miles, spending more nights than I care to remember away from home. During my absences, my wife, Lynne, has pulled double-duty, attending to the ever-changing needs of three active children. Not once has she complained about the burden my travels place on her and our family. She's always packed my bags with great care, understanding that without her support, my baggage would be too heavy to lift. My sincere and loving thanks to you, Lynne. Your support means more than you will ever know.

Our children have endured my absences as well. While I did everything possible to be present in their lives, including watching their school events via streaming media, there were times when I was not present. I owe them a great debt of gratitude for their understanding and patience. They, and now our grandchildren, have brought meaning and purpose to my life. They are a source of joy and legacy that enriches my life in such a profound way that is impossible to put into words. Without them, my commitment to NISC would have a diminished purpose. Zachary, Skylar, Quinn, Brittany, Jesse, Coraline, Thatcher and Jordan, I love you more than you will ever know.

At this moment, I am humbled beyond measure. My head is brimming with mental pictures of each individual who has contributed to the creation of *Wired Differently*. And my heart, well, it is overflowing with gratitude and love. You all have touched me and I have grown, both personally and professionally. Perhaps *Wired Differently* will also touch you.

Appendix A

NISC Employees

Following is a complete listing of the one thousand inspiring professionals who make up the current NISC family as of November 25, 2014.

Karen Abben	Loretta Auld	Pete Beeny	Danielle Bitz
Greg Aberle	David Baack	Teri Bekeris	Brian Black
Darcy Ackerman	Jesse Babbra	Danny Belaska	Holly Blair
Mary Adair	John Babin	Doug Belew	Lyla Blazer
Stacey Adams	Wardell Bagby	Deb Bell	Paul Blessing
Michaela Addison	Wendy Ball	LeeAnne Bell	Carol Boast
Jake Adducci	Paul Balogh	Darilyn Bellon	Sue Bodvig
Tim Adolf	Dawn Balzer	Sally Bellon	John Boedeker
Sadhna Ahuja	Kristen Barnett	Karla Beneke	Nate Boettcher
David Aichele	Brandy Barnhard	Arron Benne	Shanon Bogren
Ruth Albert	Frank Barnhart	Julie Bennett	Michelle Bohn
Dawn Albrecht	Joey Barone	Sterling Bennett	Scott Boies
Christian Alexander	Ashley Barth	David Bentz	Stephanie Bold
Candace Alfonso	Jim Bartholomay	Paulette Bentz	Alex Boldt
Ron Alfred	Steve Bartlow	Ashley Bercier	Connie Bolz
Sandra Allgire	Jason Bartsch	Shawn Bergan	David Bonnett
Kerri Allmaras	Jody Bartz	Jennifer Berger	Char Bono
John Alls	Linda Bass	Steve Berger	Amanda Booke
Jeff Almen	John Baucom	Troy Bernhardt	Jessica Booke
Cassandra Anderson	Charlie Bauer	Chris Beste	Brian Borr
Connie Anderson	Leora Bauer	Nick Beste	Diane Bosch
Gail Anderson	Lois Bauer	Paul Bettonville	Michelle Bosch
Kevin Anderson	Linda Baum	Chris Beyer	Kyle Bova
Kim Anderson	Ofelia Baumgartner	Joetta Bichler	Leslie Boyd
Kirsten Anderson	Brandon Beard	Troy Bichler	Kaylan Brandner
Jennifer Andre	Denise Beattie	Daniel Bickler	Jane Brass
Brandi Arndt	Carol Becher	Michelle Biegler	Kathy Braun
Sandra Arndt	Casey Beck	Phyllis Bigelow	Dirk Bremer
Jamie Atchley	Christy Becker	Jennifer Biggs	Lacey Brendel
Joshua Atkinson	Krystal Beckler	Jennifer Bird	Gary Brendes
Alan Augustin	Rachelle Beckler	Greg Birnbaum	Matt Brenneke

Ericka Brewer	Nancy Cole	Brandy Dillman	Char Feigitsch
Jon Briggs	Lisa Combrevis	Marcy Dillman	Jane Feist
Jason Brinkmann	Jennifer Conlon	Maria Dockter	Vince Fels
Jill Britton	Kevin Connor	Dennis Dolan	Jennifer Fergel
Joel Brizendine	Daniel Conrad	Gail Doll	John Ferlisi
Kevin Brizendine	Matthew Cook	Gail Domres	Amber Fetch
Ted Broadfield	Andrew Cooper	Vern Dosch	Brian Fettig
Brenda Broderick	Jackie Cope	Sheila Doty	Sheena Fetzer
Dan Brooke	Joe Cordeal	Kimberly Drury	Lisa Fields
Stanton Brooks	Larry Corder	Cheryl Dubois	Jessica Fink
Mike Brown	Karen Cornell	Tom DuBos	Lori Finnerty
Ashley Bruner	Mike Coumerilh	Kim Dudley	Heather Fischer
Sue Brunkhorst	Brian Coyner	Greg Dunn	Laura Fischer
Sarah Bryson	Matt Crile	Zach Dunn	Sarah Fischer
Andrea Bubach	Jeff Crites	Renee Dupuis	Josh Fisher
Shelly Buchheit	Crystal Crock	Diane Durkee	John Flavin
Steve Buchholz	Matt Crock	Brian Dusenberry	Lewis Fleak
Melissa Buechler	Amanda Croegaert	Berdene Dykema	Candace Fleck
Ryan Bueneman	Dwayne Cullen	Todd Eadie	Jessica Fleck
Justin Burd	Pat Cundiff	Eric Eberle	Liz Fleck
Corey Burgum	Wendy Cunningham	Van Ebert	Patty Fleck
Debra Burke	Chad Curn	Tammy Eck	Terri Fleming
Theresa Burns	Alex Dahl	Gene Edelen	Mary Fleri
Phillip Butterfield	Craig Dahle	Debbie Eggering	Michelle Flesness
Chris Calvert	Jaren Damm	Gene Ehli	Clarice Fode
Ben Cannady	Kellan Damm	Todd Eisenhauer	Jeremy Ford
Eric Capouch	Zach Danger	Jolene Emil	EJ Foreman
Shawna Carbutt	Amanda Daniel	Tim Emmerich	John Forsythe
Bob Carey	Doris Daniels	Phil Endsley	Ronda Fox
Matt Carney	Jennifer Danielson	Danay Engbrecht	Bill Frame
Brooke Carr	Wendy Danielson	Paul Engebretson	Mike Frank
Steven Carrell	Shannon Dauenhauer	Steve Engel	Damion Frederick
Patrick Carroll	Leah David	Deb Entzel	Kale Frederick
Jon Carter	Kimberly Davis	Stephanie Entzel	Brett Fredrick
Sara Carufel	Jeanne Davis	Tanya Enzminger	Dennis Freeman
Sharon Carver	Adam Day	Kristin Erdmann	Jason Frey
Sean Cato	Mari Dean	Braeton Erhardt	Ardella Friedt
Jacob Cepek	Kurt Decker	Larry Estal	Chris Fries
Jim Cepek	Janet Deckman	Charity Evers	Mike Friesen
Chris Cermak	Steven DeFriese	Grant Evers	Matt Fryman
Steve Chaffman	Jason DeKock	Tammie Falkenstein	Tracy Fugere
Ramsey Checkett	Connie Denkmann	Marty Fall	Peggy Fuller
Kevin Cherry	Gary Derby	Janine Faris	Nicole Gagner
JoAnn Christianson	Brian Derrington	Sylvia Faris	Jason Gammons
Scott Clausen	Jessica DeVaal	Elizabeth Farmer	Michelle Gangl
Brad Clawges	Cameron Dietz	Mark Faron	Ted Gardner
Brian Clemen	Ted Dietz	Eram Fatima	Carl Garrett
Brian Colburn	Erick Dihle	Tami Fearing	Haven Gauger

Phyllis Gaydon	Carol Hamilton	Laura Hood	Wes Jonas
Sharon Gebhardt	Patrick Hanna	Jeremy Hoornaert	Joe Jones
Whitney Geiger	Michelle Hansen	Derek Hopkins	Jesse Jordan
Steve Geltel	James Hardin	Alexis Horner	David Jorgensen
Jodie Gerving	Matt Harrison	Cheryl Horner	Brittani Kail
Linda Gieser	Mark Hasbargen	Jean Horner	John Kalbac
Larry Giesinger	Jason Hatton	Randy Horner	Leo Kalips
Amy Gietzen	Amanda Haugen	Keith Horntvedt	Sheena Kalvoda
Tyler Ginnever	Bonnie Haupt	Dorita Horst	JR Kasper
Jesse Ginnever	Debbie Havermann	Andrew Hough	Monica Kastner
Patricia Gisinger	Nicole Havlicek	Gail Huber	Karlee Kaylor
Lisa Glass	Darrell Hayes	Gina Huck	Scott Kaylor
Wendy Glidden	Josh Heaton	Trevor O Huck	Tammy Kear
Rita Glosier	Tom Heaverlo	Malcolm Hudson	Mark Kearney
Paul Glovik	Darryl Hehn	Bill Hudson	Jim Keller
Josh Godi	Brent Heick	Tanesha Hughes	Dean Kelly
Dianna Godwin	Zach Heidbrier	Jacob Hunsel	Michael Kempel
Dennis Goetges	Cassandra Heinert	Greg Hupke	Jeff Kempf
Allison Goettle	Rochelle Heinze	Karla Hussey	Jeff Kendall
Steven Goldade	Bob Heinzen	Georgia Hust	Lenora Kenner
Andrew Golden	Bill Heinzen	Nicole Hust	Andrew Kent
Gail Golden	Alan Heitman	Susan Hutchason	Jesse Kerzman
Christy Goodno	Wendy Helbling	Doug Huttegger	Shawn Kessler
Kim Goodwin	Larry Helfenstein	Ryan Huttsell	Amber Kilber
Wally Goulet	Evan Hellman	Chris Hyman	Jon Kilber
Jean Graeber	Melissa Hellman	Nick Iffrig	Renee Kimball
Brett Grassmuck	Mike Hembrock	Lois Ihle	Rob Kimpling
Scott Graves	Brad Hemmer	Susan Imm	Rose Kind
Allen Gray	Todd Henecke	Erik Ingebretson	Kisa Kindsvogel
Candice Gray	Spencer Henke	Suzanne Isbell	Dawn King
Travis Gray	Cathy Henn	Miranda Iwaniw	Jonathan Klecker
Mike Greene	Chris Henrich	Jon Jablonski	Angie Klein
Michelle Greve	Justin Herner	Tim Jablonski	Heidi Klein
Steve Grieshaber	Miranda Hertz	Brad Jacks	LaRue Klein
J Griggs	Kathleen Hettich	Matt Jacobs	Kevin Klemisch
Lori Grillion	Steve Hilgert	Greg Jahner	Joann Klott
Daniel Grippi	Karla Hilke	Jon Jalbert	Jay Klutenkamper
Kimberly Grube	Frank Hinds	Scott Janz	John Knakal
Colleen Gruer	Kyle Hinterser	Trish Jeske	Tyler Knebel
Mark Gurgol	Judy Hoernschemeyer	Brittany Jewkes	Valerie Kniffen
Becky Haakenson	Dawn Hoffman	TJ Jochim	Chad Knudtson
Catina Haakenson	Deb Hoffman	Troy Jochim	Margaret Koch
Ryan Hager	Niel Hoffman	DJ Johnson	Doug Koeneman
Zane Hagerott	Mary Kay Hoffmann	Jack Johnson	Tara Koerber
Christine Hahn	Wendy Hoiby	Jason Johnson	Anthony Kohler
Shirley Haider	Gerald Holt	Jill Johnson	MaKayla Kohler
Mike Haldaman	Jay Holweger	Scott Johnson	Audrey Kooker
Ben Halley	Bobbi Holzworth	Sue Johnston	Laurey Kooker

Loren Koppy
Lori Kottsick
Berkley Kraft
Kirby Kraft
Tom Kraft
Yvette Kraft
Jordan Krage
Bill Krein
Mathew Krogen
Adelina Kronberg
Anton Kuchman
Tony Kulzer
Kelley Kunnanz
Mark Kuntz
Corey Kurtz
Joe Kurtz
Kevin Kurtz
Bryce Kvindlog
Deb Lagasse
Rachelle Lakeman
Kevin LaMal
Gary Lamping
Julie Lancelle
Denise Landeis
Sandy Lane
Jeremy Lang
Kenton Lang
Nichol Lang
Tracy Langston
Roxanne Larson
Ryan Larson
Jordan Laske
Linda LaTourelle
Mark Lauer
Samantha Lawson
Lazetta Leer
Stacey Leible
Matthew Leidholm
Chad Leingang
Rich Lemons
Greg Letrello
Cindy Levi
Dave Lewis
John Lewis
Lisa Lienhard
Matthew Lievens
Tracy Liley
Ni Lin

Lorna Lincoln
Dean Lindquist
Ben Lindvall
Nick Lindvall
Paula Linke
Glen Linssen
Casey Lippincott
David Loesing
Lisa Loken
Dave Lowder
David Lowe
Channon Lowman
Kendra Lown
Elisabeth Lundstrom
Jean Lutz
Terry Lyon
Greg Machart
Justin Mackey
Kathy Maessen
Larry Magstadt
Kevin Mahoney
Mike Malkowski
Channing Mann
Dawn Martin
Jared Martin
Les Martin
Stephanie Martinez
Arylis Mason
Don Mastel
Sara Materi
Tom Materi
Laura Matthews
Paul Matthews
George Mausshardt
Matt Mays
Tammy McClain
Kathie McCord
April McDanel
Thomas McDanel
Trevor McDaniel
Jason McHenry
Jennette McLaughlin
Mark Meadows
Cory Medlin
Craig Medlock
Mary Meerbott
Kimberly Meissner
Lori Mennemeyer

Jan Merkel
Julie Mertz
Delores Messer
LeeAnn Meyer
Angela Micallef
Robyn Micheau
Curt Mildenberger
Amanda Miller
Catherine Miller
Jeremy Miller
Margo Miller
Michelle Miller
Paula Miller
Randy Miller
Scott Miller
Yvonne Miller
Eric Minard
Nick Minor
Andrea Miravalle
Matt Miskell
Peggy Mitzel
Melissa Moesch
Brad Molander
Mark Momerak
Carissa Mongeon
Thomas Mongeon
Mary Monroe
Mel Monroe
Chelsi Montplaisir
Ashley Moore
Robert Moore
Todd Moore
Matt Moorman
Rex Moorman
Rebekah Morales
Jeff Morman
Patrick Morris
Shoni Mortenson
Sarah Moss
Aaron Motter
Chris Motter
Paul Mueller
Eric Mugaas
Brian Muldoon
Bryce Muller
Diane Muller
Jody Murphy
Todd Muth

Thuy Myers
Eric Nanney
Gary Neigum
Aric Nelson
Brian Nelson
Jeff Nelson
Jon Nelson
Micheal Nelson
Brian Nengel
Shelley Ness
John Neuberger
Daniel Neubert
Shelly Nevels
Stephen Nguyen
Ryan Niederkorn
Tracie Noel
Mary Ellen Noga
Donna Norman
Andy Oberhoffer
Denise O'Brien
Pat O'Brien
Hannah Occena
Karen O'Hearn
Ken Olheiser
Christine Olson
Leif Olson
Brent Opdahl
Travis Opdahl
Joe Orf
Richard Ostrowski
Mary Pace
Becky Pack
Deric Page
Kyle Palmer
Natasha Parmley
Mark Parres
Steve Pascoe
Rick Pasker
Tiffany Pattman
Ron Patton
Ernestine Paul
Teresa Paulsen
Kurtis Pearce
Jim Peasel
Kris Pegors
Tami Peine
Tanya Peluso
Lindsay Peterson

Kelly Pfliger	Sarah Rhodes	Carol Schlueter	Sheryl Skiba
Mary Phipps	Bob Rice	Jacqueline Schmidt	James Skjod
Jack Pierson	Sherri Richardson	JoAnn Schmidt	Wendi Slominski
Karen Poetz	Chris Riggs	Katy Schmitz	Kim Sloss
April Pollard	Mark Rigoni	Carrie Schneider	Justin Smith
Barb Polzin	Ryan Rixen	Brittany Schlosser	Neil Smith
David Porter	Sarah Rixen	Greta Schlosser	Phillip Smith
Tracy Porter	Carl Roades	Kayla Schmidt	Sandy Smith
Tyler Porter	Brent Roberts	John Schock	Kristen Snow
Betty Potts-Smrcka	Gwen Roberts	Andrew Schrader	Beth Soderquist
Jennifer Powers	John Robertson	Penny Schramm	Chip Sotolar
Ryan Preabt	Mary Robertson	Natalie Schreiner	Matt Sparkman
Tim Preall	Cade Robinson	Randy Schroder	Brian Spellazza
Michele Presley	Lindsay Robinson	Chad Schuchard	Jay Srinivasan
Ryan Presley	Jackie Rocha	Dawn Schumacher	Kelsi Steckler
Cale Prewitt	Iris Rodenkirck	Ashlee Schwark	Dustan Steffan
Heidi Prewitt	Kyle Roesler	Chris Schwartz	Laura Steffan
Bill Price	Laurie Rogstad	Curt Schwartz	Dan Stegmiller
Jared Price	Tracy Rohde	Londa Schwartz	Jed Steiner
Trena Quinn	Travis Rohde	Kathy Schwartzbauer	Frank Steinmann
Rob Rabenberg	Tom Root	Chris Schwarz	Josh Steinwand
Kristi Rader	Carol Rosinski	Missy Schwerdt	Eric Stelter
Dion Rahn	Sarah Ross	Stan Scott	Jim Stenson
Sam Ramaji	Tami Roy	Tony Scott	Deb Stepanek
Stacy Randash	Dan Ruff	Twyla Scott	Sandy Stern
John Randolph	Travis Ruggles	Jesse Scrivens	Amanda Stiles
Jim Rapp	Barbara Ryan	Martha Sears	Terry Stogdill
Taylor Rash	Ron Sams	Donovan Selensky	Sandra Stoltz
Brian Rath	Calob Sanders	Fred Selensky	Misty Strilcov
John Rausch	Shelby Sargent	Eric Sellers	Steven Stroud
Matthew Reed	Konrad Sauer	Tonja Selzler	Terry Stroud
John Reede	Esther Sayler	Dan Semar	Matt Struckmeyer
Kari Reichert	Tom Schaberg	Jennifer Severson	Betsy Summers
Eric Reid	Gwen Schaffer	Pat Shafer	Daniel Sun
Janet Reineke	Connie Schaner	Lea Shalhoob	Skip Sutter
Pat Reinert	Josh Schaner	Ben Shashek	Andrea Svalen
James Reinholdt	Brad Schanks	Larue Shaw	Alexander Swanke
Greg Reisenauer	Paige Schaper	Stacy Sheeks	Dick Swann
Chris Reiser	Pam Schaubert	Denise Sheldon	Karen Swanson
Amy Remboldt	Dorothy Schechterly	Tammy Sheldon	Kathy Sweatman
Doug Remboldt	Gary Schechterly	Stephen Sheppard	Rebecca Swenson
Jamie Remboldt	Morgan Scheid	August Shultz	Jeannie Tackett
Abby Renschler	Cindy Schick	Gene Shumaker	Andrey Tataurov
Kalyn Retterath	Karen Schick	Peggy Shupp	Chad Ternes
Larry Reustle	Tracie Schiermeister	Dave Sickels	David Terry
Julie Reuter	Glen Schlechta	Carla Simokaitis	Mim Terwint
Nestor Reyes	Jay Schlenker	Ethan Sincox	Michelle Tetzloff
Kevin Reynolds	Eric Schlote	Phyllis Skager	Karen Theis

Mary Theis

Joe Theisman

Chuck Thierauf

Jordan Thilmony

Ambre Thingvold

Amanda Thomas

Marie Thomas

Mishay Thomas

Darcey Thompson

Debra Thompson

Cindy Thornburgh

Ben Thorson

Paul Thrapp

Bryan Tibor

Bev Tiefenthaler

Gail Timmerberg

Paul Tingley

Tim Tobin

Kathleen Towe

Carla Trohkimoinen

Bob Truetken

Ryan Trullinger

Lisa Tuell

Leon Uhrich

Alicia Ulferts

Tony Unterreiner

David Van Trump

Tim VanCourt

Chris Vandal

Thomas Vander Wal, Sr

Thomas Vander Wal, Jr

Brendan VanEckhout

Jaden VanEckhout

Brenda Vaughn

Nick Venn

Wayne Venn

Brian VerDouw

Shari Vetter

Steve Viehmann

Michael Virag

Phil Viton

Scott Vogel

Holly Voigt

Tige Vollrath

Jeff Von Ahsen

Joe Vonarx

Dylan Wagner

Helen Wagner

Janet Wagner

Aaron Wald

Al Wald

Doug Walker

Tony Walsh

Bruce Walth

Kim Walth

Claire Walther

Willis Walton

Brent Wangler

Jackie Warner

Tina Watermolen

Barbara Weaver

Debbie Weber

John Weber

Mike Weber

Debbie Weeke

Patti Wegner

Bill Weiand

Brenda Weiand

Stephanie Weiand

Alvin Weigel

Ken Weigel

Louie Weigel

Kristen Weiler

Mark Weishaar

Brad Weisnicht

Kayla Weiss

Mike Weltmer

Amber Wesche

Justin West

Robin West

Jamie Wetsch

Brent Wetzel

Herb Wetzel

Josiah Wetzel

Geoff White

Jaime White

Jonathan White

Shade Whitner

Jason Whitsett

Sean Wiese

Alan Wigness

Dan Wilbanks

Dan Wilding

Tammy Wilkerson

Rusty Willey

Deena Williams

Kimberly Williams

Twila Willis

Rick Willmann

Doug Wilmes

Michelle Wilmes

David Wilson

John Wilson

Vicky Wilson

Kara Winkler

Mariah Wipperling

Mary Wittry

Dave Woehler

Jesse Woeste

Jenean Wofford

Austin Wolf

Kathy Wolf

Melissa Wolf-Tveito

Cindy Wolfe

Steve Wolfe

Ed Wolff

Ryan Wolfrum

Eric Wright

Julie Yantzer

Jeffrey Young

Lisa Young

Bryan Zander

Wendy Zander

Tony Zappetillo

Mary Ziemann

Jolynn Zierden

Jessica Zimmerman

Diane Zoellner

Nick Zurovec

Connie Zuther

Appendix B

NISC Board of Directors 2000-2015

Following is a listing of the forty-two selfless individuals who have served or currently are serving as members of the NISC Board of Directors as of January 1, 2015.

Larry Adams	Roger Geckler	Mickey Miller
Marv Athey	Joe Harris	Dan O'Brien
Chet Aubin	Larry Hinz	Roberte Pflager
Larry Austin	Gary Johnson	Reginald Rudolph
Harry Barnes	Howard 'Bud' Johnson	Charles Russell
Vernon Brinkley	Mike Kays	Delbert Smith
Ron Brothen	Bruce King	John Smith
Shirley Cairns	Larry Knegendorf	Greg Starheim
Larry Carlson	Darin LaCoursiere	Larry Tade
Don Crabbe	Robert Loth	Dave Weaklend
Russell DeRemer	Jim Magnum	Wayne Whitaker
Fred Dohrman	Wayne Martian	Jerry Williams
Paul Freude	Jerry Martin	Roger Yoder
Duane Gackle	Dan McClendon	Jack Young

Index

About the Authors

VERN DOSCH

Vern Dosch is President and Chief Executive Officer of National Information Solutions Cooperative (NISC). A lifelong resident of Bismarck-Mandan, North Dakota, Vern holds a Bachelor of Science degree and a Master of Management degree from the University of Mary. He and his wife, Lynne, have three grown children, Zachary (Skylar), Brittany (Jesse) and Jordan, and three grandchildren. vernlynnedosch@hotmail.com

WALLY GOULET

Wally Goulet has served as NISC's General Counsel since 2002 and has represented cooperatives for over thirty-two years. Wally lives in Bismarck, North Dakota, with his wife, Cyndi. He has five children (Katherine, Matthew, Michael, Kristen and Nicholas) and three grandchildren. Wally and Cyndi are avid readers, hikers, travelers and golfers. Wally is a graduate of the University of Notre Dame business school and UND law school. wally.goulet@gmail.com

TRACY FINNEMAN

Tracy Finneman is a skilled listener, accredited business communicator and successful marketer who serves clients through the consultancy Integrity Partners. Tracy's family owns and operates Papa's Pumpkin Patch and Papa's Polar Patch just north of Bismarck, North Dakota. Tracy is also the founder of Papa's Granola. Tracy and her husband, Cory, have one son, Ben-Luke. tracy@ndintegritypartners.com

For more information, please visit: www.nisc.coop